Praise for *Reconnecting with Your*

"A helpful roadmap for estranged familie[...]
— Jane Isay, author of *Walking on Eggs[...] [...]g the Delicate Relationship Between Adult Children and Parents*

"*Reconnecting with Your Estranged Adult Child* is the go-to guide for parents who have found themselves in the painful situation of estrangement. The author covers many variations of and reasons for estrangement and provides both insight and practical solutions to reconnect and resolve it. The actionable advice and sample dialogues provide particular value to the parent who struggles with saying the right words to convey their thoughts and feelings. Gilbertson's process helps parents kick-start the healing process and move toward reconciliation."
— Marni Feuerman, MSW, PsyD, psychotherapist, and author of *Ghosted and Breadcrumbed: Stop Falling for Unavailable Men and Get Smart about Healthy Relationships*

"Tina Gilbertson understands the tremendous importance of the parent-child relationship and offers very practical, clear strategies for parents who are estranged from their children. This is a valuable resource for readers who are struggling and want to become self-aware and reconcile with their kids."
— Cindy Goodman Stulberg, psychologist and author of *Feeling Better: Beat Depression and Improve Your Relationships with Interpersonal Psychotherapy*

"*Reconnecting with Your Estranged Adult Child* is a warm, practical, and insightful book for parents whose adult children refuse contact with them. Tina Gilbertson helps parents with the very difficult task of finding the exact right word or phrase that can often make the difference between a door opening or remaining bolted shut. And she helps parents see what is going on in the heart and mind of the estranged child. Highly recommended."
— Joshua Coleman, PhD, author of *When Parents Hurt: Compassionate Strategies When You and Your Grown Child Don't Get Along*

"In her brilliant book, Tina Gilbertson goes beyond the kind of simplistic advice offered by many self-help books and gets to the heart of how estrangement happens, even with parents who are motivated by the best of intentions. She offers specific guidance for restoring meaningful connection to a relationship that has become painfully fractured."

— Linda Bloom, coauthor of
101 Things I Wish I Knew When I Got Married

RECONNECTING
with your
ESTRANGED
ADULT CHILD

Also by Tina Gilbertson

Constructive Wallowing

RECONNECTING
with your
ESTRANGED
ADULT CHILD

PRACTICAL TIPS AND TOOLS TO
HEAL YOUR RELATIONSHIP

TINA GILBERTSON

New World Library
Novato, California

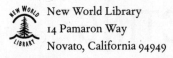 New World Library
14 Pamaron Way
Novato, California 94949

Text design by Tona Pearce Myers

Library of Congress Cataloging-in-Publication data is available.

First printing, April 2020
ISBN 978-1-60868-658-2
Ebook ISBN 978-1-60868-659-9
Printed in Canada on 100% postconsumer-waste recycled paper

 New World Library is proud to be a Gold Certified Environmentally Responsible Publisher. Publisher certification awarded by Green Press Initiative.
www.greenpressinitiative.org

10   9   8   7   6   5

To all the estranged parents who have written and spoken to me over the years, thank you for opening your hearts to me. You made this book possible. As always, I wish you healing and peace.

CONTENTS

A WARNING

Readers whose childhoods involved severe or numerous adverse experiences may find parts of this book disturbing. Some of the discussion, particularly but not exclusively in chapter 2, could trigger unwanted memories and thoughts, nightmares, or emotional distress. Please seek the support of a qualified mental health professional if you find yourself experiencing any of these symptoms while reading this book.

Disclaimers

The material in this book is intended for education. It is not meant to take the place of diagnosis and treatment by a qualified medical practitioner or therapist. No expressed or implied guarantee of the effects of the use of the recommendations can be given or liability taken.

None of the characters mentioned in this book are real people. Rather, they are composites drawn from many different stories of estrangement. All names are fictitious, and any resemblance to specific individuals is coincidental. In contrast, all quoted comments were submitted by real people — who remain anonymous, even to the author.

When it comes to relationships and what it takes to repair them, one size doesn't fit all. Instead of offering a step-by-step blueprint for every parent to follow to success, this book provides a collection of ideas, factual information, expert opinion, and tools that readers may choose to employ in approaching their unique circumstances. In the context of your personal situation, some of the recommendations may not be appropriate. Please use your own judgment, or seek counsel, before implementing any advice you read in these pages.

INTRODUCTION

Do you love your child or children? Do you want them to be happy? Have you done your best to parent them well?

If you're reading this book, I bet you'll answer a definite yes to all three questions. From the time their children are born, most parents focus considerable energy on giving them everything they need to succeed in life. New mothers and fathers look forward to watching their kids grow up and find partners, and they picture themselves holding grandchildren in their arms. They bask in the anticipation of watching their descendants continue family traditions. These dreams of the future make all the sacrifices inherent in being a parent worthwhile.

But in many modern families, the parent-child relationship goes sour when the children become adults. A divide opens up between the apple and the tree that bore it. As the distance grows, Mom or Dad's vision of a happy multigenerational family starts to fade. Many parents today feel the sting of this type of estrangement.

The word *estrangement* comes from the Latin word *extraneare*, meaning "to treat as a stranger." Becoming a stranger to one's child is one of the most painful things that can happen to a parent. If you're reeling from the shock and pain of having an estranged adult child, this book is for you. Let me add a couple of caveats.

Things to Know Before We Go

First, if your child appears to be lost in any kind of addiction, it's important to understand that addiction is a serious medical problem requiring intervention beyond the scope of this book. People with active addictions aren't emotionally available to participate in relationships. No matter how well you implement the guidelines in this or any other book about relationships, you may not be able to get through to someone whose primary connection is to a substance or process.

If this is the case with your child, please read as much as you can about addiction and seek help through your local social services. Also, team up with other people in your child's life; her addiction will affect all her relationships, not just those with family.

Second, this book assumes you have a growth mindset — that you're interested in becoming the best possible version of yourself. You're not likely to find answers in these pages if you're convinced the only positive outcome is for your child to suddenly change his mind and contact you, or to spontaneously forgive anything that needs forgiving. Those things can happen, but reunions based on spontaneous forgiveness are usually temporary, since the black box containing the cause(s) of the estrangement remains unopened. This book invites you to make changes in the way you think, feel, and behave. If reconciliation is to occur, let alone become permanent, it will most likely begin with you.

If you had custody of, and a close relationship with, your child at any time before she became an adult, and someone seems to be turning her against you now, there's much you can do to rebuild your relationship. If your child has a spouse or partner, you might end up with two relationships for the price of one, and in general your family may not look the way you once envisioned it. But if you value family as I do, that won't matter in the end.

If your estranged child is under the age of thirty or has recently left home, he may simply be undergoing a normal phase of adult development that calls for more psychological distance from parents. It's a stage that can be alarming for both parents and children, but it doesn't last forever. If you're the parent of a young adult, chapter 5 is just for you. You may also benefit from other parts of the book, especially those concerning self-care and personal development. You might need to wait a while before putting into practice some of the other ideas presented here with your adult son or daughter.

Throughout the book, I assume that both parents and adult children would prefer a loving, harmonious, and fulfilling relationship, and that such a relationship is possible with time, knowledge, and effort. But you don't have to work actively toward reconciliation to benefit from this book. Although you enter estrangement in pieces, it's a crucible that can make you whole again — not just as someone's parent, but for yourself.

There's no quick fix to be found in these pages — or any pages. Estrangement doesn't happen overnight, and it won't be healed that quickly, either. Although this is a manual for repairing your relationship with your child and creating lasting change, that undertaking will require consistent effort over time. The mature tree of your relationship has been decades in the making. It won't bend as easily as a sapling would; it will take time for you to rework your connection into something new and better. I hope to provide you with tools to do just that.

Time is limited. It can't be paused or slowed, and it keeps stealing days from you and your child. Sadly, there's no remedy for that. All you can do is to use wisely the weeks, months, or years you spend apart. When you have confidence that the steps you're taking now are adding to the relationship and will help move it in the right direction, you can settle into the work of healing the relationship from within. With all its tasks and challenges that force you to grow, the work will be worthwhile no matter what the outcome.

A new foundation poured over an old, crumbled one is not stable. Any fissures in the bond between you and your child must be carefully sealed before the next foundation can be safely poured. I wrote this book largely to illuminate as many cracks and holes as possible, and to suggest ways to repair them. Once you can seal the gaps, you'll be in a far better position to create a secure base for a closer relationship.

You won't identify with every statement or idea in this book. We're all different, and your family situation is unique. Estrangement itself constitutes far too broad and complex a topic for every circumstance to be covered here. What you take from this book and what you leave is up to you. If something doesn't speak to your situation, or if a piece of advice just doesn't feel right, trust your own judgment. But if you're interested in personal growth as well as reconnection with your child, I hope you'll find something here that resonates with you and supports you in that endeavor.

It will be most effective for you to read this book from the beginning, rather than skipping around. Each concept builds on the previous ones. If you skip around looking for sections that interest you, you won't necessarily have a firm base from which to make the best use of the practical steps outlined. I suggest that you read the entire book before taking any action. Then read it again for support while executing your strategy.

About Me

As a psychotherapist in private practice for more than a decade, I've heard from both angry, frustrated, depressed adult children and bewildered, hurting, rejected parents about their distressed relationships. The information I use in my approach to helping parents repair these bonds includes the actual experiences of people in your shoes. Although what works and what doesn't are not categorical, certain general truths can be mined and used in tackling the problem.

I've never been either an estranged adult child or a rejected parent. I have, as they say, no dog in this fight. As a stepmother, daughter, wife, and sister who is deeply attached to my own family, I have tremendous compassion for anyone estranged from someone they love. Because I haven't been subjected to this hurtful breach myself, I'm free of the bias that inevitably arises from firsthand experience. Based on a thorough review of current research and my own experience listening to the stories of hundreds of suffering parents and estranged adult children, I can take the proverbial "view from thirty thousand feet." Anyone thus removed from the fray can discern patterns that exist outside their own individual story. Free from the wounds and protective instincts born of painful experience, I help parents trace lines of opportunity for healing and repair.

I have no agenda other than to help as many people as I can who are suffering the loss of relationship with loved ones. There's a lot that's broken among modern families, and much of it can be mended. Not all, unfortunately, but more than you might think. I know, because I hear regularly from parents in the Reconnection Club (my online community for estranged parents, at https://reconnectionclub.com) who have managed to make repairs and turn things around with the benefit of an outside perspective and some heartfelt support.

I fell into this rewarding line of work quite by accident. During my internship in graduate school, I was surprised at how many of my adult clients avoided or dreaded contact with their parents. When I asked them to describe the issues that troubled them, it became clear that their parents either wouldn't or couldn't fathom their children's experience. I remember thinking, "Those parents might appreciate hearing a translation from a neutral observer." So when I built a website for my therapy practice in 2008, I posted a couple of articles designed to help parents reconnect with reluctant adult children.

Like many other writers on this topic, I was overwhelmed by the immediate outpouring of communication from estranged parents. Every article I wrote seemed to generate scores of comments and questions. Clearly this painful problem deserved a thoughtful, and much more extensive, response. I wrote my *Guide for Parents of Estranged Adult Children*, a document of just over one hundred pages, to try to address parents' need for assistance. The *Guide* sold in PDF form on my website for a number of years as part of an email-based program of support for parents. Eventually, as the sheer volume of feedback from parents convinced me that the *Guide* should serve a wider audience, I decided to expand it into a book. This is the result.

I believe in the importance, influence, and value of family. My own kin have shaped me into the person I am, and each member of my small clan is precious to me. When I think of what it would feel like to lose connection with them, the pain is almost physical.

My familiarity with the hearts and minds of adults who reject their parents, and my conversations with parents who've managed to repair the rifts, along with my training in psychology and human development, have given me insights into the problem of parent-adult child estrangement. I want to share some secrets with you so that you have the most powerful tools, and possibly new skills, with which to approach the all-important relationship with your child(ren).

I have faith that rifts between family members can be healed if just one person has the fortitude to venture outside their comfort zone. My money's on you, the one who picked up this book. With courage, change is possible even when it seems like there's no reason for hope. It's never too late for things to get better.

Estrangement Changes Everything

That question, "Do you have children?," was so easy at one time. "Yes, I have two," or "Yes, a little girl," was your automatic answer. But it's not that simple anymore. Now you've got an adult child who's not talking to you, and you're not sure what to say when asked about children. You may not even know where he lives. You may have a grandchild you've never met.

How do you answer those painful questions? I'll offer specific ideas about that in chapter 9. And what do you do with the emotions that are constantly triggered? There may be grief and despair, yes, but there might also be resentment and anger. You gave so much of yourself — time, love, money, energy — to your child. How can he repay you by acting this way?

You're reading this book because you want your relationship with your child back. But you also want to emerge from this ordeal without the shadow of all that pain. How will you heal the deep wounds surrounding this rejection? Those hurt feelings need to be resolved, no matter what happens in the future.

If you've read this far, you're likely ready and willing to do some self-reflection. You know it will benefit your personal growth, even if your adult child never comes around (though I hope for both your sakes that's not the case). A bit of navel-gazing is valuable for someone in your shoes — not to punish yourself for mistakes made in parenting, but rather to uncover and get to know your essential, lovable self. This core part of you can lose vitality when you're being held at arm's length by someone you love.

Although you know you're not perfect, you're probably ready to let go of any unnecessary shame that's been weighing you down — maybe starting before the estrangement began. I assume you want to enjoy a healthy level of self-esteem and to maintain good communication with the people most important to you. I believe you also want to be a positive role model (even if only for yourself) and a self-actualized, reasonably content, and fulfilled human being.

Change is possible, both within and without. The greatest burden for estranged parents is unnecessary shame. My purpose is not just to help you repair your relationship with your child, but also to fortify your bond with yourself. Healing from estrangement is an opportunity for intense personal growth if you're up for it. This is true whatever the outcome may be.

No One Wants This

In online forums for rejected parents, younger people are often portrayed as a generation of narcissists ready to kick their parents to the curb at the slightest provocation. Some parents who write about estrangement, especially on the internet, encourage you to view your child as heartless, selfish, materialistic, or easily brainwashed by malevolent others. But if that's the case, how can there be any hope for reconciliation? And why would you even *want* to reunite with someone like that?

Let's get some perspective. For thousands of years, older adults have lamented the selfishness, lack of discipline and sense of duty, not to mention the shameful disrespect, of the younger generation. In his book *The Vanishing American Adult*, US Senator Ben Sasse argues that for at least the past fifty years, age segregation, lack of exposure to hard work, overprotectiveness by parents, and material abundance have created generations of perpetual children — complete with childish sensibilities.[1]

If this is true, where does that leave you? It's too late to go back and try to build your child's character, reduce her selfishness, or help her develop a will toward service, compassion, and respect. The only value now in focusing on your child's (or an entire generation's) lack of character is to take a break from blaming yourself for the current state of your relationship. That's a break that might be necessary if you've been beating yourself up over it. But on the other side of that break, you'll want to seek solutions that don't denigrate you or your child.

No degree of entitlement, materialism, or lack of work ethic can strip an otherwise normal person of their emotional attachments. Even if your child *is* excessively entitled or immature, those deficits in themselves don't explain why he feels the need to reject his parents or other family members. The reasons for this behavior go beyond the limitations of his generation or personality. Believing this is the only stance that allows for solution-focused thinking about this pernicious predicament.

Both in my capacity as a therapist and as a regular citizen, I've talked with adults who are struggling with the decision to cut ties with their parents, have already done so, or have recently reconciled with a formerly rejected parent. I've also followed the research that studies the feelings and motivations of these adult children. By all accounts, these folks take parental estrangement seriously. They feel weighed down by it. It hurts them profoundly to lose connection with a parent, even by their own choice.

Here's what one estranged child wrote in response to one of my posts:

It is awful when you choose to end a relationship... especially when your parent doesn't (maybe even can't) understand what they did wrong. To turn away from them in order to move forward as a healthier person feels absolutely selfish and goes against my instincts to maintain that connection with my mother.

I've heard similar expressions of dismay from my clients, friends, and colleagues who reluctantly avoid their parents. Everyone wants to have parents they love, and who love them back, without chronic trouble or pain between them.

It Cuts Both Ways

Most parents don't get to see the vulnerability and unhappiness in their distancing child. Instead, they're presented only with heated rejection or chilly indifference. No wonder they're sometimes ready to believe they created a monster.

We humans are at our most hurtful to others — our most "monstrous" — when we're in pain ourselves. As the saying goes, hurt people hurt people. It makes sense that your child's rejection, coming as it does from a place of pain, will also be hurtful to you.

Birthdays and holidays produce hot spots of difficult emotions for rejected parents. Even the anticipation of a holiday can elicit dread and despair. But what of the adult child? For every Thanksgiving dinner you endure without your child, watching others gather with their families, she also experiences the holiday without you.

You and your estranged child also share the task of explaining to friends why you won't be getting together with the family for the holidays this year. Believe it or not, it's the same awkward conversation for him that it is for you. Estranged adult children, for the most part, feel unsupported when they share the sensitive information that they're estranged from you. Friends, relatives, and society all pressure them to reconcile.

It's clear that the vast majority of estrangers do not cut ties with their parents on a whim, for purely materialistic reasons, or just because someone else tells them to. So — please don't let me lose you here — contact with Mom or Dad has to be pretty darn painful to be worse than no contact. Don't worry: it's not necessarily as bad as it sounds, and the situation can potentially be mended if you keep an open mind. Let me share some encouraging words from a mom who's now reconnected with her formerly estranged daughter:

> I didn't know what to do, and couldn't work out why my daughter was so angry and hostile towards me, and didn't initiate any contact. I can now appreciate how complex the situation was, and feel able to look at our estrangement more from her perspective.

You and your estranged child are both in uncharted waters; he may not have the words to tell you what went wrong or what he'd like you to do about it. Even if he does, he might use language or examples that only confuse you and leave you feeling helpless. That's why I'm going to give you plenty of ideas to find your way back to him.

Keep a beginner's mind and a compassionate heart as we go forward; you'll need these to make use of the tools offered in these pages. It's a hard truth, but important to understand: for many adult children and their advocates, estrangement is considered a healthy response to an unhealthy situation. They feel better with distance — healthier, and even happier from day to day. I can't stress enough that no one should be forced, coerced, or shamed into participating in relationships that hurt them, either emotionally or physically — even with family. Trying to influence your child in these ways will do more harm than good.

Your child probably views you, your behavior, and your relationship with her as unalterably unsatisfying in some way. It's been easier for her to give up on you than to hope you're willing and able to change. This is what you're up against. If you now want to help her heal, and to be a part of her life again, you've got to convince your child that a relationship with you can be low in stress and high in fulfillment. It's not easy, but there are specific behaviors you can adopt or increase to help make it happen. I'll provide you with multiple ideas to incorporate into your reconciliation strategy.

The Problem of Shame

Healing the rift of estrangement is possible, but shame, guilt, and anger can make the work much harder for parents than it needs to be. Just about any parent, estranged from their kids or not, harbors some degree of shame, regret, or feeling of inadequacy. Some parents hide it better than others, but if you're in touch with reality, you know how easy it is to go wrong when rearing another human being. It's almost impossible *not* to feel inadequate in the face of such a monumental challenge. Nobody gets it 100 percent right — not even close — and shame is the unfortunate by-product of caring how you're doing.

Being concerned about what kind of parent you've been is part of being a good person. Only good people feel bad when they think they might have done something wrong or unwittingly hurt someone. Bad people don't care; probably that's what makes them bad people. Personally, I've never met a bad person in my work with estranged parents. But I have met hundreds of good people who have shame, whether they're in conscious touch with it or not, about not being good enough. And that shame impedes their ability to turn things around. If this is resonating with you, take your time going over the section on self-esteem in chapter 12.

Luck of the Draw

You might think that the more abusive, neglectful, or incompetent the parents, the more likely they are to be cut off the minute their children are old enough to leave. The myth that estrangement springs from only the worst possible parenting is a common misconception that keeps rejected parents up at night.

In my experience, parent-adult child estrangement doesn't occur in lockstep with terrible parenting. Some of the most abusive, neglectful, seemingly incompetent parents enjoy doting behavior from their grown children. Conversely, parents who were conscientious and tried their hardest to give their kids everything they needed can find themselves on the outs with their kids when they grow up.

Estrangement from an adult child can happen to any parent, regardless of how dedicated they were, how much they sacrificed, or how hard they tried to do better than their own parents did with them. There are innumerable factors that contribute, and from what I've seen, luck seems to be one of them. It's easy to forget this when you feel ashamed about being rejected. But shame makes the situation stickier. When you don't feel good enough, that conviction is all-consuming. You can't afford to look at specific things you might do better, because admitting to even one misstep feels like admitting you're utterly bad. One estranged parent wrote this in response to one of my articles:

> This helps a little, but I still do not understand why I am so unlovable.

Unlovable? Where did *that* come from? This comment broke my heart when I read it. Estrangement by a child can tap into dark feelings of low self-worth that were probably present before the estrangement began. The rejection feels raw, personal, and almost overwhelming. That's why it's so challenging to take a neutral, curious stance when adult children create distance. If you suffer from shame, you'll find it too painful to think very hard about any wrong turns you may have taken — until your child sends you a message of anger or silence that you can't ignore.

But wait a minute. Your child's silence may have nothing to do with mistakes you've made. Don't assume you've done anything to invite this rejection if your child hasn't said so. I talk about "normal," no-fault estrangement as part of your child's personal development in chapter 5.

Whether or not the estrangement is acrimonious, many parents become defensive when their adult children don't want to maintain contact. Shame and defensiveness are the enemies of awareness. And unfortunately, there can be no movement, no change, and no healing without awareness.

Shame says, "I don't want to know if I did anything to deserve this; it's too painful to feel that bad about myself." Awareness says, "I want to understand my part in this, even if it's painful."

In order to recover a relationship with your child, you must find a way to put shame aside and invite compassion into your heart. You need to tolerate looking at whatever your child may want to show you if healing is to occur. If there *is* something important for you to learn about the way your child experiences you, you won't be able to see it through a cloud of shame.

You have no option for a considered response as long as shame and defensiveness have you in their grip. Breaking free of these can pave the way for a closer, calmer, and more honest relationship with your child.

This is from a reader of one of my blog posts:

> I had many years of a very painful relationship with my mother. When I was thirty-five there was a breakthrough…she admitted in a letter that she had loved me, but with "white-knuckled love." That moment transformed my life, as I was finally able to know that this deep truth I knew about her love, but could not admit, was true. I became much more able to feel sane!!

Your will toward self-awareness can not only thaw your relationship with your estranged child but can also help her understand herself better. Thus it can be a gift to both of you.

Compassion Is Key

You are a loving, lovable, and still growing version of somebody's child yourself. You may be surprised by the idea that finding compassion in your heart, not just for your child but for *yourself*, can help you overcome estrangement.

Instead of approaching the problem with a right-and-wrong mentality, which pits you and your child against each other, compassion says you're in this together. I see far too many comments from hurting parents that look like this:

> My daughter chose to cut me off after having helped her through lifelong traumas with no appreciation or thankfulness on her part whatsoever. Estrangement between an adult child and a parent is usually the result of this generation's "Give me, give me, give me" attitude, and nothing is ever good enough for these selfish, self-absorbed adult brats.

The harsh tone and the name-calling are clear indications of the amount of pain this mother is in. Yet if reconciliation is the ultimate goal, this us-versus-them mentality can't prevail.

The writer of this comment appears to be hurting too much at the moment to see that she and her daughter are in this together. She's lost sight of her daughter as another unique, still-growing individual. In this comment she demonizes her daughter and an entire generation. This is what happens when we feel powerless against those who hurt us. We become frozen in our anguish, and our hearts become hard.

This parent's pain needs to be acknowledged so that she can begin to heal from the agony of being rejected. Her daughter is not the right person to help her with that, no matter how close they used to be. But that doesn't mean this mom is out of luck. She can (and must, if she wants to heal) receive the compassion she deserves. If there's someone in her life who's understanding and sympathetic, she can cry on that person's shoulder and begin the healing process.

She can talk to a friend, counselor, or cleric who will stand as a caring witness to her suffering. Whatever the outcome of the estrangement, her own healing will facilitate positive change. This mom needs no less than to be heard and cared about — not least by herself — in order for the storm to subside and the waves to calm. Once she addresses and responds with genuine sympathy to her own pain, she can better deal with that of her daughter — who has surely also endured pain, if she's willing to cut ties to her one and only mother.

Every generation needs and deserves compassion — parents, children, children who become parents, their children, and so on, and so on, and so on. We're all in this together.

1 FACES OF ESTRANGEMENT

Family estrangement, according to the researcher Kylie Agllias, is "the condition of being physically and/or emotionally distanced from one or more family members, either by choice or at the request or decision of the other."[1]

But what does that actually look like? Depending on the quality, quantity, and frequency of contact, estrangement can have many different manifestations. You may see your child frequently, but each meeting leaves you feeling empty and depressed because of the emotional distance between you. Or it may be years since you've seen your child or had any word from her at all. You don't know where she lives or whether she's married or has a job, let alone children of her own.

It seems to me that estrangement can be roughly divided into three types: total cutoff, emotional estrangement, and on-and-off estrangement. There are variations on these, and the categories may overlap. But let's look at each one.

Total Cutoff

My grandmother left home when she was still a teenager, and she never looked back. Her children, including my mother, never met their grandparents on that side of the family. It was total cutoff, physical and emotional. As far as my mother knows, her mother never spoke to her parents for the rest of her life.

It's not known how often estrangement becomes lifelong. When my grandmother left her parents' house in rural Brazil in the late 1920s, there were no private telephones, let alone cell phones, email, internet, or social media. Even if my great-grandparents had wanted to reach out to their daughter, in those days they had no way to look for her after she moved away.

With every decade in modern history it's become harder to disappear, which means it's easier than ever to find someone if you want to try to reconnect. Obviously, finding them is not the only issue. Knowing what to do after you locate your child is the most important way to ensure that estrangement doesn't last forever.

Emotional Estrangement

Estrangement doesn't always mean cutoff. Some parents feel estranged from their adult children even with regular social contact. The problem is that they begin to feel like strangers or intruders to their kids, rather than close and comfortable as they once did. Their contact lacks real emotional connection. Instead, it feels limited and even strained.

Maria and Miguel (not their real names) had three sons. Arturo, the youngest, had a special bond with his mother. As a child, he loved helping her with the shopping and often asked her to sit with him while he finished his homework. Maria was happy to oblige, as it meant spending quality time with her sweet youngest child.

As he grew older, Arturo asked Maria for advice about relationships, career, and just about anything that was on his mind. Unlike his friends who began emotionally distancing themselves from their mothers as teenagers, Arturo always seemed to appreciate his relationship with Maria.

Even after earning a degree in finance, getting a good job, leaving his parents' home, and starting to date seriously, Arturo kept in regular contact with his parents. He and Maria would often meet for lunch, take walks, go to the movies, and chat on the phone.

Then Arturo met Eva, and the two quickly married. Maria and Miguel rejoiced for their youngest son. Their family had already expanded with the marriage of one of Arturo's older brothers, and Maria pictured the next few decades filled with joyful family gatherings that included Arturo, Eva, and — who knows? — maybe a grandchild or two.

But from the beginning, Eva didn't seem interested in spending time with Maria and Miguel. Any event that brought the family together was generally short-lived. Eva would complain of a headache, or she would need to get up early in the morning the next day; there was always a reason why Arturo and Eva couldn't stay longer than an hour or two.

Soon, Arturo himself became too busy to meet Maria for lunch or shopping. He would always return her calls, though not necessarily right away, and he would decline invitations more often than not. On the rare occasions when they were alone together, the conversation felt forced. Gone was the natural, wide-ranging, and playful chatter Maria had enjoyed with her son.

Arturo refused to listen to Maria's mild complaints about his wife's aloofness. He always defended Eva, even when she did something Maria found hurtful. Maria was shocked at her son's unwillingness to try to facilitate a warmer relationship between his mother and his wife. Why didn't he seem to care if they got along?

Something between Maria and Arturo had changed, and even though they were still in touch and lived only a few miles apart, she felt she'd lost him. His dwindling availability and apparent loyalty to someone who appeared to dislike Maria threatened to make the change permanent. It was as though she and her son were destined to become strangers.

Emotional estrangement can be every bit as painful as total cut-off, though in a different way. Sometimes the solution to emotional estrangement, if there is one, is to repair a damaged relationship with your child. But sometimes the repair that's required is inside you.

Often, both may be needed, which is why we'll talk as much about you as we will about your child in later chapters.

On Again, Off Again

Somewhere between my grandmother's total cutoff and Maria's there-but-not-there relationship with Arturo lies yet another version of estrangement: the on-again, off-again kind. Agllias refers to this as *cyclical estrangement*.

A few years ago, I received an email from a formerly estranged mother. She was excited to tell me that she and her husband had managed to reconcile with their son, who hadn't spoken to them in over a year. Not only did they reconcile, she said, but apparently the son was planning to move back in with his parents! (I know what you're thinking: "Is this supposed to be a success story?")

The son did move back in, and unfortunately, less than a year later, I received a far less happy note from his mother. She reported that although her son still lived under the same roof, he'd once again ceased communicating with his parents. "He stays in his room all the time now," this despairing mom told me. "He even keeps the cat in there with him. We're not allowed to have contact with the cat."

It may be unusual for a complete cutoff to become a roommate situation overnight, as happened in this family. But this pattern of "now we're talking, now we're not" is a common form of estrangement between adult children and their parents. Pressure from social networks and the culture at large cause some adult children to reconcile with their parents even when the cause(s) of the estrangement haven't yet been addressed.

Personal ambivalence and a desire for connection with family (i.e., internal pressures) also draw formerly estranged children back into their parents' lives. However, when the underlying causes of estrangement are not attended to, the off-again part of the cycle is likely to repeat. If this pattern describes your relationship with your child, finding and addressing the difficulty with being close is key.

How to Tell If You're Estranged

There's no diagnostic definition of estrangement. But essentially, if someone isn't talking to you because of a negative relationship, or if communication between you is so difficult or distressing for one or both of you that it's minimized, the two of you are probably estranged.

Estrangement can involve an absence of feelings, negative feelings, no contact, low-quality contact (e.g., conflict), or low-frequency contact. Estranged people may see each other regularly, sporadically, or never. They might talk on the phone, only via text or email, or not at all.

In my experience, the more of the following statements you agree with in the context of your relationship, the more likely it is that you're estranged:

"I miss the relationship we used to have."

"Our contact often doesn't go well."

"I find myself walking on eggshells around this person."

"I'm worried about the growing distance between us."

"This person often misinterprets my intentions."

"I've felt hurt by this person."

"When I reach out, I don't get a response."

"I'm in pain over this relationship."

"Sometimes I'm afraid to reach out."

"This person has negative feelings toward me."

Affirmative responses to five or more of the statements above are a good indication that you're currently estranged. But you probably knew that already. If there's any good news here, it's that you have loads of company.

You're Not Alone

Most parents who consult with me about estrangement from their adult children feel as though they're the only ones with this problem. All their friends seem to enjoy close contact with their children, and so they wonder, "What's wrong with us?"

Statistically, many parents are vulnerable. Estrangement between parents and adult children is widespread and might even be on the rise as family networks shrink and geographical distance grows. A lack of data from before the present century makes it tough to determine whether estrangement is on the rise. But it's estimated that at least one in ten mothers — and possibly even more fathers — are estranged from at least one of their adult children.[2]

The definition of an epidemic is any occurrence greater than what would normally be expected. That's it. No numbers, no threshold. Just any incidence of a thing that's greater than we expect. Given that we live in a society that expects families to love each other and seek continuing contact for life, *any* incidence of parent-adult child estrangement is, by definition, an epidemic.

Because of the stigma still associated with this type of estrangement, people are often uncomfortable talking about it. But that doesn't stop them from needing to talk. Rejected and abandoned parents, and their troubled adult children, turn to the internet in droves, seeking solutions to their pain and an outlet for their thoughts and feelings.

Here are some search phrases that brought people to my website one day while I was writing my original guide:

"My son doesn't communicate with me."
"Should kids be in parents' will when they don't speak to parents?"
"My adult children have become selfish toward me."
"Can my estranged father cut me out of his will without signing it?"
"Rejected by adult child"
"Daughter-in-law won't let us see grandkids"
"Why do today's adult children not say thank you to their parents?"
"How often should I let my mom see her grandson?"

Those are just from one day. Multiply this list by hundreds, and you'll start to appreciate the scope of the problem. Thousands of such searches take place on the internet every week. If you've sought help for estrangement online, you have company.

What the Research Says So Far

Research on estrangement is sparse but seems to be gathering steam. There's virtually no quantitative information from the twentieth century, and it's only in the last decade or two that the topic's been garnering interest. That's why it's impossible to say whether what you're experiencing is on the rise. We just don't have the data. But remember my grandmother? She disappeared from her parents' lives almost a hundred years ago. If you look back into the roots of your own family tree, you might well find estrangement there, too.... Oh, and there are a couple of mentions of parent-child estrangements in the Bible, too.

Coming back to the present, here's some of what we've learned from the research so far. Prevalence estimates regarding family estrangement vary widely, from single digits to almost 30 percent. One study involving college students found that 43 percent of them reported experiencing "a definite estrangement" from someone in their family.[3] But a conservative estimate endorsed by the researcher Kristina Scharp is 12 percent.[4]

Estrangement from Dad may be more prevalent than from Mom.[5] Most research subjects in this area have been women, and we know very little about fathers' and sons' experiences of estrangement. Like most therapists, I see more women than men in my practice. But the fathers I work with are as wounded by estrangement as any mother I've sat with. In fact, it's been suggested that alienation from their children may even contribute to suicide rates among fathers.[6]

It probably won't surprise you that divorce is often a precursor to estrangement. However, in one study only 2.3 percent of adult children cited divorce as the primary reason for their estrangement from a parent.[7] Divorce per se doesn't cause estrangement. Instead, it can reveal and aggravate hidden fault lines in families. Depending on the temperature and tone of the divorce, it can intensify existing negative feelings between parents and children.[8] In addition, divorce is usually associated with other relationship stressors such as negative emotion, inadequate communication, relocation, financial restriction, and loss of support.

Adult children who report having felt close to a parent during adolescence are less likely to become estranged later on, whereas high conflict with a parent during adolescence is assumed to be a risk factor for estrangement in adulthood.[9] If you had a contentious relationship with your teenager, you've got some work ahead of you that may involve revisiting the past in a purposeful way. I'll talk about how to do that later.

Estrangement from parents may be more common among communities that are marginalized or stigmatized, such as the LGBTQ community. It's easy to understand why that would be; some parents are devastated by their child's revelation of a nonconforming sexuality or gender identity. There might be other issues as well, but accepting your child as he is, and communicating that fact clearly and often, can heal estrangement based solely on gender or sexual identity.*

Under the heading "Factors You Never Realized Would Have an Impact," is the following: having a small family, or having strained or nonexistent ties with extended family, increases estrangement risk.[10] A smaller family network makes it easier to maintain estrangement and may therefore support estranging behavior. You can't double or triple the size of your family overnight to avoid this risk, but you can begin to strengthen any ties you have with extended family. If it doesn't help with your child, it could still be pleasant for you to connect with kin.

What do we know about the causes of estrangement? For one thing, parents are more likely to blame external circumstances — such as divorce or third-party interference — than children are. Adult children are far more likely to identify personal, negative characteristics of their parents as the cause(s) of estrangement.[11]

---

* For ideas on how to support your LGBTQ child, contact PFLAG at https://pflag.org.

An online survey found that while around 66 percent of adult children say they've told their parents the reason for the estrangement, 60 percent of parents claim their child has not explained the cutoff at all.[12] That disconnect alone explains the ongoing nature of many an estrangement. I suppose it's possible that either adult children or their parents aren't telling the whole truth. However, to me it seems more likely that both are conveying the truth as they see it. If conversations between my husband and me are any indication, it's perfectly possible to be convinced you were never told something that the other person is equally sure they told you.

Major factors that contribute to distancing behavior, according to adult children, include the following:

- feeling a lack of support, acceptance, or love from the estranged family member
- feeling like their parent's behavior is, or has been, unacceptable or toxic
- choosing one relationship over another
- having different values from one another[13]

As I mentioned in the introduction, adult children often feel pressured by family, friends, society, and their own consciences to reconcile. They report uncertainty, doubt, and feelings of loss surrounding their decision.[14] This leads many to fall into that on-again, off-again pattern of communication with parents described earlier.

But as long as the factors that led your child to create distance remain in place, he will not be able to settle into an easy, relaxed, loving, and close relationship with you again. Don't focus overly on factors uncovered by researchers that may or may not apply to you. Instead, search your own relationship with your adult child for clues as to what caused — and may be maintaining — the rift between you. At the same time, keep in mind Nature's imperative for your child to strike out on his own, independent of family, as he settles into adulthood. We all have developmental needs that must be respected. I say much more about that in chapter 5.

Your Personal Clues

When parents speak with me about their estranged adult children, they often go into minute detail about character and plot: a divorce that bred resentment; an ex who turned the child against them; a new girlfriend, boyfriend, or spouse who's encouraging the child to cut himself off from his family. Sometimes there's a diagnosed or suspected mental health disorder that a parent will quietly point out as if to say, "See? My child has issues."

No matter what the story or who the players, parental accounts tend to be full of details about phone calls and emails not returned, parental generosity met with stony-hearted unresponsiveness. It's a play-by-play of cruel rejection and abandonment.

It's a relief for parents to be able to finally talk about their experience to someone who cares. There may not be many outlets for that in their social circles; or maybe they're afraid to even try to garner support. Their need to tell someone what's going on, to be heard and understood, is palpable. So is the pain that haunts their stories. There's a huge and understandable need to be seen, heard, and understood.

Estranged parents' emotional vulnerability can paradoxically create a barrier that makes it difficult for them to mend the rift. They don't quite get what their child is hurt, angry, or upset about. It's nearly impossible to listen well when it feels like you're under attack. The natural response is to close up, rather than remain open and get burned by flaming arrows flung by your child or a judging society.

Here is a typical email from a parent who feels under siege:

My daughter, age 45, has decided to be estranged...now into 18 months. She is divorced now and seems to be blaming me for that also. We were ever so close, and I don't know why she is mad. She is perceiving everything in a total unrealistic state of mind. I have been ever so patient and feel at times I just cannot take another day of this. She verbally abuses me via email.

She actually nominated me Mother of the Year when she was a senior in college. Apparently, someone or something has changed her thinking, and I can't get her thinking back on track. I am going to a counselor, but she won't go at all. I struggle daily with this, have difficulty sleeping, miss her dearly.

This obviously beleaguered and desperate mother says outright, "I don't know why she is mad," although it seems there might be some clues in those verbally abusive emails her daughter sends her. What does her daughter say in those messages? What has she said before to her mother about why she's annoyed? Whatever it is, the daughter's message probably feels too much like an enemy onslaught to be of interest beyond what it takes to defend against it.

Here's another typical story:

My daughter screamed & yelled at me over the phone, just because I asked her a simple computer question. I told her I would not tolerate this disrespect anymore, now she refuses to talk to me after I wrote her a letter saying I want us to get back to having a relationship. She didn't answer or acknowledge it.

One thing is fairly certain. Unless someone is severely mentally ill, they're not likely to scream and yell just because someone asks a computer question. While this mom may genuinely not have a clue as to what caused the outburst, chances are there's something her daughter has tried more than once to explain to her, without success. Again, it's impossible to listen well when you're feeling attacked.

A Long Fuse

Although parents often tell me they don't know why their child is angry or silent, the theme I heard constantly in the therapy room when I was

working with estranged children was "My parent doesn't listen to me."
Here are a few examples:

> "I've told my dad over and over again that Karen and I are no
> longer together, and yet he still asks me about her every
> time we talk."
> "I've asked my parents to call before they come over, but they
> continue to drop by unannounced."
> "My mother seems shocked that we stopped letting her babysit,
> even though I warned her we'd do that if she didn't start
> respecting our rules for the kids."

No matter how sudden or abrupt it might seem, estrangement usually has causes that reach back in time. Think about how long you've
been feeling under attack by your child. She's probably been frustrated
by your "cluelessness" (a word that's common in estranged children's
accounts of their parents) for much longer than that.

The full story of how things came to be this way between you almost always begins years earlier, even if the origins are not obvious.
If you're willing to dig for them, some of the roots of today's troubles
with your child are there to be found. The challenge is that what you're
digging for doesn't feel like treasure. It can feel more like something
toxic that should stay buried — or something imaginary, existing only
in your child's unforgiving mind.

Just thinking about your child's reasons for staying away can feel
like you're opening yourself up to another attack. But there's no one
here right now but you. No one can attack you if you allow yourself to
relax and let down your defenses here, in private.

As you think about the root causes of your estrangement from
your adult child, uncomfortable feelings will likely arise. They might
include the following:

- resentment
- shame

- anger
- guilt
- despair
- grief
- and/or something else

You might bounce around from one yucky emotion to another to another within minutes. Let those feelings come up, and keep all your muscles relaxed while you do this. Feelings can't do any serious damage; they're just feelings.

Don't let self-criticism or scary emotions push you into paralysis. Just notice that you're condemning yourself (or your child), say hello to shame or resentment or any other ugly feeling that pokes its head up, and let it move through you. Emotions last only a minute if you let them be. In the big picture, how you feel is not the problem; the estrangement from your child is the problem.

By the way, the more you can understand and tolerate your own emotions, the better you'll feel overall.[15] Instead of acting out feelings (by saying or doing things you regret at one extreme, or isolating yourself at the other), you'll be able to speak more calmly and honestly to yourself and others. Once you realize the truth about emotions, you'll have a new sense of freedom around them. The truth is this: your own feelings can't hurt you any more than you've already been hurt.

For now, realize that parental cluelessness about the cause(s) for estrangement is a source of irritation that sends many an adult child running for the hills when the phone rings. More likely, they'll just block your number. If you feel a little clueless yourself, I hope that reading this book will increase your understanding and confidence.

Us versus Them

As I've already mentioned, when you're hurt there's a natural tendency to adopt an us-versus-them mentality. The human brain loves black-and-white categories, and two of its favorite pairings are "us versus them" and "right versus wrong." Estrangement can seem like a case of both when your child believes something that, from your point of view, just isn't true. If only your child could see that her perception is off, this whole ugly chapter in your lives could come to an end. Unfortunately, she's convinced of exactly the same thing — only from her point of view, it's your perception that's faulty.

Here's an example of us-versus-them thinking from a mother who responded to one of my blog posts:

> For all the complaints about the grief parents may inflict on children, children inflict far more worry, stress, and pain on parents. At least parents usually love their children. They at least do it innocently and out of concern. Besides, unwanted advice and things like that are hardly traumatizing, to anyone but a millennial.

What a zinger there at the end! It can be soothing in the short term to feel like you're an innocent bystander and your child is being unreasonable. And that might even be true. But assuming your goal is reconciliation rather than placing blame, it just doesn't matter. Reconciliation requires that both parties get past the us-versus-them and right-versus-wrong thinking that keeps you on opposite sides of the problem. You can't choose your child's attitude, but you can choose your own.

Even if you accept that one of you needs to go first in opening up to the other's point of view, and that it probably has to be you, black-and-white thinking can reassert itself at any time. This parent expresses the anger and frustration that long-term rejection can propagate:

> My daughter is an adult. The things she said are out of line and unforgivable. Parents need to take back their power, at least over their own lives and happiness. It starts young. The first time they ignore a text, parents should turn off the phone. We

need to stop begging, stop being pitiful, stop needing THEIR approval, and stop worrying about what they think or if they like us.

The momentary good and powerful feeling of "us" being "right" comes at a price. As long as we indulge in viewing estrangement as a conflict between good and evil, as it were, we're stuck on our own side, with no bridge across. Yes, it can feel good and right to react to your child's behavior as this parent describes. But that makes your child bad and wrong. Ultimately, no parent delights in their child being either of those things. Claiming the moral high ground is a losing strategy for estranged parents who want to become just plain parents again.

Go ahead and feel frustrated, if you do, and annoyed at the idea of catering to your child's selfish, unreasonable, or immature whims. But if you want to get your relationship back, don't let that frustration dictate your policy toward your child. We'll revisit this notion when we talk about your "doormat alarm" in chapter 6.

Dos and Don'ts

Before we go deeper in exploring the roots of estrangement and productive strategies to heal it, here's a list of quick dos and don'ts for parents estranged from adult children. The rest of this book will fill in the details around these rules of thumb.

- **Don't place blame.** Not on yourself, your child, or society at large. Blame is not constructive.
- **Take responsibility.** Whoever wants a better relationship has the responsibility to make it better. See the section "Taking Responsibility versus Accepting Blame" in chapter 6.
- **Balance activity with passivity.** Plan to spend more time waiting than taking action. Time and silence can contribute mightily to the healing process.

- **Concentrate on the process, not the outcome.** There are no short-cuts back to your child. Assume that rebuilding the relationship will take longer than you wish, and focus on today.
- **Don't stop living.** Cultivate relationships, meaningful activities, good health, and anything else that will nurture you during stretches of silence between you and your child. Focusing solely on the problem won't bring your child back faster. And focusing elsewhere won't push your child further away.
- **Forgive mistakes.** You're only human, not perfect. You're doing your best. So is your child.
- **Embrace "I'm sorry."** Start by apologizing to yourself for what you've been through. Start viewing apologies as packets of love and goodwill rather than humiliating admissions of guilt.
- **Don't seek reassurance from your child.** If you know in your heart of hearts that you're doing the right thing, stay your course even if no feedback is forthcoming.

If some of these rules don't sit right with you now, go ahead and skip the ones that don't fit. But stay open to being convinced that these are crucial tasks to master, both for your own evolution and to repair your relationship with your child.

Risk Factors for Estrangement

The list of factors thought to contribute to estrangement between parents and adult children is long. It includes lack of acceptance, lack of support, toxic behavior, choosing one relationship over another, having different values, abuse, neglect, poor parenting, betrayal, stillbirth and miscarriage traumas, parental incarceration, drug abuse, contentious divorce, disagreements, romantic relationships, politics, homophobia, money issues, business concerns, physical or mental health problems, family size, and geographical distance.[16] Just for starters.

In counseling, I like to keep things as simple and practical as possible. Instead of focusing on a limitless field of possible contributing factors, I try to help parents drill down into the most basic, causative ones in their particular case. It's impossible to solve a problem you don't understand. And at this point, it's probably too late for you to avoid all the pitfalls that might have contributed to the present circumstances. But understanding the basic chopping blocks (as opposed to building blocks) of disconnection will help you form a strategy to change the picture.

Although every family's story is unique, I believe there are four main contributors to parent–adult child estrangement:

1. Family history
2. Communication problems
3. Unmet needs in the parent
4. Normal human development

Of these, only three involve negative feelings. Almost by definition, estrangement is a communication problem, so that factor at least is surely in play. Your case may involve only communication problems, another one or two of the above, or all four. If all four factors are influencing the tension between you and your child, things can feel pretty complicated — because they are. In the next four chapters we'll explore these factors in depth, with the understanding that none of them exists in isolation.

Before we do that, pause for just a moment and think about which of these elements — family history, communication problems, unmet needs in the parent, a phase of development — seem like they might be playing a part in your child's behavior. Your first instinct about what's going on could prove to be accurate, so remember your answer.

Even if you can't see their connection to your particular situation, each of these factors offers a line of inquiry with the potential for massive personal growth. Your growth is the fuel for healing your relationship with your child, so let's get started.

2 FAMILY HISTORY

When rejected parents ask me if family estrangement is a new thing with this generation, I usually respond by telling them the story my grandmother, who turned her back on her parents nearly a hundred years ago. Often, the parent will grow quiet. Then they'll say something like "Actually, my dad didn't talk to my grandfather for most of my childhood," or "Now that I think about it, my grandmother had a sister she never spoke to." If that's the case, I don't have to bring up the fact that estrangement is referenced more than once in the Bible. I've already made my point.

Estrangement per se isn't new, and that makes sense because it tends to run in families. For some, emotional cutoff is a fruit that grows on every branch of the family tree; it's *familiar*, in the literal sense of the word. The history of estrangement in a family can reach back many generations. It can become the default way of handling conflict, getting passed down from one generation to the next like a not-so-tasty meatloaf recipe. In families like this, estrangement may still be experienced as distressing, but it's accepted as something that happens.

Children who grow up around estranged relationships unfortunately come to see them as normal. They don't realize that there are alternatives to not speaking to someone when there's a problem.

Emotional cutoff may still be experienced as distressing in these families, but it's accepted as something that happens on occasion, whether you like it or not. If this is the case on either side of the family, an unfortunate precedent has been set for how conflict plays out.

When I'm working with parents individually, or reading their stories in the Reconnection Club forums, I often discover that they had, or still have, a troubled relationship with one or both of their own parents. They may be estranged, in which case they have an uncomfortable understanding of their child's position. But more often, they're not estranged from a difficult parent, and this presents a challenge: there's a sense of "I put up with my mother, and she's ten times worse than me; why can't you cut me some slack?" The emotional bank account (see later in this chapter) needs to be topped up.

Understanding that you and your child are part of a larger pattern can alleviate shame and dread. You didn't create the pattern, but you may be able to change it with some thoughtful, informed effort. You could be the one who ushers in a better way of relating for your family. Your grandchildren, and their grandchildren, can inherit relationship-repair skills instead of learning the art of the silent treatment. Connectedness can be your family's new legacy.

It takes energy to swim against the current. Estrangement may be such a familiar state that reuniting seems like too much trouble. I received this note from an estranged adult child:

> I cut my parents out of my life 4 years ago. I recently tried to get back in contact with them and they have decided my decision was for the best and to leave it as it is. Sometimes you can't go back....I knew when I cut them out originally that it was the right decision at that time; maybe in reflection I should not have been so hasty.

If you felt a twinge of "Serves that kid right," it only goes to show how hurt you are by your child's behavior. A little vicarious payback can feel good. But there's no real win.

While a family history of estrangement makes it more likely to occur, the past doesn't have to dictate the future. It's possible that your great-grandchildren will never have to witness estrangement firsthand, and that their kids will grow up not knowing that emotional cutoff is even an option.

Choosing Sides

A particularly dark thread that runs in families is parental alienation, in which one parent, usually (but not always) after a separation or divorce, attempts to turn their child(ren) against the other parent. The alienating parent targets the other parent by bad-mouthing them in front of the children, making visitation difficult or impossible, encouraging the children in a hundred different ways to reject them, and using a plethora of other relationship-damaging behaviors. Minors in the custody of an alienating parent often have no choice but to go along with the shunning.

Young children who suffer from what's called parental alienation syndrome may express dislike or anger toward the alienated parent, but they may not be able to give coherent reasons for those feelings. Because of a multitude of factors, including maturation, difficulties with the alienating parent, going into therapy, and becoming parents themselves, adult children may be less likely to exhibit rigid and unreasonable dislike of the alienated parent the way younger children can. But they do suffer from far-reaching problems as a result of growing up steeped in the loyalty bind created by the alienating parent.[1]

When you were growing up, did one of your parents speak ill of the other, or try to keep you from seeing them? Did you feel you couldn't speak positively about one of your parents in front of the other? If so, you may be at greater risk not only of depression, alcohol or drug problems, low self-esteem, and divorce, but also of being alienated from your own children.[2] In addition, you're more likely to experience a lack of trust in yourself and others, which makes relationships harder.

If you've been alienated from your child(ren) by their other parent, and there's no other reason why your child might be justified in seeking distance from you, don't give up, even though the odds of contact or connection might seem slim. Find ways as soon as possible to let your child(ren) know that you love them and are there for them. If they're still minors in the custody of the other parent, you may need to seek legal recourse in order to communicate with them. If you were an alienated child yourself, there could be unconscious forces at work that keep you from being able to fully embrace the relationship even after your child becomes available to you. If this was your experience and you now find yourself alienated from your own child(ren), get therapy.

You might be pleased to know that your ex-spouse's alienating behavior could very well backfire in the long run; relationships between adult children and an alienating parent are often conflicted.

Once children get out from under the psychological control of the alienating parent, assuming they eventually do, the targeted parent can continue, or begin, the work of reconnecting. Even if you were the victim of parental alienation and never retaliated by speaking ill of your ex-spouse, apologizing for your child(ren)'s negative experience is appropriate. You can express regret that they were caught in the middle, that you weren't able to be there for them when they might have needed you, and that they might have suffered because of the negative environment in their childhood home or in their lives after the divorce — none of which was their fault. See the section "How to Apologize" in chapter 8.

The difficulty is timing. Just when your kids are reaching the age of majority, getting out from under the authority of the alienating parent and becoming theoretically available to have a relationship with you, they're in the thick of cultivating the independence of adulthood. This is not a time of life when young people, as a group, are interested in solidifying relationships with parents. (See chapter 5 for much more on this phase of development.) These are the years when they need to test their wings and experience sustained independence for the first time. After all the waiting you've done, it can wear on your patience to have to wait even longer to repair those relationships.

The best you may be able to do with young adult children from whom you've been alienated is to offer them loving thoughts and emotional support while asking nothing in return. Make sure they know that you're available if they want to spend time with you, but that there's no pressure. You understand that they're busy with their lives and activities, and you hope that one day when they're ready, you'll be more a part of each other's lives.

You undoubtedly have much to say to them. There's such a lot of catching up to do. Let your messages be as enthusiastic and as loving as you wish. Reach out regularly. But don't require or expect them to respond. Be available to your child(ren), rather than expecting them to be available to you. Be consistent, but not insistent. With an alienated child, don't take silence to mean they don't care if they hear from you. They do. But reciprocating may take time.

The Emotional Bank Account

The family therapist Ivan Boszormenyi-Nagy described a process in families whereby a cycle of resentment can perpetuate itself through successive generations, based on a kind of pay-it-forward rule.[3] Boszormenyi-Nagy saw family members as having an "emotional bank account" from which withdrawals and deposits are made from outside sources — often parents and children, respectively. For instance, when a parent treats a young child like a friend (or an enemy) or helper instead of a child who must be nurtured consistently, withdrawals are made from the child's emotional bank account. To balance things out, the child might later seek deposits from his own children. Without realizing it or meaning to, we play out the story of "This was done to me, and now it's my turn to do it to you."

We're all influenced by our families' unconscious problematic intra- and interpersonal relationships. We're driven by a need to make up for withdrawals from our emotional bank accounts. There's no shame or blame in this pattern. It goes too far back to name a villain. We know for sure that if you're caught in a pattern that's negative, you didn't create it, and it's not your fault. However, you do need to understand how it works if you want to take control from here on out, and to live the life you want to live — including a satisfying relationship with your currently estranged adult child.

One of the invisible ways that emotional bank accounts affect parent-child relationships is in expectations for the relationship. Susan swore she would give her kids more attention than she got from her own parents. She would drive them to all their activities and attend their sporting events. She would be the "cool mom" who'd let kids hang out at her house and provide first-rate snacks. She'd make a point of really showing up in all the ways she missed out on as a child. Being a mother became not just a job, but a calling.

Susan's emotional bank account was depleted from a childhood blighted by an apparent lack of interest and attention from her parents. To avoid re-creating that experience with her own kids, she tried to be the best mother she could be. Unconsciously she was devising a way to try to rebalance her own emotional bank account. She invested heavily in her kids' emotional well-being, hoping on some level that her efforts would bear fruit by bringing her love, attention, and affection from her kids for the rest of her life. At last someone would give her the love she needed and deserved.

While Susan's kids did love her, other relationships called to them as they grew up. They often preferred the company of friends and sweethearts to that of their mother, and they became irritated when she "interfered" by trying to stay involved in their lives. Unaware of her own expectation of repayment for the years of generosity she'd bestowed on her children, and of her heightened sensitivity to rejection caused by her own childhood experience, Susan was dumbfounded, hurt, and angered by her children's desire for more distance. They felt burdened by her unacknowledged need for them to make her feel accepted and loved. And they expressed their resentment through complaints about a thousand small things she said or did that irritated them. The real problem could not be addressed until Susan was able to witness her own expectations, her long-standing feelings of rejection from childhood, and the legitimate but unmet needs that gave rise to them.[4]

Self-awareness, along with generous self-care, is the antidote to seeking reassurance, understanding, regular expressions of affection, and other emotional goodies from your children. Your emotional needs are important. And at the same time, asking your grown children to meet those needs can contribute to your child's estrangement. That's why we'll talk much more about self-care in chapter 4 and elsewhere.

Attachment Styles

When you were a child, your parents' level of sensitivity and responsiveness to your needs helped you feel secure in your relationship to them, or not so secure, at a very deep level.* This was your first exposure to relationships, and unless you've intentionally worked on changing the way you "do" relationships, your attachment style today is still influenced by those early years. When you cried as a child, who picked you up and soothed you? When you were hungry or cold, how long did it take before someone noticed and responded? How did your caregivers react when you were unhappy?

To the extent that a child can rely on caregivers to provide appropriate and timely responses to their needs, that child will develop a healthy level of trust and the ability to reach out to others for emotional support when needed. The lucky child enjoys what's known as a *secure attachment* to her parents. Of course, individual temperament too has an influence on how children behave when relating to others. But a child with a skittish, introverted temperament and a secure attachment will behave differently from a child with a skittish, introverted temperament who's insecurely attached. The first will be able to function better socially, emotionally, and perhaps even cognitively than the second.[5]

---

* This is a central tenet of attachment theory. For a wonderfully thorough overview of the history and main concepts of this theory, see Inge Bretherton, "The Origins of Attachment Theory: John Bowlby and Mary Ainsworth," *Developmental Psychology* 28 (1992): 759–75, available at http://www.psychology.sunysb.edu/attachment /online/inge_origins.pdf.

Are you thinking about your child or children as you read this? Try to think about yourself instead. You'll gain more insight by focusing on your own childhood in this chapter than by reviewing your parenting and its possible effects on your child. Understanding your own experience, past and present, will give you the knowledge, flexibility, and presence of mind to make the changes you want to see with your child.

In contrast to secure attachments, *insecure attachments* result from a mismatch between children's emotional needs and their parents' responses. For example, if your tears as a baby were met with frustration or anger instead of sympathy and attentiveness, that was a mismatch. If, when you were angry, food was shoveled into your mouth, that was another mismatch. Insecure attachments can be thought of as broadly consisting of two types: *anxious* and *avoidant*. These become attachment *styles* that continue into adulthood and affect our relationships with important others.

You've probably heard of the stereotypical couple where the woman always wants to be close and the man prefers to keep a certain emotional distance. In fact, the "pursuer" (usually characterized as female) and the "distancer" (usually cast as male) can be of either sex. The pursuer in a classic pursuer-distancer relationship is most likely to exhibit an anxious attachment style. This style of attachment tends to make us preoccupied with staying emotionally connected to loved ones when in distress. Anxious parents with estranged adult children are living their worst nightmare: someone they love is unavailable to them. If you have an anxious attachment style, recognize that your child's distance is only part of the problem. The other part is your intense reaction to it, which can cause you to continually (and unconsciously) act in ways that encourage your child to maintain distance. It's a vicious circle.

An avoidant attachment style is associated with dismissive behavior toward loved ones — a stance under stress of "I don't need you anyway." The distancer in the pursuer-distancer relationship often presents with this attachment style. Avoidant parents with estranged adult children are no less pierced by the poisoned arrow of rejection than their anxious counterparts. Their behavior in response may be different, but their pain is comparable. However, they may maintain or even increase the distance in subtle ways to avoid being hurt further.

Research has shown that parents with insecure attachment styles have more trouble parenting than those who enjoy a secure attachment style.[6] Their parental behavior is less consistent than that of their securely attached peers. They may also be less accepting and more intrusive than securely attached parents and may be more likely to adopt an authoritarian or permissive parenting style than an authoritative one. The latter is associated with a medley of better outcomes. Blurred boundaries and role reversal between parents and children are not uncommon when the parent is insecurely attached.[7]

Women with insecure attachments are more likely to experience separation anxiety from their children than securely attached mothers. In both mothers and fathers, anxious attachment correlates with less constructive parental behaviors, such as more yelling and less collaboration and problem solving.[8]

Insecurely attached parents are more likely to have negative thoughts about the parent-child bond, such as a belief that their children don't like them. Parental stress in general is measurably greater among those who are insecurely attached.

If you have an insecure attachment style, you're currently at a disadvantage in trying to repair your relationship with your child. Insecure attachment makes it harder to offer compassion to others and to engage in altruistic behaviors, both of which facilitate relationships in general, and reconciliation in particular.[9]

As Mario Mikulincer and his fellow researchers put it, "Only a relatively secure person can easily perceive others not only as sources of security and support, but also as suffering human beings who have important needs and therefore deserve support."[10] It's as though parents with insecure attachment styles are twice burned — once by the original wounding that created the insecurity, and again by the effects of its aftermath on relationships.

If you've been hoping for some good news in this section, here it is: attachment styles are not set in stone. You can move toward a more secure style by seeking positive relationships in which your emotional needs are not only noticed but acknowledged with consideration and appropriate care. A good mental health counselor or therapist provides a model for this type of relationship (see "Support for the Parent: Using a Therapist" in chapter 7 for details), but in theory you can have a secure attachment with any trustworthy, responsive person.

Ideally, you have a secure attachment with your spouse or partner. For many couples, however, this doesn't happen naturally. If needed, couples therapy can help you provide a secure base and a safe haven for each other, so that you can become more securely attached and enjoy all the relationship-enhancing qualities that secure attachment bestows. These include the ability to make desirable changes in the way you interact with your child(ren). Be aware, however, that changing your attachment style takes clarity, courage, information, and time. There's no overnight fix.

Anything that helps you grow and thrive as a person can have a positive effect on your relationship with your child. Don't focus exclusively on your estranged son or daughter. Instead, focus on healing what ails *you*, independently of that relationship. When it comes to relating to your child(ren), your own emotional health is of the utmost importance. So work with the resource to which you have the greatest access — yourself. Your attachment style is a good place to start or continue your personal development.

The Specter of Abuse

If you search the internet for forums where estranged parents or adult children congregate, you're bound to run into the word *abuse*. Adult children speak of growing up with an abusive or neglectful parent. Parents speak of children's abusive practices of refusing contact or withholding visitation privileges with grandchildren. The word *abuse* is flung back and forth between "us" and "them," and it often seems to be in the eye of the beholder.

But there is, objectively speaking, such a thing as abuse. Before we look at actual definitions, we must acknowledge an uncomfortable truth: abuse begins at home. About 80 percent of child maltreatment perpetrators are parents mistreating their own children.[11] At best, children who are abused by their parents or other caregivers can grow up feeling in their gut that abusive behavior is normal, even if they learn later on that it's not. At worst, such children may perpetuate abuse by treating their children as they themselves were treated.

There's also such a thing as elder abuse, and many parents unfortunately fall prey to this in their later years or if they become disabled. Parents can be abused physically and emotionally by anyone directly responsible for their care, including their own adult children.

Physical Abuse

In a health-related survey of 17,337 Americans first published in 1998, more than 10 percent of respondents reported having been physically abused as children. Known as the Adverse Childhood Experiences (ACE) study, the report revealed that childhood physical, sexual, and emotional abuse were far from rare, with over 40 percent of respondents claiming one or more of these experiences.[12]

So that we know what we're talking about, let's see what the National Domestic Violence Hotline considers abuse. According to its website, if you experienced or witnessed any of the following behaviors as an ongoing pattern in your household when you were a child, you were physically abused or raised in a household in which there was domestic violence.

- pulling someone's hair, punching, slapping, kicking, biting, or choking them
- forbidding a family member to eat or sleep

- hurting family members with weapons
- preventing family members from calling the police or seeking medical attention
- harming children or pets
- abandoning family members in unfamiliar places
- driving recklessly or dangerously with other people in the car
- forcing family members to use drugs or alcohol[13]

This is not a comprehensive list of physically abusive behaviors; it's just a sample. Do you see anything from your own childhood reflected in that list?

It can take years of conscious and concerted efforts to heal from the effects of growing up with repeated acts of abuse. If you haven't already done so, I hope you'll consider individual or group therapy to address the impact of any childhood physical abuse — not only on your parenting, but on your sense of safety, your understanding of relationships, and your self-esteem.

Emotional Abuse

The following are a few examples of emotional abuse, also drawn from the National Domestic Violence Hotline. If a parent or another adult in a caregiver position repeatedly engaged in the following behaviors toward you when you were growing up, you were emotionally abused:

- calling you names, insulting you, or continually criticizing you
- punishing you by withholding affection
- threatening you or your pets with physical harm
- damaging your property when they were angry (throwing objects, punching walls, kicking doors, etc.)
- humiliating you in any way
- blaming you for the abuse

As if that weren't bad enough, you might also have witnessed emotional abuse between your parents. If so, it's likely that your parents also witnessed such abuse when they were children. Here are some examples, in addition to those above, of spousal emotional abuse:

- refusing to trust; acting jealous or possessive
- trying to isolate the spouse from family or friends
- monitoring where they go, who they call, and who they spend time with
- demanding to know where they are every minute
- trapping them in the home or preventing them from leaving
- using weapons to threaten to hurt them
- threatening to hurt them, the children, their family, or household pets
- accusing them of cheating and being often jealous of their outside relationships
- serially cheating on them and then blaming them for this behavior
- cheating on them intentionally to hurt them, then threatening to cheat again
- cheating to prove that they are more desired, worthy, etc., than their spouse
- attempting to control the spouse's appearance: what they wear, etc.
- telling them they'll never find anyone better, or that the spouse is lucky to be with a person like them

What's considered emotional abuse of children today might have been accepted by previous generations as falling within the range of normal parenting. Being called names or being humiliated by one's parents might even have passed for good-natured teasing when you and I were growing up. The withholding of affection by parents might have been an expected consequence of breaking their rules. It's important to recognize, though, that based on recent understanding of the psychological harm caused by these behaviors, they're now classified as abuse.

To the extent that you've lived with emotional abuse yourself, you may view the behavior you've been exposed to as maybe not ideal, but acceptable. There's no shame in having accepted abusive behavior as normal. But continuing to excuse it nowadays does create trouble in relationships, especially with younger people.

Witnessing or experiencing physical or emotional abuse leaves you vulnerable to repeating the pattern of marrying someone abusive or perpetuating abuse in your own family. If your child claims that there was abuse in your household, you and she may both be abuse survivors. Disclosures of abuse by adult children are challenging not least because they require parents to confront the possibility of their own victimization.

For many parents who haven't yet acknowledged or healed from their own abuse, confronting the harm done to their child is too overwhelming to contemplate, and the conversation goes nowhere after a disclosure is made. In many families, abuse is never discussed, and the cycle may continue in successive generations. Complex trauma often goes untreated where abuse has not been recognized or acknowledged. I strongly recommend therapy with a trauma specialist for everyone who has experienced, or been accused of, physical or emotional abuse. If there are accusations of emotional abuse fueling your child's estrangement, chance are you won't be able to respond adequately without confronting your own history.

Sexual Abuse

In the ACE study cited above, 22 percent of respondents said they'd been sexually abused when they were growing up. That's one in five people.

Childhood sexual abuse (CSA) is too complex a subject to cover adequately here, so I'll limit the discussion to a few general points to consider. For a substantial number of parents with estranged adult children, abuse of any kind is a contributing factor. Even more than physical or emotional abuse victims, survivors of sexual abuse are likely to experience shame, making them vulnerable to retraumatization if and when the abuse is disclosed.

Some of my therapy clients, as well as people in my personal life, have told me about their experience of revealing to a family member that they were sexually abused as children. In a disappointingly large percentage of cases, when victims opened up about the abuse, they were subjected to anger, blaming, or denial. While it's impossible to know how often this happens, I would hazard a guess that these reactions are at least as common as less damaging ones. A parent's responding poorly to a disclosure of CSA is something that many adult children find hard to forgive.

Learning that someone you love has been harmed in any way is agonizing. If that loved one was under your care and protection at the time, the pain can be intolerable. There may be anger, remorse, shame, confusion, and other difficult feelings. These negative emotions can overwhelm, paralyze, and even traumatize you if you're the parent of a child who was sexually abused. It takes fortitude and consistent effort to marshal the presence, compassion, and proactive stance that's needed in response to a disclosure of CSA.

Like other forms of abuse, CSA tends to run in families. You or your spouse may be a sexual abuse survivor. To the extent that you've processed and healed from your own experience, you'll be able to remain more present and responsive when your child makes a disclosure. If you haven't sought counseling to help you heal from what happened to you, you could easily be retraumatized by a disclosure of CSA by your child. If that happens, you probably won't have the resources to respond in a relationship-enhancing way.

If there's a history of disclosed abuse on either parent's side of the family, there's a precedent already set for how to respond to disclosure. Try not to follow a family tradition that involves either avoidance or blaming the victim. Don't deny or question the disclosure. Remember, both boys and girls can be sexually abused, and perpetrators can be either male or female. Don't disbelieve your child. Express your sorrow, your caring, and your desire to be supportive.

Most people don't make up lies about CSA. For the vast majority, there's nothing to gain and much to lose by making accusations of sexual abuse years after the fact. You may know this from your own experience. It takes extraordinary courage for CSA survivors to come forward, both because of others' anticipated negative reactions and because of the internalized shame that so often haunts survivors.

If your estranged child claims CSA, acknowledge the disclosure, take it seriously, and please seek counseling *for yourself* immediately. Whether there was any kind of abuse in your family of origin or not, there is much here to work through before you can be expected to provide your child with what he needs from you after disclosing abuse. If the disclosure happened in the past and you don't like the way you handled it, see if you can revisit it with your child after getting counseling.

The Legacy of Addiction

There are entire books written about alcohol and other kinds of drug dependence, and as I'm no expert in that field, I won't attempt to unpack all the effects and impacts of addiction here. But whether it's alcoholism, other problem drug use, or both, substance abuse by parents deserves a mention in this chapter. Not only does it often play out in multiple generations of the same family, but it can have a grievous impact on family functioning in general and the parent-child relationship in particular.

The first public service announcement I remember seeing on TV that used the "elephant in the room" metaphor to describe alcoholism appeared in the 1970s. In it, a family of four sat in their living room pointedly ignoring a live elephant standing in their midst. Even when it lifted its trunk and trumpeted, every member of the family avoided looking at the elephant. The image has been a popular way of describing the impact of alcoholism on families ever since.

Growing up with a parent or parents who abuse alcohol or other drugs negatively affects a child's development and well-being.[14] One reason for this is that we learn relationship skills first from our earliest caregivers — generally our parents. When they're not available to us either physically or emotionally, when they engage in harmful or abusive behaviors, or when they deny the obvious elephant in the room, we find it much harder than others to develop good relationship instincts. Why? Because these rely on emotional connection — the kind of connection that happens in the very part of the brain that's hijacked by alcohol and other drugs.

Parents with problematic substance use habits don't have full availability, no matter how much they might wish they did, to bond with their children.[15] If you had a parent or parents who regularly drank alcohol or used other drugs to excess, or who were physically, emotionally, or sexually abusive, your own development was negatively affected. If you yourself used drugs, including alcohol, when your child(ren) were still living at home, their development may have been affected, along with the bond you share. Mild, occasional use of drugs by parents, such as drinking a glass of wine with dinner, appears to have far less of an impact than moderate to severe substance use.[16]

There's a difference between watching your parent have a drink while maintaining their personality, habits, and schedule, and coming home to find that parent passed out in the living room, or partying with strangers. The former may not affect a child at all; the latter is disturbing and even frightening for children. Any single event can have a lasting impact on a child's sense of safety and connectedness if it's not effectively addressed. A child who witnesses many such events can experience impairments in relationships, coping skills, and quality of life unless she seeks professional help.

There's an undeniable correlation between parental substance abuse and child abuse, including neglect. One study found that for children who grew up in a home where one or both parents had a problem with alcohol or other drugs, the risk of exposure to physical or sexual abuse was more than twice that of other children.[17] In study after study, parental substance abuse has been linked to neglect and physical, emotional, and sexual abuse.

If you haven't thought about the impact of parental substance abuse on your own childhood, or your children's, it's a subject worth exploring with the support of a counselor or other mental health professional. While you can't change the past, the present is what matters. The present is where your child is estranged from you, and where you still have ways to contribute to her well-being. And although you can't undo certain types of damage, any efforts you make to repair some of that damage today will contribute to a more connected relationship with your child(ren) tomorrow.

Changing Family Patterns

Becoming aware of long-standing patterns in your family doesn't have to mean disrespecting your ancestors, let alone rejecting your own parents. Noticing harmful dynamics doesn't require condemning your family or any of its members. You must be allowed to notice what's been true — for you, for your parents, for their parents, and so on. No judgment is needed. *All* families exist on a continuum of dysfunction. Some are more severely dysfunctional than others, but no one comes from a perfectly functioning family. Awareness of your family's particular patterns is the first step in creating change for yourself, your children, and your grandchildren.

Here are three of the most important things you can do to address dysfunctional family patterns that may be affecting your relationship with your child:

1. Refuse to keep secrets about physical, emotional, sexual, or substance abuse in your family.
2. Apologize when appropriate, even if only to say, "I'm sorry I didn't realize."
3. Listen to your child's version of your family dynamics, without defensiveness.

Harmful patterns that run in families depend on secrecy and complacency. Change begins when just one brave, enlightened soul shines a light on something and says, "No more."

When Losses Pile Up

What have you lost in your life so far? When we think of loss and grief, death is often the first catastrophe that comes to mind. But with every ending that felt premature, every forced but undesired change, each door that closed forever on an opportunity, every physical injury and illness, you lost something. It might have been a job, a person, a sense of confidence or safety, or your youthful optimism. You might have lost hope, enthusiasm, energy, or even certain abilities. The more losses you've had, both within and outside the family, the more burdensome, compelling, and confusing the present loss of relationship with your child will feel.

While it might seem obvious why it should hurt so much to be estranged from your own child, each parent struggles with a unique patchwork of losses and pain accumulated over a lifetime. Your particular history and the multiple founts of your suffering may be obscured by the conspicuous nature of the current problem.

This is why it's necessary to focus not on your child, but on *yourself* and your family of origin in approaching the problem of parent-child estrangement. Some of the most compelling clues probably lie within the family you came from, not just with your child. Examine your own experience as an individual, as someone's son or daughter, as a sibling, friend, spouse, or partner. Your own life and early relationships are a perfectly logical place to search for solutions to the puzzle of your child's behavior.

Acknowledge what you lost before you lost your child's confidence. Go all the way back, and grieve. Find a safe person or people to lean on in this process; we heal not through reading or being by ourselves, but through healing interactions with the right people. We're injured in relationships, and we heal through them, too.

Consciously working through your personal grief, pain, and loss will help you integrate any parts of your past that are affecting your relationship with your child. As you grieve in this intentional way, you'll open yourself up to profound, positive change. Emotional healing gradually increases strength, clarity, and resilience. In addition to being prizes in themselves, these are tools you can use in your campaign to reunite with your child.

Questions for Reflection

- Are there family members in your parents' or grandparents' generations who stopped speaking to each other?
- Is there estrangement in your child's other parent's family?
- Did one of your parents try to turn you against the other?
- When you were a child, did you witness or experience abuse?
- Was there substance abuse in your home when you were a child?
- What did you learn about relationships from your parents?
- What did you learn about parenting?

3 LOST IN TRANSLATION

Some parents find that their intentions of love and support don't quite translate when they try to stay connected with their adult children. A series of such breakdowns in communication can result in estrangement. "How did this happen?" parents ask themselves. "We were such a close family." But communication snafus don't spring up overnight. Like other types of interpersonal issues, lost-in-translation problems have long roots. How your family solves problems today — or fails to solve them — relates to long-standing communication patterns.

Depending on its quality, communication can be the glue that holds families together or a virus that attacks the family's immune system, threatening its well-being and even its survival. Estrangement, by definition, signals an issue with communication. By further developing your own abilities to articulate your thoughts and feelings in a constructive way, you can affect the entire family system for the better — including, eventually, your estranged child. All it takes is for one part of that system — you — to start doing things differently.

Since there are entire books out there on how to communicate well, here I discuss just a few concepts that you may find helpful.

The most effective form of communication is clear and direct. That is, messages are clear enough to be immediately understood, and they're delivered to the person they're intended for. For example, when a mother says to her teenage daughter, "I'm disappointed that you didn't call to say you'd be home late. I'd like you to call me next time," she's using clear, direct communication. Over time, this type of transmission maintains emotional bonds, facilitates problem-solving, and creates trust.

But many families have trouble with clear, direct communication. A mother in one of these families might say to her husband, "Your daughter didn't call to say she'd be home late. Can't you teach her to call when that happens?" The message is clear, but it's indirect; instead of talking to her daughter, she's handing her concerns to her husband.

These two characteristics give rise to four basic types of communication:

1. Clear and direct
2. Clear and indirect
3. Unclear and direct
4. Unclear and indirect[1]

We've looked at the first two. What about number 3? An unclear, direct version of the mother's message might go something like this: "Well, I hope you had a good time, because I was up half the night worrying." This version is direct, because she's talking to her daughter and not someone else. But the message — "I'm disappointed, and I'd like you to call next time" — is not clear from what's actually said. If the listener has to figure out the underlying intention of the speaker, it's not clear, even if the speaker believes it is.

Unclear and indirect communication can be very hard to decipher. The mother might address the room generally and say, "Some people have no consideration for others." The daughter may have no idea that her mother is talking about her, and if she does, she could still be confused as to the exact reason for her mother's displeasure.

In my own family of origin, we used clear and direct communication mostly when discussing facts, things, and logistics: for example,

"Can you pick me up at 4 PM?" This is known as *instrumental* communication. But when it came to expressing feelings and needs — also known as *affective* communication — we favored unclear communication, either direct or indirect. As a teenager, I was known for entering the living room and barking, "Why do people keep moving my stuff?" I was a genius at unclear, indirect speech.

What about the family you came from? How often, and in which contexts, did family members use clear and direct statements or questions? Who communicated with whom? Which types of subject matter were more likely to evoke unclear or indirect communication?

Since the vast majority of rejected parents who contact me struggle with overwhelming negative feelings that impair their best efforts to communicate with their adult children, I focus here on affective communication that deals with emotions.

Talking about Feelings

Families need to know that all emotions are safe to feel and to express in words. Emotional safety is something your family can work on together, but physical safety is a must. If you or other family members can't count on physical safety when expressing feelings honestly, any effort toward healthy communication is a nonstarter. I sincerely hope this is not an issue for you, but if it is, work on establishing physical safety before implementing new ways of communicating.

Assuming you're physically safe, there are still other hurdles to surmount. Even in small families there are many moving parts. Rules of engagement that include how family members communicate are affected by attachment styles and temperament as well as by rules of conduct inherited from grandparents and great-grandparents.

For whatever reason, in many families, emotions are rarely expressed directly. For example, if I'm a member of such a family and I feel sad, I might lock myself in my room and not come out or speak to anyone. I wouldn't dream of telling someone I'm sad and letting them comfort me.

If I feel angry, I might say, "You're a jerk!" (unclear, direct) rather than "I'm angry." If I'm hurt but I want to avoid conflict, I just might not say anything at all. For days.

The so-called silent treatment is a relationship-damaging maneuver that comes not from cruelty or anger, as is so often assumed, but from not being comfortable communicating about feelings. Refusing to talk with someone who has disappointed or hurt us can seem like a healthier alternative to inviting conflict by talking openly with them about what happened. Discomfort with talking about feelings often goes hand in hand with a fear of conflict and general avoidance of difficult conversations. When these are present, how could silence *not* seem like the better course of action? And in a certain sense, it almost is. Almost.

In too many households, anger is met with anger, and hurt with hurt. To express anger or hurt is to start a war of emotions. To tell someone, "It really hurt me when you…" is to risk their coming back with "Well, *you* hurt *me* when you…" Rather than effective communication, there's suddenly a competition about who hurt whom worse.

In addition, when psychological boundaries are not clear (I'll talk more about those later), family members may not know how to respond appropriately to expressions of emotion from others. They can't be certain who owns which feelings. Expressions of emotion beget outbursts of more emotion, and then there's just a soup of emotion that everybody's drowning in and no one can put to rights.

Not reacting negatively when someone initiates a potentially challenging topic is a crucial skill. One study on difficult family conversations found that although most families dreaded the prospect of difficult conversations, the majority reported afterward that the conversation had positive outcomes, including the strengthening of family bonds. However, that was true only when the initiator was met with understanding by their conversation partner. Those who received negative reactions reported tension or other problems resulting from the conversation.[2]

For families to communicate calmly and effectively, everyone has to be able to take ownership of their feelings and convey them clearly and directly. I talk about how and why to do this when I discuss the concept of differentiation in chapter 5. Weak differentiation — not being able to tell the difference between my feelings and yours, or between my thoughts and my feelings — makes clear communication extremely difficult, because ownership is uncertain and reality itself becomes fluid. Whose feelings are hurt, and who is responsible? Is behavior motivated by reason or emotion? Is it possible to be close and caring without getting swept up in someone else's emotional experience?

Boundary Issues

Clear and direct communication requires that everyone understand boundaries: the difference between you and me, and between thoughts and feelings. This is notoriously challenging, especially in families that consider themselves to be close-knit. It can feel cold, too formal, or even harsh to say something clearly and directly — even something neutral. It's as if you're holding the person you're talking to at arm's length.

The opposite of clear boundaries is fusion, in which family members all wade in the same morass of words, thoughts, actions, and emotions. For many families, this fused state feels cozy.

"Why do I always have to clean the kitchen?" is a sample remark from this fusion state, with its nonboundaried style of communication. The speaker is not explicitly taking ownership of his feelings by stating them and making a request. Instead, unnamed others are supposed to infer how he feels and do something to meet his unstated need. In the taxonomy discussed on page 56, this remark would be classified as unclear and indirect — the most problematic kind of utterance. Instead of expressing a need and making a request, the speaker is dropping a complaint in the laps of other (unnamed) family members.

The cornerstone of clear, direct communication is the "I" statement. Simply put, it's a message that starts with the word *I* and takes ownership of personal feelings, desires, and needs. Here's an example: "I'm feeling resentful about cleaning the kitchen by myself. Will you please do the dishes tonight?" Clear and direct? Check. Formal and chilly? Only if it's not what you're used to in talking to family members. There's nothing inherently unfriendly about clear, direct communication. If it comes across that way to you, that just means your default style is something else.

In this clear and direct version, the speaker owns the feeling using an "I" statement ("I'm feeling resentful"), then makes a specific request. The listener may have feelings of her own in response. If so, she can acknowledge and communicate about them just as the speaker did, using "I" statements and clear language.

Family members need to possess both the will and the words if they're to talk to each other like this. For your message to be clear, you have to be willing to put it out there, and also to craft it in such a way that it can be understood by others. The decision to increase the amount of clear and direct language you use is up to you. It might encourage you to know that adopting a different communication style yourself can raise the bar for the entire family. It takes just one person to show others how it's done. As for finding the terms that help clarify your message, there's a list of common words for feelings in the "Emotional Literacy" section later in this chapter.

Try using clear and direct communication in more areas of your life. Like many of the practices I share in this book, it's a productive use of the time that passes while your adult child isn't available. When he or she comes around again, you'll have a better grip on this cleaner style. You'll be versed in taking ownership of your feelings and making clear requests. Unclear, needy-sounding speech from parents annoys some estranged adult children.

Start with low-stakes conversations; your very first attempts to change things shouldn't be made with your estranged child. You might try a few new communication moves with a colleague, an acquaintance from your bridge club, or someone in your neighborhood. Get used to the feel of it. Encourage your spouse or partner to get on board by modeling the style for them. Once you and a few important others consciously and regularly add clear, direct communication to your day-to-day conversations, you'll be able to use it when you really need to. This particular style of communicating has been shown to help families solve problems together and enjoy their relationships more.[3]

Overcoming Fear

The price of positive change is fear. Several different species of fear may crop up in the attempt to change how you communicate. Let's look at the fears that might show up when you consider adopting a clear, direct communication style.

Fear of being vulnerable. Open and honest communication requires us to expose our true thoughts and feelings. Once those are out of our mouths, they can be criticized, ridiculed, or rejected. When we're not used to being vulnerable, it seems safer to stay a little closed off, and even to be vague at times in what we say. Without built-in deniability, we feel like sitting ducks.

Fear of conflict. What if we say something that someone else disagrees with? Or worse, what if it hurts or offends someone to hear what we have to say? Expressing ourselves clearly and directly invites the last thing most of us want in our lives: conflict. Fear of conflict is as common as conflict itself. That's probably because we humans can be pretty bad at managing it. But conflict is a necessary part of relationships. It's born out of different people having different points of view, which is inevitable. We can learn to tolerate conflict by coming through it repeatedly without lasting damage. (For more on this, see the section on developing assertiveness in chapter 12.)

Fear of the unknown. What would happen if everyone owned and openly expressed their thoughts and feelings? *Who knows?* Familiarity is a balm, even when our familiar patterns of communication are not the best way, or even the easiest. But for parents with estranged adult children, those familiar ways of communicating are often part of the problem. There comes a point when the fear of the unknown starts to be eclipsed by the fear of things staying as they are. Estrangement can create such a turning point.

Fear of intimacy. Those of us who don't like to let others get too close may feel threatened by the idea of using clear and direct communication ourselves, even if we appreciate it in others. Sharing our true thoughts, feelings, and needs is akin to letting a listener get to know our real selves. And many of us have an unconscious habit of keeping ourselves hidden unless we know we're safe from judgment or personal attacks. Intimacy is closely related to vulnerability. If we let people know us, they'll see our flaws, and those can be used against us. When it comes to sharing yourself with your estranged adult child, you will want to think carefully about what to share, when, and how. But having the will to overcome fears of intimacy and vulnerability will give you the maximum flexibility and effectiveness.

Family therapy can help you and your available family members develop healthy communication habits. Even for people who pride themselves on good communication, there's truly always room for improvement. A therapist can offer emotional safety, boundaries, and gentle corrections as you all develop new skills together. If you can't get your estranged child to go with you, take whoever you can. Even if they don't join you in the therapy room, estranged children can learn about clear, direct communication from every interaction with you, no matter how infrequent it may be.

To communicate better, most adults (at least in the United States, where I live) could use an increased vocabulary of feeling words. If you mostly use either *happy* or *frustrated* to indicate good and bad feelings, respectively, aim to add another word each week, and start using the new ones as often as you can. For examples of feeling words, see tables 1 and 2 in this chapter. A feelings vocabulary is simple to develop. However, it can be hard to put into practice because of long-standing, unspoken rules against expressing certain emotions. Again, therapy can help. But only you can supply the courage to apply these skills.

Changing the Pattern

Why does all this concern with communication matter for the estrangement with your child? Isn't it too late for the family to improve communication? Yes and no. Your child might never move back in with you (although in this day and age, you never know), but you can still be the vanguard of a new wave of clear, direct communication in your family. In every estrangement, there are emotions at play. Even if your child expresses nothing but apathy toward you, he didn't start out apathetic. Voluntary estrangement is motivated by emotion. And if you're going to get to the bottom of it and help your child heal whatever needs healing, you'll want the best communication tools you can muster, with emotional literacy as the centerpiece.

You won't necessarily begin by expressing your feelings to your estranged child, but you should be able to do so in relative safety with your spouse, your peers, or your own parents so that you can grieve, heal, and thrive again no matter what. In repairing your relationship with your child, it's critical that you be able to hear about other people's feelings without becoming emotionally triggered by them. Instinctively meeting anger with anger and hurt with hurt, as we've seen, ruins attempts at reconciliation.

To make sure communication goes well with your estranged child when you have contact, you'll need to understand how to respond if your child gets triggered even by calm, clear, direct, ownership-taking statements from you. The more adept you are at identifying and tolerating your *own* feelings, the easier it will be for you to respond appropriately to theirs. You'll also want to be able to differentiate between their feelings and yours, so you can hear that they're angry or hurt without becoming angry or hurt yourself. This takes lots and lots of practice. So why not start today?

Undoing Escalation

Let's get back to the family homestead and the example of doing the dishes. You say, "I'm feeling resentful about being the one to do the dishes. Would you please do them tonight?" And the other person says, "Well, I don't like always taking out the garbage! You always act like I'm this lazy bum who never does anything." And on and on.

What should you do if you get a response like this, one that escalates the problem rather than working toward solving it? First, take a breath. Slow things down so you can think. Recognize the boundary between the other person and yourself, their feelings and your own. Cultivate compassion and acknowledge the content of the outburst:

"I'm sorry I gave you the impression that I think you're lazy. To be honest, I don't think that at all. Would you mind doing the dishes tonight?" This response acknowledges the other person's position with empathy and reasonableness, and — importantly — returns to your original request.

Practice this technique of acknowledging objections calmly and then returning to your message. Do it with low-stakes conversations to get the hang of it. Otherwise, it will be like trying to practice a fire drill in the middle of a fire. You might get burned.

The better your ability to recognize, own, and express a feeling clearly and directly, the more effectively you can manage communication in your relationships with others, including your estranged child. If your child doesn't know what to do with his own negative feelings, you may be able to help him.

Most of us learn our basic tools and habits of communication from our parents. They did the best they could with the tools they were given by their own parents. But no parent can provide a child with skills they don't have themselves. It wasn't your fault if your child didn't learn how to navigate difficult passages in relationships without cutting people off. Like all parents, you passed along what you knew and hoped for the best.

It's also not your child's fault if she doesn't currently have the communication skills you'd like her to have in dealing with you. By developing more emotional literacy yourself (see the next section), you can engage with your child in communication that brings you closer together, instead of driving you apart.

Questions for Reflection

- What communication skills or tips did you get from your parents?
- How did your parents express disappointment when a loved one let them down?
- How did they express their needs?
- What did your parents model for you in dealing with conflict?

Emotional Literacy

Your child's silence may be sending a message that's full of emotion. But which emotions are in play, and why? Gaining emotional literacy can help you answer this all-important question.

When you learned to read, you probably began by memorizing the names and sounds of letters. Once you were familiar with those, you were able to put them together to form words. Emotional literacy entails a similar process of recognizing and naming things, but you're working with emotions (or feelings) instead of letters. Just as with letters and words, emotional literacy enables you to identify and make sense of feelings. This foundation must be in place before you can respond effectively to your own emotions and those of others. Without a basic level of emotional literacy, it's nearly impossible to solve the problem of estrangement.

Here are some of the emotions commonly expressed by parents who consult with me:

- confusion (wondering why their child is acting this way, and what they should do about it)
- desperation (feeling that something must be done immediately, or else)
- anger (at what feels like unfair treatment by the adult child)
- resentment (when they give and give, and get nothing back)

- longing (because they miss their child terribly)
- despair (believing the situation might never improve)

More than knowing and naming emotions, becoming fully emotionally literate involves taking ownership of your feelings. This means admitting to yourself that you *have* feelings (you're allowed), knowing exactly what they are, and having a good idea what caused them. If you can't do these things, you won't be able to express yourself as effectively as you otherwise might. It's like trying to write a letter when you barely know the alphabet. There's also a danger that you'll take responsibility for feelings that aren't yours.

When you own your feelings, you have the option of expressing them in a way that others can understand. "We're going so fast! I'm scared we might crash!" is a pretty clear expression of a feeling — in this case, fear. But we routinely fail to take ownership of feelings when we communicate. Instead of saying, "I'm scared we're going to crash," we might just say, "For heaven's sake, slow down!"

The problem with saying "Slow down" instead of "I'm scared" is that "Slow down" is about what the other person is doing, rather than about what *we* are experiencing. People feel attacked when we point out their behavior instead of sticking to our own experience. Using "I" statements is one way to own our feelings, and to make requests seem reasonable, not judgmental. For example, "We're going so fast, I'm scared! Would you please slow down?"

Even if we take ownership of our feelings and express them well, others may still become defensive. Welcome to Humanity. Population: everyone. Dealing with defensiveness — in ourselves as well as in others — is part of being human. We're all flawed, but we're all in the same boat because of it. Just do your best as often as you can, and know that others (including your estranged adult child) are doing the same.

Have a look at the following tables and see how many feeling words you typically use now, and how many more you might want to use regularly.

Table 1			
Some Pleasant Feelings			
accepted	confident	grounded	present
amused	connected	hopeful	proud
appreciated	content	nurtured	respected
appreciative	creative	optimistic	sensuous
aware	daring	peaceful	stimulated
belonging	elated	pensive	successful
calm	energetic	playful	surprised
cheerful	engaged	pleased	thrilled
cherished	excited	powerful	trusting
close	grateful		

Table 2			
Some Unpleasant Feelings			
afraid	despondent	hopeless	lost
angry	disconnected	hostile	nervous
anxious	discouraged	hurt	overwhelmed
apathetic	envious	inadequate	panicked
ashamed	embarrassed	inferior	regretful
beleaguered	empty	insecure	rejected
betrayed	frightened	insignificant	ridiculous
bewildered	frustrated	irritated	sad
bored	furious	isolated	stuck
confused	hateful	jealous	stunned
defensive	helpless	lonely	wary

Sharing Ourselves

Sharing how we really feel with important others invites them to know us better. It also encourages them to share their own feelings with us.

Sharing and respecting each other's feelings helps develop trust and can reduce misunderstandings, especially when everyone takes ownership of their own emotions.

But it's not easy to own your feelings, particularly negative ones, in a society where emotional literacy often isn't valued or practiced. Many children grow up not knowing the names of most feelings, let alone how to own them or express them appropriately. When they eventually have kids of their own, they can't teach them what they themselves never learned. This is how emotional *illiteracy*, like estrangement, gets passed down through generations.

Developing a rich vocabulary for feelings through emotional literacy helps us make sense of ourselves, makes us feel more normal and acceptable, and gives us something meaningful about ourselves to share with important others. Friends, family, parents, and children can form strong bonds by sharing emotions effectively. Feelings seem chaotic and dangerous mostly when we don't have words for them. A lack of ability or willingness to communicate about and through emotions hampers bonding.

Acting Out

Without being able to share feelings like anger or disappointment, or to express them in a way that preserves and enhances relationships, family members end up acting them out instead of expressing them in a reasonable, balanced way. Feelings need to be experienced to be resolved, but acting them out is an inefficient and troublesome way to do that. Acting out is the opposite of taking ownership of feelings. Here are some examples of acting out feelings, instead of simply feeling them:

- eating to suppress despair or anxiety
- driving aggressively out of frustration

- bullying others to escape feelings of inadequacy
- overachieving because of insecurity
- giving too much to avoid feeling guilty
- undermining a coworker out of resentment

Acting out feelings instead of finding healthy ways to experience and express them creates problems in our lives. For one thing, it does nothing to address the cause of the feelings. For another, those actions can have adverse physical, psychological, social, and emotional consequences.

If you came from a family that didn't express emotions well or at all, say it with me: "There's no shame in that. It's not my fault. It's not even my parents' fault." Most families, including mine and perhaps yours too, don't do emotions well. What we call family dysfunction almost always involves some degree of emotional illiteracy. Fortunately for all of us, it's possible to cultivate this relationship-enhancing skill in adulthood.

Are You Angry at Your Child?

Don't be alarmed if you experience strongly negative feelings toward your child. If you've felt hatred at times when thinking about your estranged child, that doesn't make you a hateful person or mean that you don't love him or her. Generally speaking, hatred is what we feel when we're deeply hurt and feel frustrated and powerless toward the person who hurt us.

Don't let a fear of your own emotions cause you to be dishonest with yourself. Good people can and do experience the full range of emotions, from joy and satisfaction to anger and spite. You don't have to share your feelings with anyone else if you'd rather not. But you need to know your own heart and accept your feelings as they are.[4]

More Questions for Reflection

- What messages about emotions did you receive growing up?
- How were feelings communicated among family members?
- Was there silence on the subject? If so, what did you conclude about how feelings should be handled?
- Looking at the tables in this chapter, can you find words that describe some of the feelings you've experienced in the past week?

4 UNMET NEEDS

Any discussion about unmet needs is bound to be an emotional one, because for almost all of us, the needs that go unmet are deep and personal. Inevitably, there's pain associated with unfulfilled needs. Which is to say that you've arrived at what just might be the hardest part of this book to read and absorb.

This chapter is all about you and the emotional needs that may have gone unmet throughout your life. In the interest of healing the past, so you can create a better future for yourself and your child(ren), I'll ask you to go back to times and places where perhaps you'd rather not go. It will take courage and presence of mind just to read this chapter, let alone to ponder the reflection questions. If you don't believe you have any unmet emotional needs, please read this chapter anyway; I'll refer to some of the terms and concepts later.

If you experience strong emotions as you read, or, on the other hand, if you feel yourself shutting down completely while reading it, it's an indication that there may be something here of value for you if you're willing to engage with it. Try hard to keep yourself, not your child(ren), foremost in your mind as you work through this chapter. This is not about your child's experience of you as a parent. It's all about you.

More than once in this book I've invited you to consider using a counselor for support. I do this not as a reflexive commercial for the profession, but because estrangement often highlights a need for substantial healing on the part of the rejected parent. Professional help is appropriate and necessary for healing and change to occur in many cases. This is doubly true if you have a history of trauma.

You, the Child

Before you were a parent yourself, you were someone's child. Even though you're fully grown now, with a child or children of your own, you're still your parents' child. Your parents, living or deceased, were your parents for the rest of their lives after you were born, and you will always be the child they produced. You're someone else's adult child.

Similarly, there's at least one adult out there whose parent you will always be, no matter how old they are. Here we'll look at both roles in your life: that of the Child and that of the Parent. (I'm capitalizing *Child* and *Parent* here to indicate that these are roles, not actual people.) In a perfect world, it's a heck of a lot easier to be the Child.

The primary task of the Child is to receive love and guidance. Every Child arrives with an empty bucket ready to be filled. When you were born, you didn't have the skills, competence, or understanding you have now. All you could do was learn and be cherished and protected. You came into this world ready to soak up love and learning like a little heart-shaped sponge. You had a tremendous capacity to receive. You were born ready to embrace your proper role as the Child.

The purpose of all this receiving is for the Child's bucket to be filled over time with the emotional resources they'll need in order to fill another Child's bucket one day, should they decide to become parents themselves. As children's buckets are filled, they mature into loving, productive, responsible adults.

Once the Child grows up and becomes the Parent to another Child, the new Parent's primary occupation shifts. Now, instead of receiving, the goal is to fill their Child's bucket with love and guidance drawn from their own bucket of emotional resources. The emphasis for the

Child-Turned-Parent is now on giving rather than receiving. This intergenerational system of parenting has an orderly design, with everyone getting an equal turn at giving and receiving. First you receive, and then you give.

In reality, it doesn't always work that way.

What the Child Deserves

We don't live in an ideal world. Even perfectly designed systems go awry when operated by human beings. Justice doesn't always triumph, and things that should happen often don't. Even when we apply ourselves with heart and soul, we sometimes fail. This reality forms the backdrop for all our efforts, including parenting. For the moment, though, continue to put aside any thoughts about your child. Keep the focus on yourself, and try to remember what it was like to be the Child in someone else's care.

Here's how it works in an ideal world:

- The Child behaves as she likes (she's just a kid, after all), but the Parent's behavior toward the Child is consistently guided by love and age-appropriate discipline.
- The Child is immature, self-centered, and often unreasonable (hence the negative connotations of the word *childish*); the Parent, who is literally and figuratively the bigger person, responds appropriately to the Child's behavior, rather than reacting emotionally.
- The Parent is dedicated to the welfare of the Child, and shows interest and delight in the Child. The Child is not required to show interest or delight in the parent, though he might do so spontaneously.
- The Child has every right to have emotional needs met by the Parent, but the Parent does not expect the Child to meet the Parent's emotional needs.
- The Parent helps the Child feel seen, heard, understood,

and valued as an individual, so that the Child can grow up feeling whole and generous toward others. The Child has no such duty toward the Parent.

- The Parent allows and encourages the Child over time to mature and develop into a person who is separate and possibly quite different from the Parent.
- Once the Child's bucket is full, she takes her place in the world of adults, often stepping into the role of the Parent to another Child. At this point, she may relate to her own parents from the point of view of a fellow Parent, minus the intense need with which she entered their relationship at birth. She might even have enough resources in her bucket to nurture the remnants of the Children inside her own parents.

That's in principle. In practice, plenty of us didn't get what we had every right to expect in the Child role. Our buckets didn't get filled — not even halfway. Consequently, we're still waiting for our turn. This reader's words reflect the unfulfilled needs of many former Children:

My son and I aren't all the way "estranged." It just feels like to me, that he and his wife lean towards her family. The same amount of time isn't given to me. I will hear about them doing really fun things, and I've never been included. My son has always seemed "stiff and wooden" when I try and hug him. He's even almost pushed me away at times, over the years. It's hurt for decades now. I just don't know what to do to create an atmosphere where I am loved and included too.

Most of us still feel more like the Child inside than the Parent. We have strong needs and wants, and we often feel stymied by other people and circumstances. We need recognition, encouragement, and affection as much as ever. We deserve those things, and we were supposed to receive them when we were starting out. Our buckets were supposed to be full.

Ideally, the emotional nurturing of Children, including the ones you and I once were, fills them up with love and strength and gives them the inner resources to put their own needs aside when the time comes for them to switch to the Parent role. Loving and nurturing a Child is supposed to be a one-sided undertaking, especially but not exclusively at the beginning of the Child's life.

If we're perfectly honest with ourselves, we'll notice that we're still waiting for all that good emotional nurturing we were supposed to get. It's so unfair to have to give, give, give when we're not done hoping to receive. It's as though we missed our turn at receiving, and now we have to make sure someone else gets *their* turn — at our expense!

As human beings, how can we be okay in the face of such injustice? Despite the messages you may have received telling you to "suck it up" because "life's not fair," it's perfectly normal and valid to resent the unfairness we regularly experience in life. We prefer things to be fair. That's why we have courts of law. It's why games have rules. Fairness is an ideal we strive for.

Having to play the Parent when you never really got your turn to be the Child is painfully unfair. When our buckets aren't full, it's impossible to completely set aside our emotional needs for the benefit of another human being, no matter how much we may want to, or how much we love them. The Parent is an impossible role to play perfectly because it requires complete selflessness, something most of us find, well, kind of hard.

The early 2000s TV show *Supernanny*, starring the kid whisperer extraordinaire Jo Frost, found an enthusiastic audience in the United States because Frost made it seem possible to play the Parent role after all.[1] She doled out discipline and love in such perfect proportions that children and parents alike fell in love with her.

Of course, Frost always dealt with someone else's children, which meant that technically she wasn't parenting. She was unencumbered by the projections and blind spots parents typically exhibit when dealing with their own children. Unless we had a series of visits from someone like Frost, most of us never got to experience fully the pleasures and appropriate challenges of being the Child throughout childhood.

Maybe we lost a parent when we were young and had to grow up quickly. Maybe our parents had an especially tough time in the Parent role. Maybe we even got thrust into the role of the Parent while we were still children. Whatever the case, we all have needs that continue to go unfulfilled to some degree. Again, there's no shame in this. It's normal to have emotional needs for validation, nurturing, acceptance, and appreciation throughout life. It just makes things complicated sometimes between parents and children.

The Needs We Share

Even though most parents try like heck to do the right thing when it comes to their kids, virtually nobody in the Child role gets all her needs met all the time. The very best a human parent can do is to meet his child's needs adequately, sometimes.

It's important to keep in mind that you are as much a Child as a Parent yourself. Stay focused on your own childhood as you read through this section. We're going to explore your early history, not to find fault with your parents but to get you in touch with your unmet needs. We all have them.

When you were born, your bucket of resources was empty, and your needs were great. You were totally dependent and vulnerable. For all of us, that helplessness diminishes only gradually as we become toddlers, then children. If your bucket never got filled to the brim, it's imperative now to figure out how that affected you.

To help you start thinking about your experience as the Child, I list below some of the needs we all share. This is not an exhaustive list of emotional needs, but it's probably more than enough for starters. Putting aside as best you can your experience as a parent (remember, this section is about you as a Child), try to recall how *your* parents approached these needs for you.

Safety. Children need to feel physically safe in order to thrive. Their sense of safety can be shaken by being physically harmed or threatened, or by witnessing physical or verbal violence. Loud, angry voices or frequent, bitter arguments can threaten the Child's sense of safety.

Food, Shelter, Clothing. Many children grow up in homes where basic needs such as food, shelter, and clothing are scarce. No matter how much a Child is loved, scarcity of basic resources can foster a deep sense of insecurity.

Nonsexual Affection. Knowing that they're loved comes easily to children who are hugged and cuddled by their parents. They don't have to guess or assume their parents love them in the absence of demonstrations like this. However, children who are touched in a sexual way by an adult or a much older child can suffer emotional damage that can haunt them for the rest of their lives.

Boundaries. Children crave rules and limits, and they need them to be enforced calmly and consistently. They also need help in identifying personal boundaries — theirs and others'. For example, a parent might tell a child, "That's not yours; you need to ask your sister if you can borrow it." Children whose personal boundaries are frequently violated, or who are permitted to violate others' boundaries, tend to have difficulty with boundaries as adults.

Acceptance. Everyone is unique, which means that children can be very different from their parents. Children need to know they're acceptable to other family members, whether they're similar or different. If a child is accepted as is by parents, that child learns to embrace both herself and others, and can pass this wonderful gift to her own children one day. For example, a parent might say, "It's okay that you're not into camping. It's not for everyone."

Appreciation. Children need to know they're appreciated by their parents — that the parents' lives are made better somehow by the child's existence. This happens when a parent says something like, "Thank you for helping me bring the groceries in. It would have been a bigger job without you." The opposite of appreciation is denigration: for example, "You'll never amount to anything," or "I'd have a better life if I didn't have kids." Even without denigration, an absence of appreciation can lead a child to question his worth.

Visibility. To develop a healthy self-image, children need to know that others know them and understand their struggles and delights. Parents help a child become self-aware through accurate empathy and reflection of the child's experiences, even when these differ significantly from those of the parent. A parent can help by asking, "You look down, son. Is something wrong?"

Validation. This is a kind of affirmative empathy that helps kids learn to trust their own perceptions. Validation lets them know they're not crazy or weird to think or feel the way they do. It doesn't necessarily imply agreement. A mother might say, "I can understand why you want one of those puppies; they're so cute. But we're not taking one home."

Questions for Reflection

- Which of your needs did your parents do an adequate job of meeting?
- Which of these needs seemed difficult for your parents to help you with?
- How do you imagine your grandparents approached your parents' needs when they were children?
- Do any of these needs strike a special chord for you?
- Which needs still feel unfulfilled?
- What are some ways you might try to meet your needs, at least in part, yourself?

The Child as Parent

People who become parents before they've had their buckets filled (i.e., before their emotional needs have been adequately met) in the role of the Child often attempt a compromise. They unconsciously treat their own children as siblings, friends, or even parents. They may argue or bargain with their children, withhold approval or closeness, punish them out of frustration rather than thoughtful discipline, or seek reassurance or validation from them.

This doesn't make these parents bad people. They may not even be particularly bad parents, especially if they can see what's happening and make corrections at least some of the time.

People who didn't get to be Children but now find themselves in the role of Parent might be called *Child-Parents*. Just as they didn't get to be the Child when it was their turn, the *children* of these Child-Parents don't get to be wholly the Child either, and that creates a circle of resentment. Though they may not be consciously aware of it, the Child-Parent resents having to be the (selfless) Parent, and their child in turn resents the Child-Parent for not fully relinquishing the role of the Child.

This mutual resentment is the lifeblood of many an estrangement. Abuse and neglect are painful without a doubt, but the nameless feeling of having been robbed of your turn to be the Child can be just as piercing. It's both interesting and challenging to think of yourself and your child as sharing the same type of resentment.

Now, here's the open secret: *every* parent is a Child-Parent. That's right — you, your parents, your grandparents, every parent you know, and of course, if they have kids, your children as well. We've already talked about how we've all got needs, and nobody can be the perfect Parent. So it shouldn't come as any surprise that all parenting is actually Child-Parenting. That's also why it's so challenging. As things stand, we do the best we can with what's in our buckets.

Becoming aware of your own emotional needs is one of the most helpful things you can do for yourself, your child, and all your important relationships.

Parenting Your Adult Child

Even though your adult child is no longer an actual child, and may even have children of her own, the relationship you share is a Parent-Child relationship, at least until each role has been fulfilled. The fact that there's trouble between you right now could indicate that the roles may not yet have been fully played out. Estrangement from your Child just might be a signal that it's time for you to resume the role of the Parent.

The fact that it feels like such a one-sided relationship, with the Parent doing all the giving and the Child doing all the receiving, means it's crucial for you to pay attention to self-care. To make things feel fair, you've got to get your needs met, too — just not by your child. When it comes to the relationship between you and your estranged child, your job is still to try to meet their needs.

How does this make you feel? Perhaps you agree with this reader:

> This sounds like an instruction manual for maintaining a happy relationship with a narcissistic personality disordered individual. Sometimes the demands of another are not reasonable, and wallowing at his/her feet is nothing short of feeding their pathology.

Taken out of context, this comment would be right on the money. If, say, we were talking about a husband and wife or a pair of friends, such one-sidedness would be questionable, if not actually pathological. But the relationship between Parent and Child has special rules and dynamics. Taking a detour into evolutionary biology, we might say the Child must go forward and perpetuate the Parents' genes, and so must be given every advantage, even at the Parent's expense. Most parents, if asked, will say they'd give their lives for their children without a second thought. It's instinctual.

The only thing that's fair about the Parent-Child relationship is that, at least in theory, every Parent has already had a turn to be the

Child. The joy of parenting is the experience of paying forward what was given to you. Children grow up and pay it forward to their own children. Nature doesn't demand that the giving between Parent and Child be reciprocal, only sequential. It's not mutual, but serial. Everyone gets a turn at receiving before having to do any giving. No Child is required to pay back a Parent, but instead must pay the love and caring forward to another Child.

As we've discussed, in the real world, not everyone gets a fair share of the good stuff. This creates inequality, which generates an aching sense of injustice. We resent the unfairness of being thrust into a giving role when we didn't get a proper turn at receiving. It *is* unfair. It's okay to resent that.

Parenting is therefore complicated by the inherent conflict of two universal truths:

1. Parents are givers.
2. Fairness means receiving as much as you give.

Considering the centrality of these two principles in our culture, it's easy to recognize why parents often end up looking to their adult children to help meet their emotional needs. Putting the two ideas together, you get, "I gave a lot to you when you were growing up. Won't you give at least a little back?" But wanting your child to meet you halfway is tantamount to stealing the role of the Child away from its rightful owner. Your child will resent it. She may even sever the relationship.

If you want a relationship of equals with your child, where there's equitable give-and-take, you're not walking on eggshells, and you receive as much consideration and respect as you give, it might be possible. But you probably won't get there from where you are now without first going back and putting on your Parent hat and allowing your adult child to play the Child for as long as he needs to.

An Evolving Relationship

Re-parenting in a deliberate way like this doesn't have to last forever. As you successfully re-parent your child, eventually you might receive something back, like appreciation. But beware: it will take years of consistent effort, not weeks or months, and there's no guarantee that your child will ever be ready to relinquish the Child role. What's frustrating is that the more you need it to happen, the longer it's likely to take.

Evolution of the Parent-Child relationship stalls when the developmental needs of the Child aren't met. Once you reestablish your Parent role, your child's needs can be addressed, his development can resume, and he has a fighting chance to grow into an adult rather than remaining the Child who's still waiting to receive from the Parent.

Resuming the role of the Parent at this point in your life could be the hardest thing you'll ever do. But with great challenges come great potential benefits. It could also be the most inspiring project you ever undertake, not just for your child, but for yourself. The decisive factor is how well your own emotional needs are met before, during, and after this passage.

Preparing to play the Parent role well brings you face to face with your unfulfilled emotional needs in a way that few endeavors can. But in acknowledging those needs, you can finally make efforts toward meeting them. Playing the Parent forces you to practice excellent self-care. It encourages you to cultivate closeness and interdependence in your peer relationships, deepening them. Playing this role mindfully later in life is a rare accomplishment. It can boost your self-esteem and integrity in ways that could change you forever.

You don't have to be a genius or a saint to re-parent your adult child(ren). All it takes is a dose of courage and a desire to grow. You'll need a way to fill your bucket so thoroughly that you can supply oceans of attention, forgiveness, and patience while expecting nothing in return, all with a sense of satisfaction rather than feeling like a doormat. A tall order? Of course. But the potential rewards are indescribable.

You wouldn't go into a physically demanding venture without taking equipment and supplies, and making sure you were in the best physical shape possible. So don't try to play the Parent without first maximizing your emotional health and setting yourself up with support. If you have a spouse, sibling, or friend who's sympathetic to your cause, let them know your plan and tell them you might need to lean on them more than usual. If at all possible, also consider working with a counselor, cleric, or other professional. You need to be allowed to be the Child with someone, at least some of the time. Your needs are legitimate, and it's right for you to try to have them met — just not by your child.

Don't neglect yourself in this process. Cry as much as you need to. Stay hydrated. Cut yourself slack. Get a little bit of exercise now and then; it will help your mood. I'll have more to say about self-care in the section below and throughout the book. It's that important.

Cultivating Self-Compassion

Even though you're the Parent of your child, you're still a human being and, like everyone else, an adult child yourself. We all need and deserve love and nurturing throughout our lives. If you've been wounded by your child's rejecting or disrespectful behavior, it will take time to find peace about it, even after it's over. At the same time, because you're stuck permanently in the role of the Parent with this person, your healing must happen *outside* that relationship.

The Child isn't good at delayed gratification, but the Parent must be. Be patient with yourself if you resent putting your child's need for emotional healing before your own: it's your inner Child complaining — and with every right to do so.

Get some nurturing from yourself or someone else for your inner Child while you navigate the journey of reconnection with your child. Take another look at the list of needs we all share, and get to work acquiring your share of the good stuff. Self-care is not a "nice to have" — it's a must. Your health, both mental and physical, is at stake. The medical establishment now recognizes that it's possible to die from a broken heart.[2] Please don't let this happen to you. Stress kills, and I don't need to tell you that estrangement from your child is stressful.

Self-soothing is a crucial part of staying healthy. Actively nurture yourself to avoid going downhill. At the very least, practice relaxing every muscle in your body whenever you experience fear or emotional strain. According to trauma experts, it's impossible to be stressed, let alone traumatized, in a relaxed body.[3] If you respond to stress, fear, or difficult emotions by letting your muscles go limp, you'll reduce the amount of distress you can experience in that moment. Try it and see.

What might it look like to take care of yourself? Ask yourself, "What feeds me? What makes me feel soothed, stronger, and more peaceful? What fills my emotional bucket?" Listen carefully to the answers, and make efforts to give yourself exactly what you need. Avoid temptations that aren't good for your body, such as alcohol or other drugs. Below are some healthy ideas for self-nurturing. Take what you like, and leave the rest.

Spend time in nature.
Read a book for fun.
Let yourself cry as much as you want — no limits.
Hug someone, or ask for a hug.
Spend time with animals.
Make art or do crafts.
Be with people who are warm and appreciative.
Get a massage.
Take a walk, alone or with a friend.
Join (or start) a group.
Listen to music.
Write in a journal.
Sleep late without judging yourself.
Travel.
Watch movies.
Incorporate more movement into your daily routine.
Actively cultivate your social support network.

If you enjoy communing online with other estranged parents who are actively working to improve their relationships, you'll find a friendly and welcoming community inside my subscription website at Reconnection Club.com. Whatever you do, let it be something that's just for you — not a chore, not something you "should" do. If you feel like just sitting and staring out the window, do it. Self-care is anything that answers a request from your soul. Your soul will only ask for what is good for you. The request for self-nurturing can be so quiet it's hard to hear, but listening and responding to it will help your inner voice grow stronger.

You may need to rest more than usual while you recuperate from what's happened to this point. Give yourself all the room and the time you possibly can to just vegetate, or to fall to pieces if that's what you feel like doing. Tell those close to you not to worry; sometimes we have to fall apart in order to become whole again.

By the way, if you feel like hurting someone, or yourself, that's not a request from your soul: that's pain and hopelessness speaking. You can safely acknowledge those feelings, but you don't have to obey them. All things must pass, including painful feelings. If you take the time to care for yourself well, then no matter what happens with your child, you will come to a better place than you're in now. For more on the therapeutic value of embracing negative emotions, see my book *Constructive Wallowing.*[4]

More Questions for Reflection

- Being the Child of two Child-Parents yourself, can you remember any ways in which your parents competed with you for the role of the Child?
- What withdrawals were made from your emotional bank account when you were the Child?
- Can you hold compassion for your parents in your heart because they had needs that weren't adequately met? What about compassion for yourself?
- What do you need from your adult child today? Is it something one might expect from a Parent or best friend?
- What does it feel like to reflect on these questions?

5 INDEPENDENCE

One of the more difficult passages in a parent's life may come when their children leave home. That wonderful, frustrating, fleeting period known as childhood ends, your child becomes an adult, and you're left with a hole in your day where your child used to be. Regardless of the state of your relationship, once they leave home, they're gone in a way they've never been gone before. For many parents, getting used to this takes time.

Do you have a child in the process of launching into adulthood and independence? I remember that stage very well from my own youth. I lived with my parents until I graduated from college, around the age of twenty-two. Within a few months of graduation, I moved out. But that wasn't the end of my launch.

Not only did I move out after college, I moved almost five thousand miles from Vancouver, British Columbia, to London, England. Was I trying to get away from my parents? Certainly not. At least, not consciously. As far as I knew, I was moving not *away* from my family but *toward* my own (hopefully wildly exciting and successful) future.

I remember lying awake at night in my tiny room in a shared flat in north London, aware of my parents being so far away. I wanted them to be safe. I wanted them to stay in the house I grew up in. And most of all, I wanted to know they were available if I needed them. These weren't crisp or coherent thoughts. They were sensations that only emerged in quiet moments, like the middle of the night. It didn't occur to me to share them with anyone.

Apart from carrying a desire in the back of my mind for my parents to be there "just in case," I was entirely focused on myself and my new life in London. At twenty-three, I remained as self-absorbed as a teenager, yet now I was as busy as an adult. I held a full-time job, made new friends, dated, and explored all kinds of new activities.

When my visa expired two years later and I had to leave England, I returned to the only other place where I knew I'd be welcome: my parents' home. I took a job as an administrative assistant at a small private college. I had decided just before leaving England that I wanted to be a journalist, and after a year or two back in Vancouver, paying my parents nominal rent while grumbling in my diary about still living at home, I managed to land a position as a proofreader with a local newspaper. Maybe predictably, by that time I'd changed my mind about my destiny. Ta da! Now I wanted to be an actress. So at twenty-seven, to my parents' dismay, I moved out of their home once again and drove to Los Angeles to pursue that goal. But that still wasn't the end of my launch....

It took a year and a half for me to decide that New York City would be a better fit. I drove back to Vancouver and, of course, dumped a jumble of possessions in my parents' basement for safekeeping. I asked my dad to sell my car and moved across the country. Had I needed to, I would have returned to live with my parents yet again. But as it happened, at twenty-eight I had finally, and permanently, left home.

What about you? What's your launch story? Remembering your own launch from your childhood home will lend perspective to what's happening with your child now.

Maybe your child has it easier than you did. Perhaps she's got more financial or emotional support than you were able to count on as a young adult. Then again, maybe she's having a harder time than you did. That can fill a parent's heart with a spectrum of bad feelings from anxiety to guilt and everything in between.

Consider any differences between your launch and your child's.

Questions for Reflection

- What are you giving to your young adult child that was never given to you at that age? How do you feel about that? What do you need in exchange, if anything?
- What did your parents expect from you when you were the age your child is now? How did they let you know? How did you feel about their requests?
- How much contact did you have with your parents when you were your child's age? Who initiated it? How did that level of contact feel?

Your own experience will naturally inform your perception of, and attitude toward, your child's launch. Give at least a little bit of thought to the questions above before moving on.

Developmental Factors in Estrangement

We've assumed so far that your child has some compelling emotional reason to create distance, that it pains him to be in contact with you, or that he's angry, frustrated, or disappointed in the relationship. As I've already suggested, that's not necessarily the case. Sometimes adult children's reluctance to remain close is more a function of their phase of development than anything else.

I Gotta Be Me

The task of identity formation known as *individuation* accelerates during adolescence. You can think of this endeavor as "becoming the unique person one is meant to be." Individuation is a process that, for most of us, lasts a lifetime. And although it undoubtedly looks different across different cultures, here in the United States it may begin with startling experiments that could be described as "out with the old, in with the new." Childhood friends may be dropped, new attitudes adopted. Hair, clothing, musical tastes, opinions, and habits may undergo a total makeover. Experimentation is a necessary part of learning who we are. But for parents, their children's efforts at individuation can appear far less benign. "What's happening to our beautiful boy? He's becoming so surly." "Where did our little girl go, and who is this person who holds such different values?"

One common parental reaction is to blame third parties — new boyfriends, girlfriends, or friend groups — for being a bad influence on their children. And third parties do play a role in this process. But individuation is an inside job. During this active phase of adult development, your child is engaged in a purposeful experiment, the outcome of which is still unknown. And though your child's poor decisions may set your teeth on edge, trying to control them is like trying to stop the seasons changing. Nature is inexorable, and individuation is a natural process. Cutoff from parents is not the ultimate goal of individuation or an indication of its success: the goal is a healthy balance between separation and connection. Often, however, the pendulum swings far to the separation side before a balance can be achieved. Parents who react negatively during this time can interfere with, and unwittingly prolong, the process.

I'm not suggesting that you need to be okay with your child doing drugs, hooking up with controlling partners, or running with a crowd of drag-racing delinquents. I'm saying that if your child is experimenting with choices you don't approve of, or that scare you, her behavior may be more purposeful (and temporary) than it seems. Once she reaches the age of majority, you have no power to choose for her. Your only choice is whether to accept the person she's becoming. If something terrible happens to your child during this phase, it will be awful, but it won't be anything you could or should have prevented. You still feel as much care and concern for her as you ever did, but now you have zero control. It's a dreadful and inevitable part of parenting adults.

Healthy Separation

As if individuation weren't enough for parents to deal with, that process depends on the related phenomenon of *differentiation*, which is harder to understand and achieve, but vital to adult development.

Differentiation consists of two tasks. One is the separation of thinking from feeling, and the other is the ability to retain an independent individual identity — a psychological "I" — within a collective one — a "we." The latter task has nothing to do with being self-centered or selfish: quite the opposite. An autonomous, separate self is more able to tolerate differences in others and potentially more compassionate and understanding in the face of conflict. A well-differentiated individual has no inherent need for distance from family: she can be a separate person and remain emotionally close at the same time.

The first aspect of differentiation, the ability to distinguish between thoughts and feelings, is necessary for adult functioning, especially in relationships. This grasp of the boundary between thoughts and emotions enables us to hear another person out when we're emotionally stressed, or when we disagree with them. When we can differentiate between logic and impulse, we don't confuse our emotions with reality: we recognize them as a reaction to the facts presented, rather than as the facts themselves. We realize that our emotions may not correspond with the objective truth of the matter.

For example, a well-differentiated person is able to respond calmly to criticism. She can distinguish between any pain she feels about being criticized and the actual content of the criticism. She can consider the information and come to a levelheaded conclusion about whether, and how well, the criticism fits. A poorly differentiated person, on the other hand, is flooded by negative emotions about being criticized, to the point where he can't think about the information objectively.

The second aspect of differentiation, the perception of a psychological border between "I" and "we," is also significant for its impact on relationships. A well-differentiated person is able to be near someone who's hurting or angry without becoming paralyzed or triggered by the other's emotion. The opposite of this aspect of differentiation is *enmeshment*. Codependency is an example of this. The codependent person experiences the other's needs as an imperative. It's as if they themselves are entirely responsible for the other's emotional well-being — even when the other person is an adult. In codependency, responding to others' needs is not optional. Enmeshed families not only have trouble with individual differences and separateness, but they also require a high degree of conformity of thought and feeling among members in order to keep the peace.

If you're starting to wonder how your own level of differentiation might affect your child's development and the way he communicates with you (or refuses to), you're on to something. According to the psychiatrist and researcher Murray Bowen, parents play a key role in their children's development of appropriate independence and adult social skills.[1] Parents who encourage their kids to become more independent as they grow, while also providing age-appropriate rules and structure at home, are able to strike the right balance. But in order to do this, parents must first find this balance in themselves.

Thus, the level of differentiation in a family can either help or hurt the individuation process of its younger members. When differentiation is underdeveloped in a family, it often gives rise to a state of enmeshment or *emotional fusion*, in which the psychological borders between family members are indistinct. On the other hand, when the boundaries between family members are too rigid, with too much distance and not enough emotional intimacy, families may be *disengaged*. Good differentiation in a family allows an age-appropriate balance of independence and interdependence for all its members.

The movie *Psycho* (spoiler alert: I'm going to give away an important plot element) is a fictionalized account of an extreme failure of individuation and differentiation. Not only has Norman Bates failed to separate from his mother, he's become psychologically fused with her, to the extent that at times he believes he *is* her. Norman's mother discouraged him from becoming his own person when she was alive. (Please don't take this too much to heart! Norman clearly had a lot going on under the hood, probably from birth.)

The Need for Space

In theory, physical distance is not required for individuation and differentiation. But the vast majority of us do use it, consciously or not, to help us along with these tasks. The traditions of young people moving out, going off to college, or traveling for a year provide socially acceptable space and time for a gentle separation from parents.

Though we have few reliable markers of maturity in US mainstream culture, we can think of psychological and emotional maturity as resulting from the gradual gelling of one's own thoughts, opinions, preferences, routines, and tastes, and the achievement of psychological autonomy. This includes the capacity to be connected and close with others when we choose to be, but still to remain essentially ourselves and to distinguish between facts and feelings. Real maturity of this sort is an achievement that most of us take a lifetime to attain. In fact, it can be argued that most of us don't ever become fully individuated, differentiated adults.

Normal Separation

The processes of individuation and differentiation, and their effects, can be unexpected, for both young adults and their parents. Both may be blindsided by a feeling of distance suddenly appearing like a sinkhole in their relationship, and anxiety can run high on both sides.

It's important to note here that individuation is *not* the same as estrangement. Whereas estrangement is an interpersonal process, with distance, time, and negative feelings separating parent and child, individuation is an *intrapersonal* process, without malice or even necessarily conscious intent.

Is it possible your estrangement from your child is mostly a manifestation of their developmental needs at this point in their lives? Is your child simply engaged in the normal, healthy tasks of individuation and differentiation? Is it purely Nature taking its course?

The answer could be yes if:

1. The separation wasn't preceded by regular negative inter-
    actions.
2. Your child blows hot and cold, sometimes seeking close-
    ness, other times disappearing.
3. The estrangement began within five years of your child's
    leaving home.

If all three of the above are true, you're probably seeing bona fide developmental processes in action.

Total cutoff from parents is not necessarily normal, but some otherwise loving and happy children do need to temporarily create a high level of physical and psychological distance in order to focus on this phase of their development.

If you were extremely close to your child in the past, even seeing them as your best friend, you may have unwittingly acted like an archer pulling back the string of a bow; the arrow flies farther when finally let go. A tight-knit or strongly opinionated family can have the same effect.

Contacting Younger Adults

Whether your adult child is doing fine or struggling during the first few years of adulthood, he may not want to have much to do with parents, family, or childhood friends who remind him of the past and a child-self he's trying to outgrow. The impetus is toward a more authentic, mature version of himself, one defined from the inside rather than by association.

If your child left home within the past few years, weekly or even monthly contact with people from her "old" life may be too frequent for her. Hearing from parents just a few times a year is sufficient for many younger adults exploring the wider world for the first time. If you've received a specific request for no contact, generally it's a good idea to abide by it. If you haven't, maybe send a loving note on her birthday and one other occasion, asking for nothing, but letting her know you're there for her if she needs you. Your child can always contact you if the low frequency of communication doesn't suit her.

This may not sit well with you, but technically it's not your young adult's job to make sure you aren't worried about him. He's busy making mistakes and hopefully learning from them. Of course you're concerned for his well-being, and you hope he stays safe. But no matter how much you'd like him to check in regularly, give up the notion that he owes you that. When your heart is walking around outside your body (as is often said of those who have children), you're constantly vulnerable. Breathe into the vulnerability. It's nobody's fault, and there's no escape from it. It's a paradox, but finding acceptance might afford you a measure of calm.

Safety Concerns

Developmentally motivated estrangement is likely to be temporary while the child finds his or her footing in the world. If you previously had a positive relationship, you have a basis for one in the future. But it will be forever changed. Just as you no longer belong exclusively to your parents, you must now share your child with the world. And that can feel risky. Are you thinking what this parent is thinking?

> This is all fine but how does one ensure they are safe even if they don't want to talk to you????
> From hurting mum :(

The short answer? One doesn't. It's such a difficult pill to swallow, not to be able to keep our loved ones safe! We're all in the same boat on this one. The lack of control, the uncertainty, the terrible vulnerability; what if something happens to them? It's one of the more painful aspects of being human.

If you think about it, it's an illusion to think your children were completely safe even when they slept under your roof. Things could have happened that were beyond your control back then, just as things can happen now. Your child has been vulnerable his whole life. Separation and distance merely shatter the comforting illusion of safety.

If you have specific (rather than general) concerns about your child's safety, by all means enlist the help of people close to him to watch over him. If your concerns have a basis in reality, others who care about your child will share them. His peers may be able to influence him more than you can right now.

Keep Calm and Carry On

You can facilitate your child's development into a mature adult by not insisting on frequent contact. Consciously allow him room and time to explore adult life on his own.

It's okay to remind him from time to time that you love him. If necessary, let him know that you're okay. He may worry that you're wasting away without him. No child wants to have to fret about his parents' well-being, especially when he has so much work to do right now becoming a functioning adult. Do your child the favor of not giving him reason to be concerned about you. Worry can become resentment if it goes on long enough.

If you were close before in a way that worked for your child, there's nothing to stop her coming back around to you when she feels psychologically separate enough to have a more mature relationship. No matter how long you both live, or who may be diapering whom, you will always be fixed in the roles you began with, of Parent and Child. Her needs will always trump yours, as far as you, the Parent, are concerned. Fortunately, this is the only relationship in your life that absolutely has to be this way. Make sure you have other relationships from which to draw the sustenance you need and deserve.

Since virtually no one succeeds in differentiating completely (as I said, a lifetime is not enough for most of us to achieve that), our parents have a unique ability to influence us throughout our lives. Have you ever visited your parents and felt younger after a very short time in their presence? It's a common experience. It's as though we never quite "graduate" from being our parents' children.

Let that give you comfort now as you face being separated — temporarily, I hope — from your own child. Let's turn now to some common scenarios that can create extra anxiety and pain during this phase.

If You and Your Child Were Best Friends

It's natural to experience a sense of loss when your child leaves home. But if, when they were younger, it was you and your child against the world, you will also experience the deep grief of losing your best friend and constant companion. Perhaps there was a time when your child was your *only* close friend. If so, separation from your child represents a tremendous loss for you.

You'll be shocked when your child stops responding the way she used to. You may become convinced she's being unduly influenced by new, shady figures to whom she's inexplicably become attached. Why would she choose these hostile new people over the special friendship you shared? It doesn't make sense. Something feels terribly wrong.

In truth, friendship between parent and child is not necessarily what Nature intends for young children. Friendship between a parent and an *adult* child is certainly possible once the child is established in adulthood. But such a friendship is not normally at the center of the adult child's social life, and there are good reasons for the maturing child to leave behind an early parent-child friendship.

When a close friendship exists between parent and child, the child experiences ongoing internal pressure to be a good friend to the parent. In order to be the best possible friend, he may try to suppress the natural impulses and desires that children typically have — to explore the world in increasingly independent ways, to spend time with peers, and to experiment with different identities. *This is true whether or not the parent wants or intends to contribute to such pressure.* In fact, the parent might not even realize it's happening.

The child's desire to be a good friend to Mom or Dad can be so binding that when it's time to grow up and away, only a wrenching, painful break, or else creating a great physical distance, can loosen that bond and allow the child to concentrate on the necessary processes of individuation and differentiation.

Nature's Way

You might remember the PBS special "My Life as a Turkey."[2] It's a documentary about a man who raises a brood of turkeys from hatchlings. They imprint on him the day they're born, and they follow at his heels throughout their youth.

The man becomes emotionally attached to them. He gives them names and learns to make sounds they recognize, to which they readily respond.

One day, when the turkeys are in their late adolescence, their human "mother" takes them out to the woods as usual. As the turkeys begin to stray, he calls to them to come back. The turkeys, who have always responded before, ignore the man's calls and spread out into the forest without him. They never obey his calls again. They still know him, and occasionally visit with him, but always on their own terms.

The man is caught by surprise when the turkeys stop responding to him as a parent. He feels injured by their abandonment, and the loss of their constant companionship leaves a hole in his life. But he understands.

Nature seems to have a plan for social development, and it calls for a separation from parents at the appropriate time. The turkeys didn't turn their backs on the man because they were ungrateful for all that he'd done for them. It wasn't that he'd failed as a parent. Quite the contrary. Because they'd been well parented and were healthy, the birds were able to do what all young adults do in the natural course of things: take their places in the world as independent adults.

It may be as natural for parents to grieve as it is for their offspring to leave the nest. Give yourself permission to have your feelings about the loss of closeness with your child. Seek support from an understanding person or people who will listen and understand. Some people may respond by attempting to explain to you that kids need to leave home in order to thrive. Tell them you understand that, but you have your feelings about it all the same. You're allowed.

Letting Go

If you're extremely concerned about the company your young adult is keeping, you've joined a club with millions of members. There's nothing you can or should do to drive a wedge between your now-adult child and his new friends or romantic partners. The more you try to interfere, the more the child and his friends will unite, possibly against you and other family members. If your child's friends are truly awful, give your child room to figure that out for himself. He trusted you to take care of him when he came into your life; now it's time for you to trust that he can take care of himself, or at least that he has the capacity to learn and grow.

The first few years away from home will be full of trial and error. Think of this phase as your child's enrollment in the New Adult Learning Academy (informally known as the School of Hard Knocks). Meanwhile, you'll be spending that time in the members' lounge of the White-Knuckle Club. Let him make mistakes, not because it's good, right, or easy, but because you have no other choice. The more you try to help your estranging young adult avoid mistakes when he's not requesting help, the more he'll feel the need to pull away from your guidance.

Drop the rope. Give your child nothing but slack. Let him run with it. And yes, I'm aware of how much more easily that's said than done.

You may be aware that your child is at a disadvantage in some way — he may have a learning disability, a medical condition, or trouble making or keeping friends — but if he wants to venture into adulthood without a concerned parent looking over his shoulder, he must be allowed to make those attempts. Cross your fingers for his eventual proficiency, despite his disadvantages. It beats the alternative, which is needing you for the rest of his life. Letting him try means letting him fail. Meanwhile, you must tolerate the inevitable fear, concern, and any feelings of dread, loss, or panic. Your child has his work to do, and you have yours. It's not clear whose is harder.

If letting your child go feels like someone has died, there's nothing wrong with you. You're grieving. It's okay to experience a sense of bereavement when a child and former companion starts to pull away. If the relationship was close enough to meet many of your emotional needs in the past, you'll feel that loss all the more sharply. Just feel it, and survive it. You will heal eventually.

If your child is busy individuating right now, there's no reason you can't have a relationship again on the other side of that process. It will necessarily be a different relationship, but perhaps on the other side of your own grief, you'll be ready for that. Use this time to continue your own personal development, especially individuation and differentiation. There's always more work for most of us to do in that realm.

Attending to Your Own Development

The departure of a child can be a time of upheaval for families, and it can also be a catalyst for parents to make necessary and positive changes in their own lives. Letting go of the active role of mother or father can open up possibilities for self-expression that had to be set aside when parenting was your focus. If you find yourself constantly thinking about your child, and about how you can stay close, ask yourself this: What are you *not* thinking about? What are you neglecting while you focus on that one relationship?

Your child's young adulthood is a good time to explore and address the multitude of emotions triggered by this stage of life. You can do this on your own; with a spouse, partner, or friend; in a support group; or with a counselor or other mental health professional in therapy.

If you're extremely lonely without your child, bring compassion and curiosity to the loneliness. Have you ever felt this way before?

When? If you become aware of feeling unlovable because your child isn't visiting, have you felt unlovable before? How far back does that feeling go?

Are you jealous, as many parents discover themselves to be, of your child's freedom from family responsibilities? What was it like for you when you were their age? What obligations stood in the way of your own freedom as a young person? What responsibilities do you have today that your child could help with — if only she would?

Does your child seem ungrateful for all that you've done for him? Ask yourself what you need from him. Is it gratitude? Or do you need to know he still loves and needs you? Let yourself experience that need in yourself, if it's there. You have a right to feel your feelings, whatever they may be.

These are just a few examples of emotions that can arise when young adults distance themselves from parents. It's helpful to be aware of, and compassionate toward, all your feelings, even if you don't expect your needs to be met. *Someone* should know and care how you feel. You deserve that compassionate attention and concern. It's not appropriate to ask your child to meet that need right now, but that doesn't mean someone else can't be there for you.

At the very least, show up for yourself. You can seek support from peers or even your own parents if you need it. You don't have to go through this alone. Don't ignore your painful feelings. Give them names — grief, loss, despair, fear, anger — and experience them willingly, so that they can move through you, and you can move forward.

While the challenging work of individuation affects all families and can contribute to a kind of temporary estrangement, remember that a relationship hiatus that's motivated mainly by the maturation process is more about the child moving *toward* the wider world than *away* from you.

When estrangement is clearly intentional and accompanied by complaints or animosity, there might be more going on than just a developmental phase. Or not. Some adolescents unconsciously seek excuses to push parents away in order to feel better about "abandoning" their parents. In those cases, children may become irritable around their parents; everything Mom or Dad does annoys them.

Whether or not there's more to the estrangement, your child's need for autonomy while transitioning to adulthood will trump any desire they may have to strengthen their relationship with you. Just like the young turkeys in "My Life as a Turkey," they're being called away by developmental forces. It's time for them to test their wings, not to return home. Your fear that this separation will be permanent is just that: a fear, not a fact. Feel it fully, but don't let it bully you into chasing a reluctant child.

Time for Yourself

There's nothing unnatural about children growing up and leaving home, psychologically as well as physically. But the other three factors that contribute to estrangement — family history, communication problems, and unmet needs in the parent — may create extra tension during this phase. These can be addressed and potentially overcome, but you might have to wait a few years before starting the process in earnest. No matter what you do, if your child is working on independence, your efforts will not bear fruit right now. Nor should they. But read the rest of this book anyway, for your own edification. When adult children are launched, the time is ripe for parents to return to learning and growing.

Your main assignment if your child is recently launched is *not* to get them back or make sure to stay in regular touch; it's to grieve the loss of regular contact. Your son or daughter will never be a child again. Their childhood, along with your central role in their lives, has come to an end. If you feel you made mistakes, I'm sure you're right, because everyone does. But even if they feel like strangers at the moment, it doesn't mean you've lost the opportunity to know them as adults. Estrangement is not about mistakes made in the past; it's usually about continuing to make the same mistakes in the present.[3]

The parent of an adult child has a different role from that of a toddler or teen. You must define that role for yourself, with an eye on your adult child's evolving needs and desires. But personal healing is paramount. Grieve what's gone so that you can focus on the future instead of the past. Spend this time parenting your *own* inner Child. What does that child need from you? At least recognize your own grief by saying, "I see that you're hurting, and I'm terribly sorry." Give yourself time and compassionate attention.

Reengage with the job of differentiation yourself. Try to separate your thoughts from your feelings, and your own experience from that of your adult child. Develop your sense of self, and celebrate your individuality. Reconnect with your spiritual side, the one that puts you in intimate contact with your highest self and brings you peace. Anything you can do that encourages you to focus on yourself as a growing individual will help. Deepen your appreciation for who you are, independent of being a mom or a dad. It will lend you the strength to embark on a future campaign of parenting your adult child in ways that work for both of you.

More Questions for Reflection

- How did you separate psychologically from your family of origin? Did you go away to school? Get married? Leave the family business?
- How did you want your parents to treat you as you were becoming an adult?
- In what ways are you and your parents similar as people? How are you different?
- How did your parents relate to the ways in which you're different from them?
- How is your child different from you? How do you relate to those differences?

6 RE-PARENTING

Long ago, when you were a younger adult and your child was still a tot, she took her cues entirely from you. You, as the adult, set the emotional tone for your parent-child relationship. Having been born with no social skills besides smiling, your child could only follow your lead.

As she grew up and ventured farther from home, there were other influences. She started taking cues from teachers, friends, and eventually lovers, bosses, neighbors, and coworkers. Gradually your child became her own person — an adult like you, with the power to contribute to the emotional tone of relationships.

Your child is now an adult, entirely responsible for her own behavior. However, you are still and always the Parent in the relationship you two share. That will never change — which is both to your detriment and to your advantage.

It's to your detriment insofar as your child will always desire, at some level, for you to be the selfless Parent, offering unconditional love and needing nothing in return. You may not want to be in that role anymore. However, as the Parent, you also have an inalienable, permanent advantage. You're more powerful than you realize when it comes to your adult child, even if that isn't evident right now.

An analogy might help illustrate this point. When I was studying to become a psychotherapist, I was taught that therapists are likely to be perceived by their clients as more powerful than the clients. Even though I don't feel *at all* as though I have more power in the therapeutic relationship than my clients, the facts are suggestive. Clients come to see me, rather than the other way around. They pay me for my time, rather than the other way around. They look to me for support and guidance, rather than the other way around.

For all these reasons, the relationship may feel unequal to my clients. They're likely to perceive me as having more power than they do. If I didn't know this, if I allowed myself to be guided by my own feelings about my relationships with my clients, I might not realize the impact of my words and actions when I sit with clients in session.

Knowing myself to be just a regular human being, with many flaws and limitations, I don't experience having any more power or influence with my clients than I have in my other relationships. It's only through my training that I know my perception is mistaken. Thanks to that training, I weigh my words and actions carefully when dealing with clients in therapy.

As a parent, you have more power and influence over even fully grown children than you probably realize. From what I've learned in conversing with rejecting adult children, if your child is refusing to talk to you, no matter how they behave toward you, they don't feel like they have more power in the relationship than you have. They don't *want* to have it, either. Children feel most at ease when their parents are securely, and benevolently, in charge.

This is another secret that estranged children won't tell you. They still see you as the Parent, and they may just be ready to take their cues from you again.

Commit to the Role

Re-parenting your adult child is a viable action plan for reconnection. To do this, you'll need to commit to being the "bigger" person, even if your child is now a head taller than you.

Are you ready to take on the challenge of the Parent's selflessness? You may or may not have been ready for this difficult task when your child was born. Are you willing to allow your child to resume the role of the Child with you, so that you can take the reins and set a new tone for the relationship?

You don't have to be the perfect Parent. That wasn't required the first time around, and it isn't required now. Just play the Parent as often as you can, keeping the role responsibilities and your adult Child's needs in mind. Apologize when you get it wrong, and do it sincerely. For tips on how to apologize well, see the section "How to Apologize" in chapter 8.

To prime the parenting pump, first go back over the list of role responsibilities that was presented in chapter 4. These are repeated below for your convenience, but with slight alterations that take into consideration the fact that your child is now an adult. These will give you areas for focus as you re-parent your child.

- The Child behaves as he likes (he's still a kid on the inside, after all), but the Parent's behavior toward the Child is consistently guided by love and discipline. Now that your child has his own rights and responsibilities, your "discipline" will take the form of boundaries. You'll respect his and make sure he knows yours. See "Holding Your Boundaries" in chapter 11 for more on this topic.
- The Child is immature, self-centered, and often unreasonable. The Parent is, figuratively, the bigger person and responds calmly to the child's behavior rather than reacting emotionally.
- The Parent is dedicated to the welfare of the Child and shows interest and delight in the Child. The Child is not required to reciprocate.
- The Child has every right to have emotional needs met by the Parent, but the Parent does not expect the Child to meet her emotional needs.

- The Parent helps the Child feel seen, heard, understood, and valued as an individual. The Child has no such duty toward the Parent.
- The Parent allows and encourages the Child to mature and develop into a person who is separate and possibly quite different from the Parent. The Parent celebrates and shows appreciation for the child's differences, including respecting stated and implied boundaries.

As you go back over these slightly modified responsibilities, and also the needs of the Child from chapter 4, examine the Parent's responsibilities and note which ones you already do well. These are the tools you can and should pull out often when dealing with your child. Write down the ways you already act as the Parent, even if you aren't always consistent. Let those actions be the main tools in your toolkit. The more you focus on what to do, rather than what *not* to do, the more skillful you'll be in your new relationship with your child.

Note any parts of the Parent's role that were especially hard for you the first time around. These areas will improve as you work on them, while making sure your own emotional needs are met.

Practice treating yourself as the Child; offer visibility and validation when you're feeling hurt or down. This happens inside your own head, so there's no need for embarrassment. No one has to know you're re-parenting yourself. Be kind to yourself so you can be even more patient with your disgruntled or inconsiderate estranged child.

Your Doormat Alarm

Do you feel victimized by your child's behavior? Does it feel wrong to take all the blame and all the responsibility? We all want the same things when we feel hurt: compassion and understanding. But again, unless we're saints, we find it nearly impossible to offer these to the person who's hurt us, at least before our own pain has been acknowledged.

Many parents aren't consistent in their efforts to revive their relationship with an estranged child, even though they would love to be, because their "doormat alarm" keeps going off. They hate feeling like a doormat when they've been giving and giving and getting nothing back. The Child inside the parent feels attacked and vilified by the person they parented. Their own needs for acceptance, visibility, and validation are going unmet.

The Child-Parent resents the Child for rejecting her; she digs in her heels against continuing to apologize. She doesn't want to hear any more about what she's supposed to have done wrong, or what she has to do to fix it. She feels misunderstood and mistreated, and she wants things to feel more balanced and fair.

Whenever your doormat alarm goes off with your child, you can take your power back by first nurturing yourself, and then consciously stepping into the Parent role.

Parents (with a capital P) are never doormats. If you're changing a baby and he pees on you, is he treating you like a doormat, or is he just being a baby? How much power does a baby have in your relationship with him? If he can't even control his bladder, he's hardly a peer (no pun intended), let alone someone more powerful than you.

A doormat is someone trampled on by a more powerful person. Here's a message from an estranged child. How dominant does this child sound to you?

> I would literally feel dizzy and sick and drained when I would see that missed call [from my parents], and if I got 2 or 3 voice messages, I might be physically ill and unable to attend work.

Your texts, emails, or letters are not going into a black hole; every one of your communications has an effect, either positive or negative. Parents aren't powerless; they have virtually all the power to set the tone in their relationships with their children, and this hardly wanes over a lifetime.

Even though the Parent role is a thankless one when feedback is absent, limited, or negative, if you play it consistently, you might get results you never knew were possible. There's no guarantee; but if you don't step back into that role, your inner Child could do battle with your actual child for the rest of your life, and the results are almost certain to be disappointing for both of you. It's a matter of choosing a possible win over an almost certain loss.

Reframe every interaction in which you feel resentful as one in which you are generously and responsibly re-parenting your adult child. Your self-image will soar when you can see yourself as mature and giving, rather than as someone who's being walked on. Remember that your child is nowhere near as powerful as she may seem. Also remember to fill your bucket of emotional resources elsewhere, or re-parenting will be impossible.

Being willing to try to meet your child's needs is not the same as giving them the shirt off your back. The needs we're talking about are emotional, not material. As the parent of an adult, you're no longer responsible for their material well-being. In my opinion, in making decisions about material support for adult children after they graduate from college, you should always put your own financial health and well-being first. If you have extra, you have the option to help. See the section "Financial Assistance" later in this chapter.

Guidelines for the Parent

Here are a few pointers to keep in mind when you're feeling strong, peaceful, and ready to play the Parent.

Be Consistent

You have to be consistent if you want to build trust. And that takes time. When you first start conscientiously playing the Parent with your child, he won't necessarily buy it. He might even see it as a ploy you're using to get your way.

Don't be discouraged if your new behaviors don't produce immediate results; they almost certainly won't. In the face of lack of results, continue to be consistent in every way you can while making doubly sure to get your own emotional needs met elsewhere. Fill your bucket regularly. Be seen, heard, and understood by someone. To use another analogy, don't try to drive this road while you're running on empty.

It's a drag to keep at something when you don't get feedback, but if you're being consistent, you are having an effect. Even if it appears that your efforts aren't accomplishing anything, don't be so sure. You can't give out energy and not make ripples somewhere.

Delayed gratification is still gratification. Did you ever make deposits in a bank account and watch it grow? Each deposit in itself may not have seemed like much, but when you compared the opening balance to the closing one, you could see how much you'd saved. Add a penny to a piggy bank consistently, and count the results in dollars.

Decide on your personal rules of engagement. This is one of the many areas in which it's helpful to think about your boundaries. There's no right or wrong answer to what your boundaries should be: you can set them wherever you choose. But you do need to make conscious decisions about what's workable for you in the context of being the Parent. Will you continue to pay your child's phone bill or car payments, no matter what? Can you do that consistently without feeling resentful? Will you send her a letter every three months, even if you never hear from her? Can you keep that up regularly without feeling resentful? Will you stop reaching out at a certain point? If so, when will you know you've reached your limit? How will you respond if she approaches you after you've given up?

Make decisions now about your boundaries. Get help with this if you're not sure what's reasonable. Setting boundaries will help you regain a sense of control. When you've decided on your rules, stick to them. If it seems appropriate (i.e., if your child asks), you can share these. But do so with the Parent role firmly in mind, and don't use your rules as threats or punishment. Think "calm" and "consistent."

Activity: Figure Out Your Boundaries

Spend some time thinking about how you want to be consistent about the following:

Money: Will you give any, and if so, how much? Loan or gift? (Gifts are simpler.)

Language: What's acceptable and what's not, when your child is talking to you?

Witnesses: Who in your circle is allowed to know about the estrangement?

Contact: When are you available? How much notice do you need?

Other: What else can you draw a boundary around, without encroaching on your estranged child's emotional needs? With family members, whenever you draw a boundary, it will be tested, and more than once — I can absolutely guarantee it. Maintain your calm with boundary-protecting words like the following:

"I'm truly sorry to say *I don't have any more money for you this month.*"

"I don't like being called names. *Please stop it.*"

"*I'd prefer it if you didn't* mention the estrangement to _____."

"I would absolutely love to see you, and the sooner the better. But *I'm not free tonight.*"

"I'm heading to bed. Would you *please turn the television down?*"

"*I'm not angry*, I'm making a request."

If you expect your boundaries to be tested repeatedly, you might not get quite so exasperated when they are. Plan to be tested, and have your words (and your patience) at the ready.

Why Not Calling Isn't a Boundary Violation (or Abuse)

In typical online forums, estranged parents frequently refer to their children's lack of contact as abusive. While it can certainly feel that way, technically abuse always involves either a boundary violation from a position of power, or the withholding of something to which the victim has a right. Not responding to a text sent by someone for whom you're not responsible, while it may be rude, is not a boundary violation. And although you might wish for a return text from your child if you've sent him one, his right not to respond trumps that wish.

The boundaries we set up around ourselves determine whether others are *allowed* (not *required*) to approach us, and what happens if they do so in ways we don't like.

I was once yelled at by the owner of a coffee shop for bringing in a cup of soup from outside. I shouldn't have done it, and if he'd spoken to me in a normal tone, I would have apologized sincerely and either put away the soup or left, undoubtedly feeling ashamed of myself. Instead, reeling from the shock of his unexpected verbal attack, I didn't say anything at all. I just picked up my soup and left without a word. He had violated a boundary of mine that says, "If you speak to me, it should be at a reasonable volume, or I won't engage with you." Feeling I was the victim and not the perpetrator, I never went back to that coffee shop. I discouraged my friends from going there, too. Boundary violations often have consequences.

In personal relationships, we don't get to make rules for other adults that say things like "You must call me" or "You must respond when I reach out to you." Boundaries protect us from invasions, not from lack of connection. Of course, you have the right to decide for yourself what the consequences will be if your child or anyone else hurts your feelings with their behavior. Keep in mind that reaching out to your child if she's requested that you not contact her *is* a boundary violation. And it will likely have consequences, whether or not they're immediately apparent.

Respond, Don't React

Imagine how a pair of young parents might respond if their toddler tried to shut them down by ceasing all communication with them. You can bet the "estrangement" between a two-year-old and her parents would end when the parents decided it would. With toddlers it's obvious who's in charge and who's the bigger person. When a young child throws a tantrum, parents don't think, "Well, I guess I can't have a relationship with my toddler anymore. I hope he forgives me one day."

You're going back to that phase of parenting with your action plan. Your aim is to *respond* rather than *react* to what your child is doing, whether it's differentiating, throwing a tantrum, or simply ignoring you.

His silence or her stubbornness may drive you crazy and hurt your feelings, but an emotional reaction will only yield more of the same. Instead, get your need for soothing met elsewhere, wait until you're calm, then figure out how best to respond (not react) to the situation. Never send an email the same day you write it unless it's 100 percent positive. Here's an example:

> Thank you so much for writing. I'm thrilled to hear that you've found a new place to live, even though I wasn't able to help you. Congrats and lots of love from Dad.

When in doubt, stick with your action plan and the boundaries you set for yourself early on. If you choose your boundaries with integrity, don't regret sticking to them later, even if you feel bad for your child.

Focus on the Child's Well-Being

Every decision you make in dealing with your child, after you've set your internal rules of engagement, should pass the test of promoting her well-being. This doesn't mean enabling destructive behavior or helplessness.

If you're wondering whether your good deeds are enabling rather than beneficial to your child, consider this definition: *Enabling* (outside the context of addiction) means doing things for your child that she can and should do for herself, such as paying for her phone or car when she has a full-time job and otherwise supports herself, or writing a letter on behalf of a literate adult son.

As the re-parent of an adult child rather than a first-time parent of an actual child, you can't be responsible for the logistics of your child's life, such as getting to work on time, eating, or taking a shower. Your behavior and words should focus on meeting his *emotional* needs, including the need for visibility, validation, and acceptance. Here are some examples of how to address those needs.

Visibility

Let your child know that you know who she is, and what she's going through.

"You're a good friend to Marjorie."
"You have a lot of responsibility at work."
"It sounds like you're looking forward to your trip."

It's important to reflect your child's words and opinions back to them rather than offering your own take on their situation. For example, don't say "You have a lot of responsibility at work" unless your child has indicated that she does.

Validation

Understanding plus empathy equals validation. We'll take a closer look at this in chapter 7.

"You've got a full plate right now; it must be hard to manage all of it when you're not feeling well."

"Your boss is so hard on you, no wonder you hate going to
work."

"I know I wasn't there for you when you needed me to be, and
that must have been frustrating/disappointing/hurtful."
[Use your child's words.]

Same tip here as above: don't editorialize. Reflect only. It's fine to
apologize if you feel so moved.

Acceptance

Show your child that you accept and appreciate him for who he really is.

"You have better taste in clothes than I ever did. It's fun to see
what you're wearing."

"I know you and I are very different when it comes to [fill in the
blank]. But I appreciate where you're coming from."

"I haven't expressed it enough, but it's okay with me that you
didn't go to college. I'm proud of what you're doing with
your talents and your life."

Meeting your child's needs for visibility, validation, and acceptance
will require you to pay close attention to him. Even if he's accused you
of overinvolvement in the past, it might be okay to offer quality attention now. Overinvolvement is more about you as a parent needing to
have input, whereas quality attention shines a light on the person of the
child. Most of us enjoy having someone show genuine interest in us.

Remember: *reflect*. Say back to your child, in slightly different
words, exactly what she says to you. Stay positive. Or if she's being
negative, be negative with her. The important thing is to reflect her
views, without judging or trying to change what you're hearing. Don't
worry about amplifying negativity by agreeing with it: negative feelings are soothed, not compounded, by empathy.

If you're in therapy, that experience will help you with expressing empathy. Notice the way your counselor or therapist listens and talks to you, and try paying it forward with your child whenever possible. In many ways, good therapy has a lot in common with re-parenting.

Be Curious, Not Defensive

If at any time your estranged child complains about something you're doing or have done in the past, guard against reacting with defensiveness. Instead, be compassionate and curious. Empathize, and collect more information. When you're dealing with unwanted estrangement, knowledge is power.

Even if your child's anger stems from past interactions, what he needs from you now is in the present. Here's a fictitious phone conversation between a college student and his mother, whom he accuses of being "too involved" in his life.

Conversation A is how the interaction usually goes. In conversation B, Mom employs curiosity rather than defensiveness. Check out the difference:

Conversation A

Mom: How are your classes going?

Son: (*instantly irritated*) Fine!

Mom: You don't have to yell at me. I'm just trying to —

Son: I know what you're trying to do, I know! *Okay?*

Mom: What? What have I done now? All I said was —

Son: Mom, I don't want to talk about this right now. I have to go study.

Mom: You have to go? It's been two weeks since I talked to you.

Son: (*Sighs.*) Mom, don't be so dramatic.

This conversation escalates, ending shortly thereafter with Mom in tears and Son getting off the phone not looking forward to the next call.

Conversation B

Mom: How are your classes going?

Son: (*instantly irritated*) Fine!

Mom: That's great, honey.

Son: They're going *fine*, okay?

Mom: Okay. That's wonderful.

(*Long pause*)

Son: Is that it?

Mom: What do you mean?

Son: I can't believe you're not going to ask for details about my classes. That's your usual MO.

Mom: I know. I usually do ask, don't I?

Son: It's fine. I don't need you to ask. In fact, please don't.

Mom: (*Laughs.*) Okay.

Son: How are you?

Conversation B, while tense, continues without escalating and ends peacefully.

The son is used to being closely questioned about school, and he's reactive to the point of being rude. In conversation B, Mom's lack of interrogation catches him off guard. When he says something about it, Mom doesn't jump to explaining or defending her behavior. She responds with the most useful, versatile response ever: "What do you mean?" That particular phrase is a good one to keep handy. It serves to elicit more information. It also invites others to hear what they themselves are saying.

When the son points out the old behavior, Mom just validates his observation by admitting, "I usually do ask." The conversation can now take a fresh direction. There's no bad taste left in anyone's mouth, no new incentive to avoid future contact.

Conversation A keeps Mom and Son stuck in a painful pattern of bickering. Conversation B is not exactly full of warm fuzzies, but it's different from the norm, and it doesn't escalate. When there's tension in a relationship, sometimes the best possible way to handle a given interaction is to avoid escalation and keep things peaceful. Small victories like this add up over time. Be proud of yourself whenever you achieve one.

Taking Responsibility versus Accepting Blame

When emotions run high and out of control instead of being owned and tolerated inside, estrangement becomes a blame game. Your child blames you, you go back and forth between blaming yourself and blaming them (or someone else), and everybody feels worse and worse. Responsibility is passed around like a hot potato, because it seems to imply blame.

I received this comment from someone, presumably an estranged parent, on one of my posts about estrangement:

> This so biased against parents, I cannot begin to believe it. Parents are NOT always wrong...and they should NEVER admit to being wrong if they are not. That is what abused people do.

Abused people may indeed admit to being wrong when they're not. However, that doesn't mean that apologizing for harm done, even unwittingly, is inherently unhealthy. By the way, the very same post elicited another angry comment accusing me of being biased in *favor* of parents.

For many estranged parents, finding a way to reconnect with an estranged child takes a backseat to the emotionally charged goal of not being wrong. The specter of abuse is often raised by estranged parents, either to say, "I didn't neglect or abuse my kids," or to claim abuse by the child. In these cases, estrangement is usually prolonged.

As I acknowledged in chapter 2, elder abuse does happen. Physical and verbal abuse are perpetrated every day against aging parents by their own children, and it's ugly. But it's not the same as estrangement, even though both situations are deeply wounding.

Taking responsibility for making peace with your child is not the same as accepting blame. The difference between blame and responsibility is that blame is destructive, and responsibility is creative. You don't have to accept blame in order to take responsibility.

To really appreciate the difference between the two, imagine that a burglar breaks into your locked home and steals your laptop. Whose responsibility is it to buy a new one? The theft was not your fault, yet it's still your responsibility to buy yourself a new laptop if you don't want to live without one. Is that fair? Of course not. The burglar gets a free laptop while you have to pay for another. But if you don't buy yourself a new one, you'll be the one who suffers.

Taking responsibility, not blame, is what's required to solve the problems that come up in our lives. You already know what it feels like to be responsible. As a parent, you've had many responsibilities over the years. By reading this book, you're already taking responsibility for the evolution and protection of your relationship with your child.

Another way of looking at this is through the lens of intention. Being "intentional" in life is a popular concept these days, and for good reason. We can't create what we want without forming an intention to do it. And we can't be intentional about anything unless we first accept that we're responsible for creating the life we want. To me, this feels empowering. It means you can choose to work on repairing the relationship with your child and take informed action in that direction. Even if the outcome is ultimately disappointing, it won't be because you sat on your hands waiting for things to get better.

Should You Tell Your Child What You're Doing?

When parents assume the obligation of re-parenting their estranged adult child, they sometimes wonder whether they should let their child know. It depends. If you tell your child that you've read a book on parent-child estrangement and you're going to try re-parenting them, it may or may not go over well. Your child might think you're trying to manipulate them.

However, if you say something like "I haven't always listened to what you need, and I'd like to try to correct that," you're more likely to score a hit. If you do, don't expect your child to show it. Most estranged adult children need to see consistency before they're comfortable acknowledging positive changes. And again, that takes time.

If they suspect that you're up to something, either because you're behaving differently or you're using words you don't normally use, you can be honest if they ask you about it. Make sure your explanation focuses on the unstated emotional needs of your child. You could offer one of these responses:

1. "I saw something on the internet about being a good listener, and I realized I haven't always been that for you. I'd like to try to do better." [*Yes! Meets needs for visibility and validation.*]
2. "I'm trying to avoid making you angry." [*No. Gives too much power to the child by placing the parent in a subordinate role.*]
3. "You said you wanted me to listen more, so I'm listening more." [*No. Same as 2.*]

Explanations 2 and 3 both make the speaker sound like a child and cast the listener in the role of a powerful parent who can't be pleased. Avoid subtle role reversals like this. They drive adult children nuts, and understandably so. Despite appearances, deep down no Child has the desire — let alone the need — for power over a Parent.

Even if your explanation is assertive, generous, and balanced like example 1 above, your child might seem unimpressed. Take any lack of a negative response as positive at this point. Do be honest if you're doing something different and your child asks you about it. It's important to be trustworthy. You might say:

"Yes, I'm using a new word."
"I thought I'd experiment with being less defensive. I'm not sure how well I'm doing, but it's something I'd like to get better at."

"Yes, it feels different to me, too.... I think I like it. What about
  you?"

In order to strike the right tone in every interaction with your
estranged child, it might help to think of a mantra or keyword. For
example, try *humble*. This is something only a powerful person can be.
If you're powerless, you have nothing to be humble about.

Feeling *humble* comes across as *giving* (whereas, unfortunately,
feeling *hurt* comes across as *grasping*).

Coming across as giving should be doable. But don't attempt
re-parenting until you feel strong and peaceful enough to keep a keyword like *humble*, *selfless*, or *compassionate* in mind when dealing with
your adult child. Reread the section "Cultivating Self-Compassion" in
chapter 4 if you don't feel ready yet.

Financial Assistance

One issue that comes up for many parents of young adults who are
estranged is the question of financial assistance. Should they get any if
they refuse to engage with their parents? Before taking any action, consult your financial adviser about any potential decision that involves a
substantial amount of money. You need to understand the implications
for your own financial health.

New adults who are away at college or have not yet entered the
workforce may continue to rely on your financial support even as they
shun you socially. For better or worse, extended adolescence, with its
mixture of dependence and autonomy, is the new normal. Young adults
today may need financial assistance until they can support themselves,
despite surrounding themselves with a moat of psychological and physical distance. Insisting on contact as a condition of financial assistance
during this vulnerable phase in your young adult's life may leave scars
on the relationship.

It's perfectly acceptable to put realistic, noncoercive boundaries on financial support for your estranged child. For example, if you provide a monthly stipend that's sufficient as long as she manages the money well, then poor judgment that leads to a shortfall is not a situation from which you're required to rescue her. Just make sure you tell her right up front what the limitations are on your financial support. Your boundaries should never catch your child by surprise. If you communicate that there will be no further help in case of a shortfall, then it's up to her to make the arrangement work.

If you haven't been clear and consistent with boundaries of this kind in the past, expect new limits to be tested, and prepare to squirm while you witness spectacular failures. Be compassionate in your speech, but keep the boundaries consistent. Just because you're being generous enough to give your child money while expecting nothing back right now doesn't mean you're an ATM. Give him the support he absolutely needs if you can afford it without risking your own financial well-being. But when he makes mistakes, let him figure out how to deal with them.

Micromanaging a new adult's budget is as problematic as it is tempting. If your now-adult child is generally honest and tells you she needs a certain amount from you each month, and the amount seems reasonable to you, take her word for it. However, if she comes back a month later and says she underestimated, then it's only natural to ask questions about her income and expenses to help her clarify her needs. Once an amount has been agreed to, don't be quick to increase it. Young adults benefit from learning to manage on a specific income. It's a skill few people nowadays can do without.

If your child's past behavior has damaged your trust to the point where you can't be sure about his financial needs, but you know he requires *some* help, suggest a reasonable amount and ask for his input. If he says it's not enough, ask for details. If he says something like, "Just trust me, I need more than that," you can remind him gently that the last time you trusted him, he wasn't honest with you. Reinforce the idea that you want to help him, but you need him to reestablish your trust with accountability. Administered calmly and with kindness, this can be a valuable life lesson.

If your child becomes angry and says, "Keep your money. I don't need anything from you," respond with love. "If you change your mind, let us know. We're here for you if you need us." Then retreat. Don't use money to tie your child to you. Allow him to make do without your financial assistance if he wants to. You might be tempted to offer him money later, when he hasn't asked for it, just because you miss him and regret not helping him when he asked for it. But he needs to know that you mean what you say. In the long run, basing your connection on money will not sweeten or strengthen your bond. On the contrary, it introduces unnecessary complications to an already complicated relationship.

You'll need to tolerate feelings of guilt, remorse, and uncertainty around financial decisions and your child. It's not easy to be consistent, or even to know what's right in the first place. When reviewing your past interactions with your estranged child, you will inevitably see different paths you could have taken. But only a few of those regrets signal serious mistakes that should be revisited. Holding appropriate, well-thought-out boundaries with your child, while painful for both of you at times, is rarely a mistake.

Expect young adults to act like very large, long-distance boomerangs. They may appear to move away from you for years before coming back around. In some cases, they won't come back on their own. But you won't know what's going to happen until they're on the other side of adolescence — as a "guesstimate," let's say in their late twenties, or at least five years after they leave home for the last time.

Whether or not your relationship with your child is on a strong foundation, young adulthood is not the ideal time to go back and make repairs. Instead, focus on staying calm and consistent during this difficult phase. Turning your attention to your own personal growth is a better use of your time than trying to pull your child closer while they still want to move away.

7 FILLING EVERYONE'S BUCKETS

Gaining perspective is one way to wiggle things loose when you're feeling tied up in the estrangement knot. It will help you nurture the compassion you feel toward your child. This is obviously very hard to do when you're reeling from hurt feelings yourself, but the pathway to reconciliation begins with compassion, which in turn enables you to offer validation and a good apology to your child.

The Challenge of Gaining Perspective

If your child has cut you off for some perceived wrongdoing on your part, their reasoning may seem petty, ungenerous, or downright wrong. You may even think it's based on a lie: if only you could set the record straight and get them to see the truth, they would have to take everything back and apologize. But they won't give you that opportunity.

It's no picnic trying to drum up compassion for someone who's being stubborn or believing lies about you. But that is the task before you. This is not about who's right and who's wrong. It's about mending fences. The reason to seek your child's point of view is *not* that you were bad or wrong, but because you need to understand it to achieve the goal of reconnection.

Let's step outside the emotionally loaded scenario of parent-child estrangement to better understand the psychology of connection in the presence of conflict. Imagine that a complete stranger approaches you on the street and accuses you of stealing his car. In tears, tearing his hair out, he yells at you, "I was going to visit my dying grandmother. Because *you* stole my car, I had to take the bus, and by the time I got there, she was already gone. I never got the chance to say goodbye!" He dissolves into tears, adding, "I *hate* you for what you did."

Watching him sob, how do you feel? You know you didn't steal his car. Can you put aside his anger and blame in order to respond to his grief? Can you find compassion for him in light of his loss? If you find that you can let his criticism roll off your back and feel sorry for him despite his unprovoked verbal attack, why do you think that is?

I think it's because he's a stranger. You don't need anything from him, and you know in your bones that you're not to blame for his troubles. It's therefore a relatively simple matter to put aside his accusations and respond to his pain. You might even find yourself murmuring, "I'm so very sorry," and offering a hug.

But let's raise the stakes. What if you *did* move his car, but only to save it from an oncoming mudslide? How easy is it for you to stand there now and take his angry, hateful accusations? You were doing him a favor. How much do you need him to understand that?

Seeing things from another person's perspective is easier when you don't have to defend yourself. You can readily put yourself in their shoes and empathize with their pain. But when someone accuses you of hurting them and shows no interest in hearing your side of the story, your defenses can activate automatically and block your ability to respond effectively.

Now suppose that you moved the stranger's car, and you have only ten minutes to make him either your friend or your enemy. You might try telling him about the mudslide that almost swallowed his car. But what if he doesn't care about that right now? What if the loss of his grandmother eclipses any concern he might have about the car? Sure, you did him a favor. But he can't appreciate that right now. What he *can* appreciate is empathy. He wanted to see his grandmother one last time, but because he couldn't find his car (regardless of the reason), he lost his only chance. He's devastated.

If you've only got ten minutes with him and you want to make him your friend, you must let go of any need for gratitude or appreciation for your good deed in moving the car. The best use of your limited time is to respond with compassion to the feelings he's sharing. He needs nothing but kindness from you right now. Can you provide that?

If you show empathy, apologizing profusely for moving his car and sitting with him in his grief, you have the best chance of continuing the relationship. You will have succeeded in seeing things from his perspective and, in so doing, made him your friend.

Once he's had some time to heal, your new friend may come back to you and ask about your reasons for moving the car. You can tell him then about the mudslide. He'll be in a much better place to hear about and appreciate your good deed, and the friendship will grow stronger.

Metaphorically speaking, you may have only ten minutes to respond to your child's complaints. If those ten minutes don't go well, she might give up hope of ever getting the understanding she's seeking from you.

When your child complains about your current or past behavior, the best thing you can do to enhance your relationship is to try to see things from her perspective. Drop your defenses and take her side — not because hers is the "right" side, but because she needs you on her side if she's to heal and become available to connect with you again. Wait until she's calmer and happier before expecting her to try in her turn to see things from your perspective.

You probably won't be able to respond well to criticism or complaints unless you're feeling strong and peaceful. You shouldn't have to try to fill anyone else's bucket when you're emotionally injured and in pain. That's the time to rest and recuperate, surrounding yourself with people — and filling yourself up with experiences — that nurture you and help you feel better.

On the list of people who might be willing and able to understand where you're coming from, your estranged adult child comes in dead last. He's coming from the point of view of the Child, who has every right to expect more than he gives.

If he hurt your feelings the last time you had contact, he could hurt you again next time. To keep disappointment in check, try to come from a place of no need (i.e., with as full a bucket as you can get with the help of appropriate people) when you reach out to your child. The less you need him to understand and sympathize with you, the easier it will be to reconnect.

Validation (It's Not Just for Parking)

Validation is one of the most healing gifts you can offer to your estranged child. Over time, words of understanding and acceptance can cut through the thickest walls of alienation and anger. Consistent, sincere validation provides a foundation for a new and more fulfilling relationship.

As an example of how to use validation to mend a tear in your relationship, let's consider the case of Peggy and her estranged adult daughter, Margo.

Margo's grievance against her mother is that after her parents' divorce, her mother seemed interested only in men, leaving twelve-year-old Margo, an only child, to fend for herself. She felt abandoned.

Peggy remembers it differently. She remembers the sacrifices she made to put Margo first. For example, she often clocked out early at work to make sure she was there when Margo got home after school. She put money aside for Margo's college education, even though she could barely afford to do so. Peggy didn't ignore her daughter as she's accused of doing. She remembers worrying about Margo at the time and making efforts to ask her how she was doing. In her recollection, Margo rebuffed her, seemingly not wanting or needing to talk.

In order to restore the relationship between them, which Margo has now indicated she no longer wants, Peggy has to find a way to meet Margo's current emotional needs. If they were friends, sisters, coworkers, or anything else to each other besides Parent and Child, this wouldn't be Peggy's responsibility. But because she is the person in the Parent role, if she wants to make repairs, she must put Margo's needs ahead of her own.

Peggy leans on her new husband and another good friend for support, then tries to put herself in Margo's shoes. She lets herself imagine what it might have been like for a twelve-year-old girl to lose close contact with her father and move with her mother to a new town where she knew no one.

Peggy remembers dealing with the aftermath of the divorce herself, complete with financial problems and injured self-esteem. She couldn't be there for Margo as much as Margo needed her to be, because she was still recovering herself, feeling empty and in survival mode. She dated several men (unsuitable, in retrospect) in an attempt to reassert her feminine confidence, and there must have been times when Margo felt abandoned.

Looking back, Peggy can see that although she did the best she could at the time, she simply didn't have the confidence, time, or emotional reserves to give Margo all the support and security she needed as the child of a divorcing couple.

Peggy can understand both her own limitations back then and their causes, so she doesn't need to chastise herself. But yes, she can see how Margo didn't get enough of what she needed back then. Margo needed an adult to help her process her feelings about the divorce, the move, her new school, and all the vagaries of being twelve, though she couldn't express those needs at the time.

Margo was still a child, with a right to expect that she would be taken care of. Although she's now an adult, Margo, in the Child role, still needs an acknowledgment that she was an innocent bystander who got hurt when her mom "abandoned" her after the divorce.

Peggy can't change the past, but that doesn't matter because the problem between them exists in the present. Peggy can help heal Margo's wounds by meeting the needs today that went unmet yesterday — primarily the need for visibility. She can help meet this enduring need by acknowledging now, in so many words, that:

1. Margo deserved more than she received (this is also true of you, me, and all Children).
2. It's understandable that Margo felt abandoned.
3. Peggy is truly sorry for not being able to give her what she needed back then.

As the Child, Margo doesn't need to hear Peggy's side of the story; the only facts that are relevant to her healing are the three above. Peggy may know in her own heart — and she may also have peers who know — that she was a conscientious mother who did a very good job as a single parent, but she doesn't have to try to convince Margo that "it wasn't like what you're saying."

Refer to the role responsibilities whenever you're in contact with your child: the Parent should seek to understand the Child but should not seek visibility or appreciation from the Child.

It's extremely important, however, that Peggy acknowledge to herself and appreciate the sacrifices and efforts she made on behalf of her daughter. Although Margo doesn't have to offer her mother validation, Peggy does need to offer it to herself. If necessary, she can seek validation from her peers and, if possible, her own parents.

At the heart of the estrangement, as painful as it may be to think about, is your child's belief that you let him down in the past and that, in some way, you're still doing so now. I mentioned in the introduction that unnecessary shame can get in the way of addressing this sad truth. All parents let their children down, because all parents are human. No one can always be as selfless as the Child needs the Parent to be.

Like Peggy, you may need to develop an exceptionally thick skin to validate your child's view of what happened then and what's happening now between you. In the encounter with the man whose car you saved, you had to put aside your own hurt feelings in order to gain his friendship. To win his heart, you first had to give him yours.

You deserve validation as much as your child does, but in the interest of repairing this relationship, you must seek yours elsewhere. Get it from yourself, your parents, your spouse or partner, your friends, or your therapist. But make sure you get it. Life without validation is like a life lived in a remote desert: lonely and barren.

Validation with Apology

If you have no idea whatsoever why your child has stepped away from you, start with what you do know. "I'm not good with emotions," or "I was never really sure how to handle our relationship," or "I don't say 'I love you' very easily" will go a long way, if true. By leading with what you know, you signal that you're open to discussing things that are real and true, and that you recognize some of your personal growing edges.

If you do have some idea why your child is cutting you off, look beneath the surface to make sure you understand it at its roots. A single incident that seems to have led to the estrangement should be understood as the final straw, not the sole cause. What is the theme of the incident? Did your child feel criticized, neglected, or misunderstood? When has this happened before? See also the section "If You Don't Know What to Apologize For" in chapter 8.

When it comes to providing validation as the Parent, you don't have to feel like a doormat. Validation doesn't mean they're right about what happened, that you're a bad parent, or that you need to grovel. *Validation is attempting to understand their point of view, with empathy.* Your child just needs to know that you want to understand how she feels, and that her feelings matter to you.

The fact that you care about her may seem obvious to you, but don't assume it's obvious to your child — especially if your first response to the estrangement was to be hurt, to protest, or to try to smooth over your child's complaints by asserting your good intentions. These normal reactions can convey that your child's feelings don't matter to you as much as your own feelings do.

Some people will disagree with me about this, but I believe it's perfectly okay to apologize for things you know you didn't do. Your child might just need to know you're willing and able to apologize. Saying you're sorry about this, that, and everything else costs you nothing, does no damage, halts downward spirals, and could reap large rewards. Your child may be surprised, and might even reconsider his accusations later, if you claim full responsibility for something you don't feel responsible for. It's your child's *experience* of what happened, rather than what you intended or what really happened, that had a negative impact.

Although that kind of magnanimity may be beyond the reach of most of us, let me offer an example of what can happen if you're able to put resentment aside and embrace apologizing for something you didn't do. I have a therapist friend who worked for several months with a client who had substantial difficulties in numerous relationships. One day, she came in and told him that the advice he'd given her was bad, and she was very upset about having taken it.

Here's the interesting part: he hadn't offered a single word of advice. In fact, he'd been very careful to avoid doing so for therapeutic reasons. He knew he had only asked clarifying questions and had let the client come to her own conclusions about how to handle the imbroglios she talked about in their sessions.

When the client accused my colleague of foisting bad advice on her, he was taken aback. "Had I felt guilty," he told me later, "I would have gotten defensive. I might have suggested that her behavior was *her* responsibility, regardless of the advice she received." But knowing he was innocent, and wanting to avoid conflict, he apologized instead. To sweeten the deal, he even expressed sympathy and regret for the bad experience she'd had, following his supposed advice. Treating it as an act of relationship maintenance rather than an admission of guilt made the apology relatively easy for the therapist to offer.

That same client later told my colleague that his apology had had a profound effect on her. She'd been expecting him to defend himself (which made him wonder if she realized at some level that her accusation was unjust), but when he apologized instead, she experienced an unexpected moment of healing. She realized that she herself didn't need to be defensive in relationships, she told him. She could simply apologize and, in doing so, smooth troubled waters. I suspect she also felt heard, accepted, and validated by this therapist's compassionate response.

Staying open to your child's point of view and allowing yourself to be vulnerable will almost undoubtedly strengthen your relationship over time. Be open to criticism, even if it's unfounded. With your child, that may be the only path to reconnection right now. I know it's tough, but try not to take those stinging barbs personally. Try instead to see them as an opportunity to be the wise and compassionate Parent. Afterward, you can go and cry to a spouse, parent, or caring friend, and let them soothe you.

If it lightens the burden for you, think of re-parenting as a hobby. Or imagine you're punching in and going to work. Keep your emotions out of your re-parenting as much as possible. I know it's impossible, but do your best.

Support for the Parent: Using a Therapist

Compassionate counseling will nurture you in these lean times, especially if it focuses on emotions rather than just on changing behavior. Even — and especially — if you're not in contact with your child, you'll benefit from a relationship in which your emotional needs and well-being, and not the other person's, are paramount.

A good therapist embodies aspects of the Parent; they help you feel seen, heard, understood, and cared for. They model good boundaries around things like appointment times, payment, and roles. For example, sessions begin and end on time, the counselor holds you to the payment schedule agreed upon, and she won't ask you to babysit her kids or go out for coffee with her. The roles are clear, and there is both "love" and "discipline" in the form of caring and respect on the one hand, and expectations for common courtesy on the other.

An effective therapist doesn't act like a critical or needy parent. He helps you see the good in yourself, providing appropriate validation and appreciation of your Child self, while gently challenging your perceptions when appropriate. Because of how he treats you, he helps you know what it feels like to have some of your emotional needs met.

Being in the receiving role, in which someone else both sets the tone for your relationship and caringly acknowledges your needs, will provide you not only with emotional support but also with a model for how to approach your estranged child with compassion. It's helpful to experience what the Child gets to feel like, so you can give the gift of parenting with your whole heart, from a full bucket.

There's nothing selfish about the Child role; its purpose is to fill you up with inner resources so that you're capable of being selfless when you need to be. Go ahead and receive. You need it. You wouldn't expect to drive a car forever on a half-empty tank, would you? No matter what happens between you and your child, the right kind of counseling will help you get your inner Child's important needs met — to fill the tank.

Therapy should provide a time and place for you to be reminded of who you are, in all your marvelous, messy, and unique humanity. It should especially help you to realize that your feelings and needs are important, that you have an inner Child who needs your loving kindness, and that there's nothing inherently wrong with you.

Some of us are prone to a quiet but persistent feeling that there's something wrong with us. We think that if others got to know the "real" us, they too would discover that ugly fact. This fear keeps many estranged parents away from the very treatment that could wipe out this dreadful lie once and for all. It may feel risky to expose your vulnerable self to a therapist, but if you choose wisely, therapy can be life-changing.

I recommend in-person counseling whenever possible. Even though distance counseling is becoming more widely available, sitting in the same room with a person who knows you and cares about you is more visceral than gazing at a kind face on your computer screen or hearing a soothing voice on the phone. If you possibly can, physically go see someone. If you live near my office, I invite you to come and see me.

Pay attention to how you feel when you sit down with a new counselor. If you've found the right one, you should feel understood, accepted, and respected most of the time. Meet with more than one therapist if possible, and compare how each makes you feel. Extensive research has shown unequivocally that the relationship you have with your counselor is the most important clinical factor in how helpful your therapy will be — more important than the techniques they use, the credentials they hold, or anything else about them.

Here are a few qualities of a therapist with whom it's comparatively easy to form a relationship:

- nonjudgmental
- focused on you and your needs, not their own agenda
- interested in understanding you, rather than telling you what to do
- warm, kind, compassionate
- treats you like a person, not something growing in a petri dish

For more tips and a sample dialog, see chapter 10, "How to Choose a Therapist," in my book *Constructive Wallowing*.[1]

Estrangement Specialists

People at a distance often ask me for referrals to estrangement specialists in their city, state, or country. The truth is, you don't need a family estrangement specialist to get good therapeutic support.

Some fascinating research came out a few years ago about compassion for distress — that is, the ability of others to sympathize with what you're going through.[2] This is obviously a desirable quality in a counselor. The findings, however, turned common sense on its head.

Researchers found that, as a group, people who have successfully navigated a difficult situation actually have *less* compassion for folks who are having a hard time with exactly the same thing. This means that if you find a therapist or coach who used to be estranged from their own child and succeeded in repairing the relationship (arguably a proven expert), they might feel *less* compassion for you than someone who never had that problem in the first place.

If the findings reflect a general truth, I think this is wonderful news. Whether you're talking to a therapist or another parent on the street, there's really no need to despair if you can't find someone who's been estranged from their own child before. There's a subtle but important point to understand about the research, which I'll illustrate with the example of bullying.

The same study concluded that people who've experienced bullying are generally more compassionate toward those who are bullied than are people who were never bullied. Not surprising, right? They know what it's like. They can relate. But that compassion plummets when the person being bullied fails to overcome the situation. If instead the victim acts out in distress, cries all day, gives up, or otherwise fails to overcome the bullying, their harshest critics are those who were bullied in the past and ended up in a good place. These happy former victims see the current victim as failing to endure the bullying.

The researchers hypothesized that previously bullied people either forget how hard it was to overcome the bullying and move on, or they place too much emphasis on the fact that they themselves endured (so of course it's doable!), or both. This combination of knowledge and experience appears to result in lower compassion for the distress of current sufferers.

Extrapolating from this finding, the most compassionate supporters of parents with estranged adult children should be people who are currently experiencing estrangement themselves; they're in the thick of it and can readily identify with your pain. The catch is, of course, that you're talking to someone who doesn't necessarily know how to solve the problem. They can empathize, but they can't pull you out of the hole because they're in it themselves. And if they get out first, they may lose patience with you if you remain stuck.

Although the conclusion is counterintuitive, all this research seems to indicate that if you're having a hard time with your child's estrangement, the *least* compassionate helper will be someone who has experienced the problem in the past and solved it. While individuals differ in their levels of compassion, as a group these folks came in dead last. The most compassionate group of people you can find are those currently in the same boat as you, unless you're doing just great in implementing your strategies. In that case, your biggest supporters are those who overcame their own estrangements. Just don't fall off the success wagon, or they might lose their patience with you.

A reasonable choice when you're looking for help would be a therapist or coach from the second most compassionate group, which according to this research consists of people who have never experienced estrangement from an adult child. Hopefully, helpers in this category are in the majority.

So take heart if you can't find a therapist, counselor, or coach who's been down the same road with an estranging adult child. Just look for a kind helper who makes you feel understood, not judged.

Action Plan

We've seen that the emotional tone of the Parent-Child relationship is set early on by the Parent, and I've suggested that with the relationship off the tracks, the time has come for you to take back the power and responsibility inherent in that role.

It bears repeating that it's perfectly all right if you still feel like the Child inside. Becoming a parent doesn't turn off your own inner Child. The key is not to be controlled by your inner Child in your relationship with your actual child.

You can experiment with playing the Child with your spouse, friends, therapist, or — here's a crazy idea — your own parents. There's no shame in having emotional needs, in wanting to be seen, valued, and cared for. Good for you for wanting that. You deserve it.

What I have to say next might make your inner Child cry, and I'm sorry for that. As heartbreaking or mystifying as this may be for you, your estranged child doesn't completely trust you. They're likely using distance as a protection against feeling hurt in some way. That's the most common reason given for estrangement from family: for some reason, it's too painful to be close.

I know the idea that they're protecting themselves from you is difficult to accept, especially if you're feeling hurt by *them*, but that's what seems to be true. They didn't ask for it, and they don't want it to be this way, any more than you do. That's just how they feel. There's something about the dynamic between you that hurts them, and they're not yet convinced that you know how to make it right.

To be clear, hurting your child is as easy as falling off a log. All you have to do is not meet all their needs as the Parent. You don't have to be neglectful, careless, heartless, or stupid not to meet all their needs. You just have to be human, with needs of your own. Come to think of it, even a robot programmed never to hurt a child's feelings would almost certainly fail. There just isn't an algorithm sophisticated enough to perform perfect parenting.

As I've emphasized, I assume your child is a person with normal intelligence, not lost in addiction and not seriously mentally ill (e.g., suffering with schizophrenia or experiencing a psychotic break).

Assuming we're dealing with a basically good and reasonable person whose needs have not been met (a hurt person who's hurting people), our action plan has one objective: re-parenting. Your child is already acting the part of the Child, wanting their needs to be met and not knowing how to fix the situation if they're not. Use that as your inspiration.

Don't confuse trying to meet your child's needs with walking on eggshells around them. Those actions may feel the same, but delivering on your child's need for a Parent is purposeful, while walking on eggshells is just a description of feeling awkward. Now that you know that they may be upset because of needs that have not been met, you know what to do. Review the list starting on page 73 and go to town. If you don't know what specifically to *do*, just memorize the Parent and Child roles, then think about being the Parent in every interaction.

While you can't make anyone act a certain way, you definitely have the power to help your child *feel* differently than they do now. They'll feel either better or worse depending on how interactions go with you. Use your considerable power for good. It takes an abundance of patience, so get support and find outlets for your inner Child to be needy and to receive.

If you're not in contact at all with your child right now, we'll discuss how to get back in touch in the next chapter. But maintain focus on your own self-care while you finish reading the rest of this book.

8 CONTACT

When it comes to contact, I can't think of a single rule that applies in 100 percent of cases. Answers to questions like "How long should I wait before contacting him again?" depend entirely on your individual situation. Still, there are a few general guidelines. Whenever I make specific suggestions, I'll provide a rationale. Use the explanation to decide whether any given suggestion makes sense for you and your child.

Take a No-Contact Request Seriously

If your child has asked you explicitly not to contact her, in general, the very best response to a no-contact request is to send a brief acknowledgment and then respect her wishes. (For suggestions on how to respond to such a request, see "If They Asked You Not to Contact Them" in chapter 9.) Don't contact an adult child who's asked you not to. It will worsen relations between you and possibly prolong the estrangement. A child who might have come around by himself after a few months of silence may feel so disrespected, or even harassed, by unwanted texts, emails, cards, or gifts that he'll continue to keep his distance for years in the hope of one day getting the space he asked for.

As discussed in chapter 2, one possible exception to this rule involves young adults who were exposed to parental alienation as children (usually, but not always, surrounding divorce) who have continued an unjustified campaign of rejecting you out of loyalty to the alienating parent. Some research suggests that these young adults might appreciate attempts by the targeted parent to reach out to them, even if they don't respond.[1]

The picture is complicated by the fact that even a child with an alienating parent may have her own reasons for rejecting the targeted parent. Parental alienation syndrome is the most likely culprit when the child's complaints are unjustified, and when there's no evidence of ambivalence or guilt about cutting off the relationship.[2] Any sign of uncertainty or guilt therefore can indicate that the child's estrangement is not wholly the result of parental alienation. Signs of ambivalence may include expressing uncertainty or regret to other family members or friends about the estrangement; sometimes responding and other times not, to the same sorts of communications; and expressing positive sentiments about the rejected parent, e.g., "I love you as my mother, but I don't want to have a relationship with you."

In most cases, the adult child is acting as a free agent. If they ask for no contact, it's because that's what they really want. Take the calculated risk of being absent from your child's life for a while. Don't worry that your child will forget you unless you reach out to him. He won't. Don't assume she'll get comfortable not having you in her life. As a member of a society that values and celebrates family ties, she won't be comfortable living with estrangement from family. Have you ever heard the expression "Absence makes the heart grow fonder"?

I'm not suggesting that respecting your child's request for distance will be easy; it may seem inconceivable. It goes against the grain of being a parent not to be connected to your own child. But your options are limited: you can either honor or ignore your child's stated wishes. Which do you think bodes better for your long-term prospects of connection?

It's a harsh reality, this no-contact business. I wish I could offer you just the right words that would melt your child's heart and change his mind. But when he's requested silence, it doesn't matter which words you use. Only the fact that you're still contacting him when he asked you to stop will get through. The message he'll receive, loud and clear, is, "I don't care what you want; *I* want contact." And that message will not break through the defenses your child has erected.

If you're *not* on the receiving end of a no-contact request, read on.

Find Your Voice

Read this sentence:

I hope you're happy.

How do you interpret that? Your reaction to those words will depend on what you know about me, your best guess as to my state of mind when I wrote them, and your own state of mind when reading them. If I leave those words as a voice message on your phone, you'll gain more information about my intent, and you're more likely to interpret the message accurately. (For the record, I do wish you happiness.)

If you can't get together in person or for a video chat, the best form of contact is a voice message. Yes, I realize nobody makes calls anymore and that your child prefers texting. Yes, it's much easier and more convenient to send a text or an email. But "easy" and "convenient" are not always the best avenues for repairing troubled relationships. And if your child rarely or never receives calls, it just means your voice message won't be competing with a dozen others in her voice mailbox.

Voice messages convey layers of meaning through the tone, pace, pitch, and volume of your speech. Your spoken words are less likely to be grossly misinterpreted than written ones that lie unmoving on a screen or a page.

The fact that your emotion shows in your voice can present a problem. "I don't want my child to hear how insecure/angry/desperate I feel," you might think. The solution? Don't leave a voice message when you don't like how you're feeling. Wait until you're in a calm, generous, loving, or otherwise decent mood before sharing your voice with your child.

The exception to this is if you've been accused — or suspect yourself — of having been emotionally distant with your child(ren). A heartfelt message about missing your child, offering an apology, or both, can be very effective if your child has never heard you express those emotions before. Let your voice betray your feelings if this is you.

If there's even the faintest hint that your child has ever viewed you as needy, self-centered, immature, or anything along those lines, wait until you feel strong, calm, grown-up, centered, and generous before leaving a message on her voice mail.

Writing is the riskiest form of communication. Texting is the absolute worst, followed by email, then letters sent via regular post. The word choice you agonize over, the heartfelt message you craft over the span of hours or days — these are skimmed at lightning speed by someone whose mind is already closed to what you have to say. Their interpretation of your carefully constructed missive, which probably already skews negative, is further debased by the difference between the time it took you to write it and the time it takes them to read it. They can easily fail to absorb the import of your words. Even your sincerest sentiments can come off as banal and not worthy of attention, let alone deep consideration.

Texts tend to be too short to convey your true meaning, and they might pop up at the worst times for your child to read them. Longer texts are likely to be scanned, not read. Handwritten letters are somewhat better than texts or email because handwriting slows the reader down. It also adds a personal touch and evidence of greater effort, which might or might not be appreciated.

Scripting Your Call

When you call your child, you'll either leave a message, or he'll pick up and you'll talk to him. In either case, it might be helpful to have a cheat sheet so you don't stray from your goal for the call. And yes, your call should have a goal. When you're estranged, calling "just to say hello," or to find out what your child is doing, doesn't go over well.

Your cheat sheet should not be a word-for-word script but rather a very short list of bullet points. Or, better yet, a single bullet point. It's fine to write down a word or phrase that you want to be sure to use, but don't plan out whole sentences. It's hard to sound genuine when you're reading.

If your child answers the phone (or calls you out of the blue), you might feel unprepared to deal with an actual conversation. Many parents tell me they worry constantly about saying the wrong thing. Concentrate on listening, not talking. Affirm your child's thoughts and feelings, even if you don't agree with them. She's an adult; your ear, your acceptance, and your empathy are far more valuable to her these days than your opinions. Here are a few examples:

"That seems unfair; no wonder you're upset."

"Yes, it is frustrating (or discouraging) to try and get by on a low salary."

"That's exciting that you got an interview at the dispensary."

"It's disappointing when a friend lets you down."

"You sound relieved about not having to take that exam."

Keep It Short

The more tension there is in your relationship, the more advisable it is to keep all contact brief and positive. Particularly when you're first practicing visibility, validation, and appreciation, keeping emails and phone calls short gives you less opportunity to say the wrong thing. Think "short and sweet" whenever you write, dial, or answer the phone.

If you call your child and leave a message, be positive and focus on the needs of your child, not your own preferences. For example, you might say, "Just calling to say happy birthday. I hope you have a wonderful day. I love you so much. Take care." The End.

On every occasion, if you think you've messed up and said or done something that didn't go over well, apologize immediately and then drop the subject. Saying, "I'm sorry; I didn't mean that," is a fine way to deal with it. Going on and on about your mistake serves no one.

On the other hand, if your child wants to focus on a mistake you made, go with it. Tell yourself, "To love is to be open to feedback from those I love. I am open." Let your child decide how much time she wants to spend going over something she feels like talking to you about. While you're estranged, any conversation is a positive development if you handle it well enough. If you can let go of defensiveness, all your interactions with your child can proceed more smoothly.

Making mistakes is part of living, and it's definitely part of being a parent. If your child tells you he doesn't like something you did (or do), try not to take it personally. Fall back on your apology skills and give yourself a pat on the back for not being defensive with your child. Then go have a cry with someone who loves you. You're allowed to have hurt feelings — just not in front of your child as long as the relationship is strained.

Be Predictable

When contacting your child, one of the most important qualities to demonstrate is predictability. That builds trust, which in turn allows your child to take the risk of being close again. Being consistent (a core aspect of re-parenting) will make you predictable, as will following through on what you say you're going to do.

If you've been sending a card or an email every other month, keep doing that. Don't jump around, taking them by surprise, sometimes emailing three times in one day, then being out of contact for six months. Decide on how often to write or call, let them know about the schedule, and unless they object, stick to it.

Predictable doesn't necessarily mean *frequent*. A once- or twice-a-year schedule of contact is just as consistent as a once-a-week schedule (which I usually advise against, since it's much too frequent for most estranged adults).

If you decide to change your contact routine, let your child know what to expect so that they can mentally prepare for the change. Sometimes parents get tired of putting out effort and getting little or nothing back. They need a break. In such cases, letting the child in on the change preserves predictability.

Here's an example of a voice message you might leave your child if you're planning to change the contact schedule:

> Hey _____. I hope you're well. I wanted to let you know that I'm thinking of maybe calling a bit less often than I have been. So rather than calling next month as usual, I'm going to give it until your birthday. But please know that I'll be thinking of you, and I'm always here if you need me. So if I don't talk to you before then, I'll give you a call on your birthday.

The importance of doing what you say you're going to do can't be overstated. If you say you'll call your child on her birthday, do it. Also, if you tell your child you're going to give them space, *do not contact them at all.*

I spoke to a dad who agreed to give his twenty-four-year-old daughter the space she asked for — only to write her a month later when he heard through the grapevine that she might need a loan. Except in the case of a true emergency (e.g., a serious illness or death in the family), do not contact your child during a period when you said you wouldn't. If you're a member of ReconnectionClub.com, you can download the flow chart in our online library titled, "Is Contact Necessary?" In most cases, the answer is no.

If you knew for a fact that contacting your child when you've promised no contact would ruin your chances at reconciliation for at least another year, would you do it? Contacting him after you've said you won't makes you unpredictable. You'll have to start all over again with basic trust building. If you have trouble waiting now because of how much you miss your child, imagine doubling or tripling the waiting time with one poor decision. Forewarned is forearmed. Not contacting your child when you said you wouldn't, as hard as it may be, is an investment in your future relationship.

The longing to contact your child outside of your planned contact regimen will come and go, just like waves of grief. Ride them out. Tell a friend, your spouse, or your therapist how hard it is for you not to reach out. Soak up as much compassion and sympathy as you can, because those longings can be excruciating. But as the saying goes, there are no shortcuts to any place worth going. When it comes to truly reconnecting with your child, there's only the long road.

Definite No-No's

Like anyone else, estranged adult children react negatively to what they see as invasions of their personal space or privacy. Boundary violations are an easy mistake to make, especially when a child's need for space feels unreasonable to you. It's crucial to be aware of this danger so you can avoid missteps.

Go out of your way to show respect for your child and her domain, as in the sample emails later in this chapter and in chapter 9. Once you've done this consistently, the consideration you've shown may begin to be reciprocated. (Be patient; it could take a long time.)

If you have doubts about something you're thinking of doing, or saying to your child, err on the side of caution and avoid it. Your gut is telling you there's something wrong, either with what you want to say or the fact that you want to contact your child at all right now. Listen to your gut. It's your best guide.

Here are some common pitfalls, all of which many estranging children find disrespectful:

- posting on their social media page without asking them first
- pointing out their flaws, inconsistencies, or poor treatment of you or others

- sending long emails or texts, or leaving rambling voice messages
- involving yourself in their relationship, finances, or parenting
- giving advice without being asked
- giving food or gifts to grandchildren without asking their parents
- initiating contact with people in their lives

The list above is not exhaustive; it's meant to give you just some ideas of the kinds of unremarkable acts that lucky parents can get away with but will probably cause trouble for you. Respect their personal boundaries to help them feel safe enough to get close again. Be predictably (i.e., consistently) respectful to encourage movement toward you, rather than away.

Giving Advice

For parents who must tread cautiously, giving unsolicited advice to an adult child is usually a no-no. Unless you've been accused of offering too *little* advice in the past, resist the urge. Make them pull it out of you if they want it. If you're used to offering advice freely, practice restraining yourself with other people you talk with regularly. It can be a hard habit to break.

Meanwhile, think about the emotional need that giving advice might be meeting for you. Is offering advice a way for you to feel close or useful? If so, consider these questions carefully: What else do you have to offer, besides advice? How might it feel to just sit on your hands and watch things play out, without making any attempt to influence the outcome? These are not rhetorical questions. Try to answer them if you're more comfortable giving advice than not. Try to make advice-giving optional, something you can turn on and off at will.

Contacting Their People

When it comes to talking with others about the estrangement, beware of unintentionally violating your child's privacy. Feel free to talk to people who are *your* people. But when you talk to *their* friends, partner, spiritual adviser, coworkers, or neighbors about your relationship, you're encroaching on their territory. Where your social circles overlap, follow the motto "When in doubt, leave it out."

Claiming Access to Grandchildren

Naturally, you'll wish you could spend time with any grandchildren who may exist behind that wall of silence. It's very sad when children become involved in adults' relationship troubles. Everyone loses. But as we've seen, it's not uncommon for children to grow up in a milieu of family estrangement.

Where visitation rights are concerned, grandparents take a backseat to parents in most courts of law. You're unlikely to win a visitation suit in the absence of overwhelming evidence of child abuse, and drawing your child into a legal battle could very well push your relationship beyond the point of no return. If there's child abuse, report it to the authorities. Otherwise, let your child be in charge of everything concerning his kids, and think carefully before proceeding with legal action.

Let yourself grieve if you're losing time with grandchildren. While there may be no immediate remedy, you're allowed to have emotions about the situation. Don't bottle them up inside; protect your health by letting yourself feel those feelings. Whether you tell others how you feel is up to you, but don't hide your feelings from yourself. Practice constructive wallowing.

Ignoring Boundaries

Keep your ears open for specific requests from your child. Though boundaries can sometimes make your relationship feel like a battlefield, your child's boundaries present opportunities for you to make peace with her. Does she want you to call before coming over? Do it every time. No presents for the grandchildren? Disregard this rule at your peril. Must wear a costume to their Halloween party? Wear one, or skip the party. Keep in mind that sometimes boundaries are hinted at, rather than stated openly. It's fair to ask for clarification if you're not sure, but implied boundaries are just as sacrosanct as stated ones.

If you have negative feelings about a boundary set by your child, address them with your counselor, partner, or trusted friend. But don't act on those feelings by failing to respect a boundary you see as frivolous or wrong-headed. Your pushback will violate a tall stack of your child's emotional needs. That could send you back to square one.

We all have the right to set personal boundaries that feel appropriate for us. If you're irritated by your child's boundary setting, consider whether you've been exercising your own prerogative to set boundaries. If the answer is no, it's no wonder your child's effort to do so is rubbing you the wrong way. You'll benefit from the discussions of boundaries in chapters 11 and 12.

What to Say When You Write to Them

As I've said, email is riddled with prospects for misunderstanding and should be used with extreme caution. Many an estrangement has sprouted from an email or text exchange that got out of hand.

I know it's harder to place a call to someone who's rejecting you than it is to write a note from behind the protective shield of time and distance. But in your most important relationships, the path that's hardest to follow is often the right one.

Many times, when people tell me about the mean thing someone wrote to them in an email, they recite the words from the email in an angry, critical tone. Sometimes I can imagine the words without the withering interpretation and can believe that the writer's intention was likely very different from what came through.

If you insist on writing instead of calling your child, perhaps because you don't have a phone number for them, use extra words to slow the reader's pace and make the email sound friendlier. Instead of writing, "Your dad wants to know if you've got a job yet," you might write, "Your dad and I were wondering, given that you've been looking for work recently, whether anything has come through yet?" Better yet, don't ask about sensitive topics that might put your child on the defensive. If getting a job is one of those, nix it from your conversational repertoire. The short, concise sentences that make for good writing in just about any other context don't work well for this kind of email. Throw in those extra words to slowww the reader dowwwn and convey more warmth.

It's often best to make your email about your child, not about you. Children, including adult children like you and me, generally respond better to parents' acknowledgment and interest than to complaints, requests, or arguments. Feel free to offer praise if it's due, unless you've been accused of criticizing or trying to control your child. In this case, positive feedback can make your child feel pressured and uncomfortable, since praise and criticism are both forms of evaluation — two sides of the same coin.

It's usually not a good idea to talk about your emotional needs (e.g., "I miss you so much") when contacting an estranged child. Writing to let them know they're breaking your heart will only push them further away. Instead, tell them they're *in* your heart, that you love them and wish them well. And don't do this too often. Sugar is sweet, but toxic in large quantities.

Lead by meeting important needs such as visibility, validation, and valuing. If they responded to your last attempt at contact, you can express some gratitude if the mood takes you. But if your child does respond to you, and if there's nothing in her response that needs to be addressed, resist the temptation to write back again. Your child needs to be able to respond positively to you without escalating communication. Replying will reinforce her belief that she can't write to you without inciting a frenzy of contact from you in response. You're unlikely to receive a second reply, and your joy will quickly turn to disappointment.

Not responding may provoke anxiety in you. It feels wrong not to reinforce your child's communication. That's okay. Just remember that you're doing it to give your child what he wanted: some space in the relationship. Obviously, if his response contains a question or a complaint, you'll send an appropriate reply.

Here are some examples of responses from your child that, depending on context, of course, don't necessarily require another response from you:

> "Okay."
> "It was nice to see you too."
> "Fine."
> "I will."
> "Jeff and Fido say hi back."
> "Thanks for letting me know. I'll follow up."

Be a Mirror

To make it easier to focus on your child when writing or calling, you might want to keep a picture of her or him nearby, either physically or in your mind, as you ask yourself questions like these:

- Who is he?
- What does she like?
- What makes him tick?
- What's important to him?
- What does she enjoy?
- What frightens her?
- What's meaningful to him?

The more you think about these questions as you write to your child, the more you will come across as a Parent who can be relied upon to keep the Child's best interests foremost in mind. As long as you seem to be centered on him in a patient and compassionate way (rather than a grasping or judging one), it will feel emotionally safer and thus more appealing for him to be in contact. Remember, trust takes time. Be patient and fill your own bucket while you do this.

Sample Email

The following email offers copious and respectful validation, visibility, and valuing language. It's relatively short and sweet and has the emotional tone of the Parent, who can self-soothe if necessary. Imagine receiving this email yourself.

> Dear Ken,
>
> I was happily surprised to see your name in my inbox back in May [*valuing*]. Obviously, it was difficult to learn that you'd rather not hear from me so often, but I do understand your request for distance, and I want to respect that [*validation*]. I hope these past six months have given you enough time that this note isn't unwelcome [*respect*].
>
> I want to honor your understandable wish for space [*validation*] and at the same time, if it's not too late, at some point I'd like to try to be the father you deserve [*valuing*]. I let you down in so many ways because of my own limitations, and you didn't deserve that. Of course, you don't necessarily need a dad the way you did when you were younger [*visibility*]. But I'd like to be a source of positivity for you — someone you can talk to and feel built up by, not torn down. I don't blame you if you're not sure you're ready to give it another shot [*validation*]. But I'll be waiting patiently if you ever decide you're open to it [*respect*].
>
> I'd like to send you a hello via email every three months or so if that's okay [*respect*]. Good luck with your llama farming — it sounds like interesting work [*visibility*].
>
> Love,
> Dad

This email assumes that Dad didn't send an immediate acknowledgment to his son's request for no contact as recommended (see chapter 9). He's picking up the ball now, after some months. If you received a request for no contact and haven't yet responded, it's appropriate after a minimum of, say, six months to send an email like the one above.

Email Subject Lines

If your child is peeved enough to delete an email from you without reading it, it's doubtful that a good subject line will change her mind. However, if she's ambivalent about opening it, an inviting subject line might offer a nudge in the right direction.

In general, use the subject line in an email as a preview, to tell your child what she'll find inside. For example, the email to Ken above might bear the subject line "Acknowledging your request for no contact." A subject line like this may reduce anxiety by allaying uncertainty about the contents.

Be as accurate as possible. If your subject line is "Saying hello," and the email contains information that the dog has been ill, your subject line isn't accurate. A better subject line would preview the contents: "Rosco is ill but should recover." Think of your subject line as a news lede, with the most important information right up front.

If your email conveys bad news, don't shout it in the subject line, but do provide a preview. For example, "Difficult news about Grandpa." This shows respect for the fact that your child may wish to choose a time when she can read the email undisturbed.

In short, an email subject line should:

- accurately describe the contents of the message
- convey good news in a nutshell
- offer a description of bad news, not the news itself

If you're wondering what to title an email that discusses six different topics, that's easy: don't discuss six different topics in the same email. It will be way too long.

Don't Overanalyze Wins (or Losses)

Parents predictably measure progress by whether their child responds to a particular attempt at contact. If they send three emails and then all of a sudden receive a response to the fourth one, they study the email that elicited the response. They assume that whatever they did differently in that last email, it must have had a positive effect. They become Sherlock Holmes, searching for clues to their sudden success. Obviously, they want to stick with a winning formula.

The fact is, it could easily have been all the emails combined that finally brought about a response, or something in the child's life that has nothing to do with his parents. It's possible that their most effective communication was the one they tried a year ago, which their child is still processing and which finally had its effect. Don't drive yourself nuts trying to figure this out.

The time for analysis is *before* you contact your child, not after. When you understand the role of the Parent, every contact attempt is designed to benefit your child. Receiving a response becomes irrelevant; you already know you've given your child what she needs from you. Don't look to her for reassurance. Your new approach may have softened her attitude toward you, but your own need for acceptance may not be met right away. Have faith that silence is not necessarily rejection. For more on the various meanings of silence, see chapter 9.

Unless you receive specific instructions to the contrary from your child, keep doing what you're doing. Playing the Parent role is a marathon, not a sprint.

How to Apologize

I suggested early on that adult children don't feel powerful when they estrange themselves from parents. This makes sense if you think of keeping one's distance as the last refuge of the defenseless. What do you do if you come face to face with a tiger in the jungle? You run.

The tiger can easily kill you if you don't have the means to protect yourself.

Apart from expressing generosity and providing validation, apologizing is a way to show your adult child that you're no tiger: you're as vulnerable as he is. He doesn't have to run away to protect himself from you.

But how you apologize makes all the difference in whether an apology will slow your child's retreat. "I'm sorry you feel that way" is one of those statements that don't exactly leave your child, or anyone else, falling all over themselves to forgive you. If you're looking for forgiveness, or trying to repair a damaged relationship, there are three elements to a great apology that you can't afford to leave out.

Before I enumerate those, let me assure you, in case you think it might be too late to apologize for something that happened years ago, it isn't. A good apology has an impact in the present, not the past. Today and tomorrow are your only options, so take your pick.

What You're Apologizing for, and Why

An effective apology conveys that:

1. You understand *what* you did.
2. You know *why* it was hurtful, inappropriate, or wrong.
3. You're very sorry.

These convey the three most important aspects of a good apology: ownership, understanding, and remorse. The *why* in the second part isn't why you said or did the thing you're apologizing for; it's why it was hurtful or wrong. Don't offer explanations for your actions unless you also address the *what* and the *why* above. Your child will see them as excuses for poor behavior, and they won't help your case.

A good apology starts with "I'm sorry I..."

A poor apology begins with "I'm sorry you..." (unless it's "I'm sorry you had to put up with *my*...").

Some Good Apologies

"I'm sorry my tone was so harsh when I asked you to do the
dishes. I was frustrated, and I took it out on you. I shouldn't
have."

"I shouldn't have borrowed your car without asking. I'm very
sorry."

"I'm sorry for quarreling with you yesterday; looking back on
it, I was being unreasonable."

With these apologies, you're taking ownership of your words and
actions, which helps to melt the other person's defenses. You're not at-
tacking them, you're offering validation. You can see things from their
point of view. Importantly, you're also demonstrating remorse.

Some Poor Apologies

"I'm sorry you felt I was being rude."

"I'm sorry your feelings got hurt."

"I know I'm not perfect, and I'm sorry."

The first two admit no responsibility, and the third is too vague.

Delete the opening "I'm sorry you…" from your lexicon. You can't
apologize for someone else's negative reaction or mistaken belief. Always refer in your apology to something *you* did. You might have been
inconsiderate or impatient, or made a snap judgment. At some point
you fell prey to any of the myriad imperfections to which we emotional
humans are prone. But never apologize for not being perfect.

"I'm not perfect" isn't satisfying to the listener. They need to know
that you recognize what you did. The implication that they're upset
because you aren't perfect is insulting: no reasonable person expects
perfection in others. Most of us just want to see an appropriate level
of accountability when someone hurts us, even if it wasn't intentional.

While the hurt we cause each other often isn't intentional, a good apology always is.

Setting the Tone for the Future

After you've apologized, you might choose to add some words about how important your child is. If your family isn't verbally expressive, you may think of saying something like "I'm glad we were able to clear the air." But that would be underdoing it. Now is the time, if ever there was one, to turn up the dial on expressing affection. Here are some examples:

> "I love you, and I hate hurting your feelings. You're so import-
> ant to me."
> "I value our relationship so much; I hope I haven't damaged it
> beyond repair."
> "Hurting you is the last thing I want to do."

If forgiveness is important to you, consider the advice of Harriet Lerner, author of *Why Won't You Apologize?* According to Lerner, "A true apology doesn't ask the other person to do anything — not even to forgive."[3]

If you offer a fabulous apology, don't be surprised if your child feels compelled to say, "It's okay." But if no such affirmation is forthcoming, wait until the issue seems resolved. It might take some time, and multiple conversations. Later, you can ask if your child needs more from you on the subject before asking whether you're forgiven.

If you apologize well and it doesn't seem to mean anything to your child, consider the context. If you've had nothing but negative responses from her up till now, and your excellent apology gets a neutral response, isn't that an improvement? Don't count on your relationship changing on the spot if you get it right. An excellent apology is merely the beginning of a long road of trust building.

If You Don't Know What to Apologize For

The cluelessness that adult children complain about is a real thing. Even if you're raring to apologize, you may genuinely have no idea where to begin.

If you're stumped, ask yourself, "Is my child on the cusp of adulthood?" This is more than just a function of age. If a thirty-one-year-old was addicted to alcohol or other drugs from age fifteen to twenty-five, then got sober, she may only now be catching up with people ten years younger in terms of emotional development. She may currently have the sensibilities of a twenty-one-year-old. A forty-year-old man who's only recently found the wherewithal to move out of his parents' home can be thought of as reaching the cusp of adulthood as well.

If your child is recently launched or in the process of becoming independent, she may simply need benevolent distance. No apology may be required. Even if she's irritable with you and nothing you do is right in her eyes, her impatience could be simply Nature's way of helping her create space to ease her departure. Wish her well and let her know you'll be there for her if she needs you.

If the biggest complaint you ever hear from your child is "You treat me like a baby," that's a tip-off that a developmental need for independence has taken center stage. A response that might net you a bit of grudging appreciation is something along the lines of "I'm sorry. It's hard to know when to stop parenting and let you be an adult. I'll try to be more mindful. It might take some time for me to get used to your independence."

If you've miscalculated and fail to offer an apology that's due, you'll find out later when the dust of your child's departure has settled. Since it's never too late to apologize, you won't seal the door shut by missing the opportunity now.

But let's imagine there's more to the estrangement than a phase of development. Let's say you sense (or have been told by your child) that you need to make amends.

Search your memory for clues from your child. Think about

accusations he's made, including ones that baffled you or simply didn't seem true. Interpret his needs from his words and behavior, reading between the lines. Don't get caught up in the details of any one incident; rather, look for themes, such as "You don't make me a priority," "You don't understand me," "You criticize me," or "You always make things about you."

Once you extract a theme from the arguments, criticisms, and eye-rolling declarations you've received from your child, you can fashion an apology using specific examples. Use the diamond model: Picture moving from left to right along a diamond shape laid on its side. Start at the leftmost point with specifics. In the middle part, you search for broad themes out of those specific incidents. Then, as you reach the opposite point of the diamond, you narrow your focus down to specifics again to craft an apology that takes into account both broad themes and specific injuries.

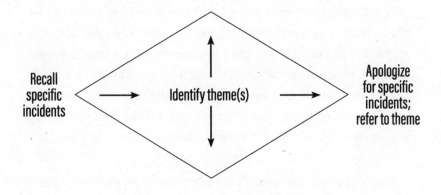

Figure 1. The Apology Diamond

Example: "You don't make me a priority."

Devon's dad worked hard for decades to provide for his family. He remembers his son's disappointment whenever he wasn't able to attend Devon's hockey games. When Devon graduated from high school, Dad was traveling on business. But Dad remembers attending many of Devon's games, some of which required considerable juggling of his schedule. Dad feels he didn't get enough credit for the things he did. He got grief when he wasn't able to follow through, but no kudos for showing up.

Still, in shuffling through the history of his son's complaints, Dad recognizes the theme "You don't make me a priority." Whether he agrees with that assessment or not, to make an effective apology he must acknowledge it. He searches his memory for an incident that embodies the theme, and crafts his apology.

Sample Apology 1

I'm so sorry for all the times I didn't make you a priority. As just one example, I should have canceled the trip I was on when you graduated from high school. At the time, I thought it was more important to close that particular deal than to attend your graduation. But I was wrong. I regret that, especially now that I understand how hurt you might have been. I can't believe I let you think you weren't my top priority. But I can see how you got that message. It was the same message I got from my own father, which is maybe why I thought it was okay. But it wasn't. You *are* more important to me than anything else in my life. You deserved better than what you got. I'd like the opportunity to make it up to you, if it's not too late.

Dad's apology contains all the elements of an effective one: ownership of mistakes ("I should have canceled the trip"); understanding ("I can see how you got that message"); and remorse ("I regret that"). There's also hope for a different future, given his insight into why he behaved the way he did ("It was the same message I got from my own father"). He uses the specific incident of Devon's graduation to anchor the apology in Devon's reality and keep the message from being too general. General apologies are less effective than ones that refer to specific injuries.

Use this formula — starting with specifics to uncover broader themes, then returning to some of those specifics in the apology — to craft your own unique amends message.

When There Are No Clues

You may have a trove of complaints from your child to draw on when you're formulating an apology. But what if you don't? What if you're completely in the dark about the source of your child's resentment?

Review the needs of the Child in chapter 4. Compare them with any complaints you've *ever* received from your child, or through someone in whom your child confided. What needs in your child might conceivably have gone unmet?

You might get clues by reviewing the needs that your parents weren't quite able to fill for you. Sometimes we unwittingly mimic the parental behaviors from which we ourselves suffered. Other times, parents overcompensate in certain areas where they themselves experienced neglect, regardless of what their own child needs.

An apology needn't be motivated solely by your child's concerns or complaints, especially if you don't know what they are. You can offer remorse for things *you* wish had gone differently, based on your own understanding of how they might have affected your child.

Example: "I treated my child as if she were me."

Theresa's path of personal growth has made her aware of the ways in which she treated her daughter, Sarah, as an extension of herself. When Sarah had trouble with friends at school, Theresa experienced acute anxiety. She would lie awake at night, worrying about Sarah's social life and trying to figure out what her daughter should do. Only later did Theresa understand that high school had been an especially painful time in her own adolescence, and she was reliving those years through Sarah. She wanted to do things differently this time, to have a better experience. But it was Sarah's life to live, not hers.

Now that they're not speaking, Theresa regrets the pressure she put on her daughter and the anxiety she imposed on their relationship. Though Sarah has never complained about those particular things,

Theresa feels she owes her an apology. Her own anxieties blinded her to Sarah's actual feelings during high school, denying her need for visibility.

Sample Apology 2

I can't begin to express how much I regret inserting myself into your affairs, especially in high school. I pressured you to take my advice whenever you had the slightest issue with a friend. My anxiety must have been hard to be around, though you didn't complain. Still, it seems to me you didn't get to just be a teenager, figuring things out for yourself, because I was too emotionally involved. For example, you could have worked things out with Bethany yourself, but I couldn't stop myself from calling her mother. You did talk to me about that, and rightly so. You told me it wasn't a big deal until I made it one. I'm afraid I couldn't separate myself from what was going on with you, and I'm terribly sorry for that, now that I understand it.

If you identify an issue that your child never complained about, you might discover that your child does recognize it once you put it into words. Interestingly, it may dovetail with something your child has complained about before. Their words may have been so different as to make the issue unrecognizable to you. So examining your own regrets about her childhood can lead you to insights, healing, and productive lines of conversation with your child.

When it comes to apologies, start wherever you can. Your will to uncover the truth is all that's needed to find fodder for reparative discussion. Of course, that assumes you have any contact with your child at all. If you don't, the next chapter offers some ways to cope with the pain of silence.

9 SILENCE

So far we've talked about the roots of estrangement and how they can reach deep into the past. We've seen how communication often goes off the rails, especially when emotional literacy is not yet fully developed. We've discussed the destructive role of shame and how reprising the role of the Parent can allow you to reestablish trust with your adult child. Chapter 8 offered some points to remember every time there's contact, along with a few sample messages.

But all of that assumes there's at least some contact between you and your child. What if complete silence is all you have?

Coping with Silence

When your only answer is no answer at all, you may experience a kind of separation anxiety. We all get anxious when we're cut off from people who are very important to us; we seem to be designed that way. The three phases of the separation response are familiar to many parents: protest (trying in vain to make contact); despair (feeling hopeless, grieving); and detachment (numbing out, giving up). You might cycle through all three repeatedly.

There's nothing wrong with you if you miss your child. Your

feelings are telling you that something's gone wrong, and it has. Some of your options for dealing with silence are the following.

Seek to understand what happened and why. It's unlikely that this breach is a random occurrence. Unless your child has a serious and severe mental illness, is deep in the belly of addiction, or is finding his way in the world for the first time as an adult, the estrangement has something to do with how the two of you relate to each other.

Try not to let shame, hurt, or bitterness stop you from gaining a clear understanding of how this happened. Has it happened before in your family? Did your child learn to cut people off when she was young? How has the communication been, not just with her but in the family in general? The more you understand, the more avenues there are for change.

Even if you never hear from your child again, gaining understanding of the factors that played into this complex and painful plight will afford you a "cleaner" grief and help you heal. When grief is muddied by confusion, denial, or second-guessing, healing and growth are stalled. Commit to fully becoming the person you're meant to be, with or without your child in your life.

Don't compound neglect with silence. If your child's complaints revolve around the idea that you've never really cared about her, you are the parent who needs to think twice before respecting a no-contact request.

There are estranged children out there who, after failing to respond to their parents even once, find themselves abandoned. Their parents give up on them, even though all the child wanted was to improve the relationship, or take a break from it — not to leave it. Ask yourself two questions: (1) Has my child accused me of not caring enough? and (2) Am I keeping my distance in order to protect myself from being hurt?

Get counseling. You don't have to cope with this alone. In counseling you can attend to your own evolution as a human being with a heart, a mind, a soul, and a purpose on this earth. Why are you here? What is your life project about? What qualities of the Parent do you want to bring to your own experience, regardless of your relationship with your child? Which of your own inner Child's needs have yet to be met? What might you be capable of, given enough support? Your personal growth is not a consolation prize. It's *the* prize. And when you're winning, your child can win, too.

Dare to hope. The majority of adult children are not happy about being estranged from parents. They wish like crazy for even one small reason to thaw. They may be afraid to hope that things could be different, but you don't have to be. You have the power to set the tone for the relationship for the rest of your life. Can you believe in yourself enough to try?

Make a plan for reestablishing contact. First, decide whether you feel strong enough to make an attempt — or several attempts — at contact that may be rejected. If this is the way it's been, it's not likely to change right away. If you're not sure you're ready, find ways to fill your bucket until you're stronger. If you feel you're ready, see the section "Resuming Contact" later in this chapter.

If They Asked You Not to Contact Them

Frequently, estranged children ask their parents not to contact them. They might or might not explicitly say, "Don't contact me." But they also might say something like, "I'll contact you when I'm ready," or "I need some time to figure myself out." For the majority of cases, here's what I suggest if you've been asked to cease and desist from contact.

Throughout this book I advocate respecting a child's no-contact request, but if you have a compelling reason to disregard this advice, please go with your instincts and do what feels right. You know your child and your overall situation; I don't. And as a reminder, if your child has accused you of not caring about him enough, a no-contact request may be a test of how much you value him; do you love him enough to pursue him if he runs away? The right answer is yes. But for most other cases, here's what I suggest if you've been asked to cease and desist.

Acknowledge the Request

Immediately respond with a *very brief* statement (no longer than this paragraph) that you're genuinely sorry your child needs to ask for no contact. Take responsibility for that. Assume that if your relationship were different, they wouldn't feel the need for distance. Say that you hope to be able to rebuild the relationship in the future, but you understand their desire for distance and will of course respect their wishes. Wish them well in the meantime. Let them know you're always there if they need you, and that you love them.

Here's an example:

> I'm so sorry to have put you in a position where you need distance from me, but I understand and will respect your wishes. It will be hard not to reach out on your birthday and holidays, but I will silently send my love on those days, as on other days. I hope to repair our relationship in the future, but for now, just know that I'm here if you need me, always.

Mentioning special days when you would ordinarily send a card, a gift, or a note will make it clear to both of you that no such acknowledgment of the day will happen.

As soon as you've sent your acknowledgment, observe a cooling-off period of an absolute minimum of six months. In most cases, planning on a year of no contact is appropriate. I know that's a long time, but if your child has requested no contact, it will behoove you to honor that request for as long as possible. The longer you can hold out, the more likely you are to be rewarded with a response when you eventually reach out again. Or your child may contact you first. Time heals. Your prolonged silence is proof that you respected her request. You're more likely to err by contacting her too soon than by waiting too long.

Tie yourself to a piece of heavy furniture if necessary, but do not contact your child *at all* during this period. No email. No calls. No letters. No messages carried by friends, relatives, or pigeons. No gifts, baked goods, or birthday or holiday wishes — including anonymous ones. No returning belongings they left in your home, cottage, or boat. Make zero contact of any kind.

Observing the cooling-off period is the only way to show your child that you respect his wishes. Talk is cheap. Showing respect through your actions — or in this case, your inaction — begins the repair phase of your relationship.

You may want to use this period to cool off yourself if you've been hurt by your child's behavior. Just think: you don't have to figure out how to deal with him. There'll be no unstated expectations, no walking on eggshells, no hurtful words, no messages that go unanswered.

Mark the day on your calendar when you'll reestablish contact, and then decide how best to spend your time in the interim. After an appropriate period of demonstrating your respect for your child by honoring her request, it will finally be time to take charge as the Parent and attempt, gently, to resume the relationship.

Resuming Contact

The cooling-off period shows caring for the adult child. Resuming contact shows caring for the Child within him, who would most likely prefer to have a true Parent in his life, even if he's not yet sure that's possible.

Reestablishing contact is a delicate process: technically, you're violating your child's request for no contact. But as the Parent you don't have to give the Child everything she demands. Sometimes what the Child wants is less than what she deserves. Everyone is worthy of parents who will love and cherish them in ways they can appreciate. You might need to make a few changes in the dynamics to help your child feel that way about you, but I'm betting you're up for the effort.

Your child didn't desire any more contact with the old you, but he hasn't yet met the new you — the parent who has spent time grieving, healing, and growing, and has come out the other side a more whole person. The new you is calmer, more mature, and committed to taking responsibility for the relationship you share with your child. Let that image of a new you inspire you to move forward with confidence, and become the finest Parent you can be.

When reestablishing contact, your best chance for success is with a message that comes from a place of calm, caring, and humility — the opposite of self-centeredness. Remember that humility is the prerogative of the powerful. Those with no clout have nothing to be humble about.

Your reconnection message should do the following and little else:

- Acknowledge the no-contact request.
- Apologize for not being able to fulfill the request anymore.
- Validate the child's desire for no contact with the old you.
- Assert your own responsibility to create a better relationship.
- Communicate your openness to criticism.
- Avoid laying claims to grandchildren.
- Let the child know when they can expect further communication.

Here's an example of an email from a mother accused of narcissism by her thirty-year-old daughter, who has a two-year-old son:

Dear Jenny,

I'm truly sorry to be violating your wishes for no contact with this email, but it's been just over a year now, and I'd like to know if you might be ready to talk again sometime soon?

I've been doing some soul-searching, and I think I understand why you asked for distance from me. In the past, I treated you more like a friend than a child, and that must have been hard for you. You needed a mother, not a friend, and I so regret putting you in a position to support me emotionally, with everything both of us went through. I should have been there for you, not the other way around.

This past year has been one of personal growth for me, and I'm ready to be responsible not just for myself, but for the quality of our relationship. And that depends on my seeing you as the individual you are. I'm afraid I might mess up from time to time, but I want to try to be there for you in a different way than before, and to have the mother-daughter relationship you've always deserved but didn't have.

Please let me know if and when you're ready to talk. If I don't hear from you, I'll write to you again in six months, if that's okay.

Take good care in the meantime. I love you.

Mom

Notice the tone of this email. There's nothing here that a reasonable person would label overbearing, narcissistic, needy, or disrespectful — hot-button words I've heard from many estranged adult children.

You may have been horrified by the promise to wait another six months if Jenny doesn't answer. After a whole year of silence, how can Mom willingly sign up for that? But suggesting this long time frame will encourage Jenny to respond sooner if she's on the fence. If Jenny is inclined to crack the door open now, she'll need to do it herself. Mom has already demonstrated that she can go a year without reaching out. Jenny's probably starting to believe that if Mom says six months, it will be six months.

There's a paradox here: in order to waste as little time as possible getting your child back into your life, you have to behave as if you had all the time in the world. Pressuring estranged children pushes them away and can lengthen the estrangement. Giving them loads of time provides them with the room and incentive to reach out.

Do yourself a kindness: assume that you won't hear from your child within the six months and that you'll have to send the promised follow-up email. Don't wait six months to write it. Write that email right now, just like this one. Better yet, write a dozen of them. Then sit on them until it's time to send them.

Every email to your child should evince the same calm, caring, humble tone. Here's a possible follow-up to the first email above, though I hope you won't need it.

> Dear Jenny,
>
> I hope this email finds you happy and healthy. I mentioned that I'd check in with you again in six months, and that's why I'm writing. I'd like to try to repair the damage I did to our relationship by treating you like a friend instead of a daughter. I'm eager to make changes in how I communicate with you and to work on creating a positive and loving relationship.
>
> I do understand that it may be easier not to try having a different kind of relationship with me. I imagine it's hard to trust that it could be different between us. And of course, you have a life of your own to live. I'm sure it's busy and full. But if you ever find that you're ready to talk, I'll be eager to listen.
>
> In the meantime, I wish you and your son much love, peace, and happiness. If you don't mind, I'll check in again in six months if I don't hear from you.
>
> Lots of love,
> Mom

This humble yet assertive email reminds the daughter why she's receiving it and reiterates that Mom desires contact. In addition, it conveys that Mom understands Jenny's reluctance and is taking responsibility for making things better; Jenny need only open the door when she's ready. Again, it establishes a schedule for the next contact.

Did you notice that Mom refers to "your son" rather than "my grandson"? With this choice of words, Mom is demonstrating that she respects her daughter's autonomy as the head of her own family, that she's not stepping in where she's apparently not welcome, that she's not viewing the world as revolving around herself, and that she's generous enough to forgo her desire to claim her grandchild as "hers."

The more you respect your child's boundaries, the sooner you're likely to be invited in. If you say you're going to write after a specified amount of time, mark your calendar. Being trustworthy means keeping your promises.

Although I've provided sample emails for attempts to revive contact, breaking the silence with a phone call can be more effective. Make sure you feel at your strongest and most peaceful when placing a call to restart contact.

But what if you don't have *any* contact information for your child? No phone number or email address? Or if you know you've been blocked? Find out their mailing address and send a letter. You may need to get creative, you may even need to pay a service, but unless they're living in a tent in the woods, you can dig up an address for just about anyone. If you know where your daughter works, you might consider sending a letter to her at her workplace, but please note: workplace missives are an absolute last resort. Mark anything you send "Personal and Confidential," and think long and hard before exercising this option. Your child could deeply resent the intrusion, and if by chance it's opened by someone else, the damage could be devastating for both of you.

If you send a letter to your son's home, don't write your return address on the outside of the envelope. It's easy to delete an email without reading it when you know who it's from, but a handwritten envelope from a mystery sender is hard to resist opening.

If your daughter hasn't blocked you from her social media accounts, go online, look her up, and see if you can send her a brief, positive, *private* message. Keep the needs of the Child in mind when you write it.

If you have to contact someone your child knows in order to locate him, identify yourself as "someone who wants to get in touch with him," not as his mom or dad. This protects your child's privacy as well as your own.

Even if the initial contact goes well, be prepared to give it time. The most common response to positive contact is more silence. Chalk it up to ambivalence and a need to see consistency; don't be confused or discouraged by continued silence. Reconciliation is a process, not an event.

The Pain of Silence

Silence in response to your efforts at reconnection is part of a vicious circle. You feel a wave of love and understanding toward your child. You feel strong enough to give without taking, so you reach out. It might be a little gift, a note in the mail, or a brief voice mail message with a heartfelt apology. You figure, "I know he won't respond, and that's okay."

But then one day turns into two. Two days turns into three, and then it's been a week without a response. Even though you've tried not to expect anything, you can't help but feel rejected. The hurt may be dull or piercing, constant or intermittent. Maybe it compels you to try again. And again. But eventually you have to take a step back. You retreat and nurse your wounds for a while. In the course of time, you reclaim yourself; you begin to feel stronger. You're ready to try again... and the cycle repeats.

What Does Their Silence Mean?

Maybe the silence itself doesn't have to hurt quite so much. Maybe the cycle can be converted into a steady, less painful campaign that's part of the natural rhythm of life.

Getting no response when you reach out to your child hurts because of what it seems to imply. It feels as though it must mean something like

"I hate you."

"You're not worth a reply."

"I don't want to hear from you anymore."
"You mean nothing to me."
"I'm never going to talk to you again."

With interpretations like that, it's no wonder silence is so painful. But that's all they are: interpretations, not facts. Your child's lack of response might mean something totally different. Here are five other ways to interpret that silence.

1. "I need some space right now." Some adult children find it hard to ask for space directly. Others feel they've already done so more than once. In either case, they may turn to silence to get the message across.

Needing space from someone doesn't mean you hate them, or that they don't matter to you. It means that for some reason, you simply need some time for yourself. With young or recently launched adults, time and distance are often required for individuation. It's a natural process that needn't be taken personally.

If it's clear your child wants space, the best thing you can do for your future relationship is to tolerate missing them right now. The fact that time's a-ticking is a cruel fact of life, but it doesn't change what works. The most respectful response to a request for silence is silence.

2. "I'm ambivalent about getting close." If you sometimes get a response and sometimes don't, ambivalence is likely at play.

Ambivalence is characterized by loving and needing someone on the one hand and wanting to keep a certain distance on the other. Children who feel criticized, misunderstood, immature for their age, or too needed by parents may experience ambivalence.

Ambivalence is easier to understand and forgive than disrespect or antipathy. In my experience, it's also more common.

The antidote to ambivalence is emotional safety. Make it easy for your child to be close by letting them control the frequency and content of contact. Resist the temptation to extend or multiply any contact they initiate. Treat an ambivalent adult child as you would a deer that wanders into your yard. Let them come to you on their own terms, and enjoy them when they're there.

3. "I don't know how to respond." I once spent considerable time crafting what I thought was a very nice email, and got no response. I was miffed. Fortunately someone who knew the recipient told me she'd been "blown away" by the email and felt incapable of responding at the same level. She thought anything she had to say in response would be "lame" by comparison, so she didn't respond at all.

Given that you might be communicating a little differently than expected since reading this book — and given that your child is the Child and you are the Parent in the relationship — your child may think, "I have no idea how to respond to this. Fortunately, I don't have to."

If you offer your child a voice mail or note that you know is wonderful, don't be put off, as I was, by not getting a reply. It's not easy to respond to heartfelt messages even in an untroubled relationship, let alone one in which there's tension.

4. "I'm busy." Especially if they sense that you have a strong need for connection, silence may be an adult child's way of indicating that they can't give as much time and energy as you can to your relationship. Work, new relationships, and other responsibilities usually take precedence over connecting with parents in young and middle adulthood, no matter how healthy the relationship.

It's not that they're too busy to take thirty seconds to respond to your text. It's that they're hoping silence will convey that they're too busy in general for frequent contact — even though they love you. From their point of view, anything but silence would reinforce unwanted behavior.

Don't become an item on a chore list. Give busy adults enough time to miss you.

5. "Is this for real?" If you begin communicating with your child(ren) in a very different way, they may not know what to make of it. Even though they might genuinely like your new modus operandi, how do they know it will last?

Estranged adult children don't want to be lulled into a false sense of security only to be disappointed when positive changes fail to stick. They may fear that if they respond right away, they'll get hooked into an interaction that feels disappointingly familiar. They might feel safer taking a wait-and-see approach to new developments.

No matter what changes you make in the way you relate to them, trust requires consistency, and consistency always takes time. Silence is just another interval in the necessary passage of time. Try not to think of it as a waste. It's not. Maintain your course and remember that the only constant is change.

Don't be hurt unnecessarily. Think twice before interpreting silence as one of those awful statements in the preceding list.

Time Is Relative

When the relationship breaks down, parents are usually in a hurry to reconcile. Being older and more invested in their children than children generally are in parents, they're aware of the limitations of time and the distressing fact of mortality. Also, they just plain miss their kid(s).

Parents tend to believe that the longer the estrangement lasts, the harder it will be to reconcile. With every day of no contact, their child seems to slip further away. But the feeling of a positive outcome diminishing with time is just that — a feeling. Especially with very young adults, it's often not the case. While prolonged silence could make it awkward to begin again, such a hiatus may just as easily provide a time-out that allows intense emotions to dissipate, thus making reconciliation more, not less, feasible and manageable with the passage of time.

In some families, the longer the estrangement goes on, the more the child questions her decision. She becomes more inclined, not less, to reunite. For some parents, just waiting it out can bring reconciliation. But the uncertainty can make waiting excruciating for parents, who would rather *do* something to create change as soon as possible.

When adult children intentionally build a wall between themselves and their parents, the only thing they're in a hurry to do is to solidify that wall. Therefore, contact that feels barely enough to parents can seem too frequent on the other side.

If your child has said that your neglect or apathy as a parent is the primary reason for the estrangement, and especially if your child is older, by all means start your campaign for reconnection as soon as possible. But if perceived neglect is not the problem, balance your need to reach out to your child with a clear awareness that for them, five months with no contact could feel like five minutes.

The image of sand rushing through the hourglass is never far from an estranged parent's thoughts, especially if you're older, retired, or widowed. But unless you've been diagnosed with a terminal illness that your child needs to know about, the cruel reality of a diminishing window of opportunity is a problem with no good solution. The estrangement can heal only when your child starts to trust you again. That takes time. Every anxious parent is in the same boat, discomfited by this harsh, unyielding fact. Cultivating trust is like aging whiskey in a barrel. It takes the time it takes, regardless of how much time you personally have left.

Remind yourself that respecting a request for no contact by staying silent is a constructive activity. Yes, it feels like you're doing nothing at all to repair the relationship and wasting time to boot. But in fact your silence, as a direct response to your child's request, is actively building trust and thus helping to reset the relationship.

What to Say When Asked If You Have Children

Our society doesn't understand parent-child estrangement. We don't have social conventions established for it or a shared vocabulary to use when talking about it. The word *estrangement* itself is becoming more widely known as increasing numbers of people search for answers. But a continuing sense of stigma associated with rejection by your own child makes it awkward for everybody when it comes up in conversation.

On top of society's confused discomfort about it, parents themselves don't always know what to think. Until you've reached a coherent understanding of the problem yourself, it's impossible to sum it up for someone else. Not that you would necessarily share this information with just anyone. But once you have a coherent narrative of what's happening, you won't necessarily be threatened with a mini meltdown inside every time the subject is raised.

Develop a short, simple answer that you can deploy calmly as needed. It will be one that makes sense to you — perhaps something like one of the following, or perhaps something completely different.

> "I do have a son, but unfortunately we're estranged." (When the other person makes sad noises, follow up with: "Yes, it's hard. But I'm hopeful that it won't always be this way. What about you? Tell me about your children.")
>
> "I have two, including a daughter I'm not in touch with, sadly." (When the other person reacts, agree with them, and then start talking about your other child.)

You can also use variations of these if you're asked whether you have grandchildren, such as:

> "Yes, but unfortunately we're not in touch with their mother, so it's quite a hard thing for us."

If you don't know whether you have grandchildren, the answer can simply be "No." If for some reason you want to share more, you can say:

> "I wish I knew. My son and I are estranged, and I haven't heard from him in a long time."

This assumes, of course, that you're willing to display your family's business in public to some degree. You could also pretend you don't have children, or tell people your child died, but only if you're sure you're comfortable with that story. Claiming the death of a child could come back to bite you.

Deal with the circumstances in whatever way is most comfortable for you. There's no one right way that works for everybody. You get to set your own rules here about whom you tell, and how much and what you share.

One possible benefit of admitting that you have estranged children is encountering someone else in the same boat. You may have already had dealings with other estranged parents without knowing it. Until one person speaks up, everyone remains isolated.

The Rule of Ten

As I've said, most parents I work with express the fear of losing their adult child forever. They worry that if they don't fix what's broken as soon as possible, their only window of opportunity will close. The younger or more recently launched your child is, the less likely this is to be true.

If your child is already a mature adult, you can get started today with the work of making repairs. However, even in these cases, it's usually necessary to allow some time to pass between outreach efforts. Adult children need time to orient themselves to your new approach, and even after a good start, relationships take time to rebuild.

Experiment with thinking in terms of tens:

- Try to wait ten times longer than you'd like to before contacting your unresponsive child again.
- Realize that time passes ten times faster for your child than it does for you.
- Be ten times nicer than you believe your children (or you) deserve.

- If you write your estranging child a letter, edit it to one-tenth of its original length.
- When leaving a voice message, aim to speak for only ten seconds.
- Assume reconciliation will take (*gulp*) ten years.

This Rule of Ten is not based on research; it's simply a mindset I suggest to counterpose the desperation and impulsiveness that can dominate the behavior of rejected parents. In fact, it's less a rule than a set of ideas to keep in mind in order to slow things down. Anything that reminds you to do less, rather than more, in response to the estrangement can be helpful.

From what I've witnessed, actions taken instinctively by estranged parents are based in emotion and impulse, not strategy. Emotion is inevitable, but it should not guide behavior. A well-founded strategy is more likely to produce desirable results.

There's timeless wisdom in holding the situation loosely despite its provocative tension. Desperate measures don't fit the role of the calm, secure, and reliable Parent. Mindfulness beats haste every time. Think of Yoda from *Star Wars*. Surely he, the Rule of Ten, would endorse.

Feel free to add your own tens to the list above. And use the time and space to get centered in yourself, so the contact you initiate will set just the right tone.

10 SPECIAL CIRCUMSTANCES

Certain types of circumstances come up again and again in my sessions with parents who are estranged from their kids. In this chapter I discuss some of the most common scenarios and how to address them.

When Someone Has Turned Them against You

Even a child who is beaten black and blue by his parents will cry when Social Services comes to take him away from them. He'll feel lost without them, and will continue to miss them even if people try to turn him against them. It takes a *lot* to turn a child against a parent.

One notable exception involves parental alienation, which is briefly mentioned in chapters 2 and 8. Parental alienation can be described as one parent turning the child against the other to secure the child's exclusive loyalty. This destructive parental behavior is commonly associated with divorce, but it can happen in intact families as well.[1]

Once children who have been alienated from a parent grow into adults, they typically become less dependent on the alienating parent. Many factors can contribute to the child's realization and rejection of the alienation, including differentiation and individuation, intervention by others, reaching personal milestones, and the return of the targeted parent into the child's life. This new understanding can transform the relationship with the targeted parent.

In general, no spouse, no ex-husband or ex-wife, no sibling, friend, or lover has the power to permanently ruin an affectionate, respectful relationship between an adult and his parents. It's only when that relationship has already deteriorated — or was never fully realized — that adult children may remain susceptible to negative influences.

If you believe a third party has poisoned your child's relationship with you, it may be counterintuitive and deeply painful, but it's essential to recognize that estrangement that continues into adulthood requires your child *himself* to abandon your relationship. It is your child, not the third party, whose affection and trust you must win back.

But what if your child isn't free to have a relationship with you because they have a controlling spouse or partner? If you suspect that this is the sole reason for your child's distance, it implies that your child is in an abusive relationship. This is devastating news to most parents, and if this is you, my heart goes out to both you and your child.

Abusers control their partners. They monitor their activities and are jealous of other relationships. They often put their partners down in front of other people, and their partners go to great lengths to avoid making them angry. Not just parents, but friends, coworkers, and even neighbors can be held at bay by a controlling spouse. If this sounds like your child's relationship, your best course of action may be to put down this book and call the National Domestic Violence Hotline.[2]

I sincerely hope that your child has other reasons for not wanting to pursue a relationship with you right now and that her partner is, at worst, supporting her choice, not insisting on it. Whether or not your child is a victim of abuse, your action plan can remain essentially as described in chapter 6. You've got to establish yourself as the trustworthy Parent.

If the interfering third party is someone other than your child's spouse or partner — perhaps a friend or coworker — it should be safe for you to ignore them and focus on rebuilding that one-on-one relationship with your child. If the negative influencer is one of your other children, however, then there are two relationships that need your attention. Do your best to avoid talking to either one of your children about the other, except to say nice things about them. Calmly resist invitations to gossip by saying, for instance, "That's something for your brother and me to talk about; it's not something you and I need to discuss. I'd like to focus on our relationship."

If you're pretty sure your kids tell each other everything you say to them, be specific in your separate apologies, and consistent in your messaging to each. As long as you act with integrity and keep firm boundaries around each relationship, don't worry about the fact that they talk to each other. If one of them appears to be telling the other one lies about you, you can't make them stop. All you can do is be honest and direct in all your communication with both of them, and let them know you're open to any questions they may have for you.

Never ask your child to choose between you and another person. Love shouldn't be a zero-sum game; there's enough to go around and, in theory, it multiplies when given.

When You're Rejected by Your Child's Spouse

When your adult child marries someone you don't like, or who doesn't like you, it's as though your child is hanging from a cliff by a rope — with his spouse and in-laws attached to him. If you don't want to lose your child, you have to pull the rope up, with all of them hanging on. It's hard work.

If you don't get along with your child's spouse or in-laws, I genuinely feel for you. You don't get to choose your in-laws, and some people are just harder to get along with, let alone love, than others. Some sons- and daughters-in-law seem to have no interest whatsoever in meeting you halfway. They don't make any effort to blend in to the family, and they may even come across as hostile. It's as if the very notion that their spouse already has a family is distressing to them — as if your child can't possibly be shared with you. I like to think that most sons- and daughters-in-law are *not* like this, and that if they seem unfriendly, there's probably been some miscommunication between you.

As for getting along with your child's partner's parents, I've heard of many variations of terrible in-law combinations, from cops and all-but-robbers to conservatives and self-described hippies. There is such a thing as luck, both good and bad. Statistically, someone's going to lose the in-law sweepstakes, and it might be you. But no matter how the odds may seem stacked against you, your options remain the same.

If you want to enjoy a relationship with your grown child and any grandchildren who come along, I hate to say it, but you must learn to get along with your child's spouse — yes, even if that spouse is Attila (or Priscilla) the Hun. I feel the need to point out that I don't make these rules; I just report on them.

Your child's other half has taken the position of number one person in his life. As hard as it may be to do, if harmony is your goal, you've got to win that person over. If you don't find a way to get along with a daughter- or son-in-law, unfortunately it's you who will likely lose. As long as that person is in your child's life, he or she has power over where your child spends holidays and how much time you get with your grandchildren, if any.

When There Are Misunderstandings

So how do you get along with someone you don't get along with? The first thing to do is to realize that conflict and tension can easily arise from misunderstandings. When people from different family backgrounds come together, the situation is ripe for mix-ups. One person mistakes another's reticence for silent judgment. Unexpected behavior is interpreted in an unflattering light, based on the observer's fear of not being liked.

Each family has its own rules of engagement. Maybe in your family, teasing is what you do to feel close and connected. But in mine, teasing may be seen as thinly veiled criticism. If you start teasing me, I might wonder why you're being so hostile.

The first rule, according to Deanna Brann, the author of *Reluctantly Related*, is not to take things personally.[3] Look for possible misunderstandings instead. Wherever there's conflict between in-laws, there's usually a misinterpretation or two in the mix. Give daughters- and sons-in-law the benefit of the doubt. When you're not sure what's going on with them, feel free to ask. For example, "You didn't seem enthusiastic when I mentioned we could babysit next weekend if you need us to. Did I read that right?"

If your differences are truly irreconcilable, and you just don't see how you'll ever like this person, well, somehow you still need to stay on their good side. Yes, even if they don't have one.

POP Goes the In-Law

How you do stay on someone's good side when the two of you don't get along? The short answer is "Very carefully." Over time, you'll develop your in-law survival toolkit. For starters, try the following technique.

Look for opportunities to ask your son- or daughter-in-law for one of three things: permission, opinion, and preference (POP). All of these questions communicate respect, if not affection. Permission, opinion, and preference are a paint-by-numbers formula for warming up relations.

Permission. Whenever you're thinking of doing something that will affect or involve your child's family, ask permission first. "I just wanted to call and make sure it's okay if we send a gift for [grandchild]. We were thinking of [item]. Would it be okay for us to send that?" If there are no grandchildren, ask for permission to buy a gift for the couple's home, to do something in particular at or for a wedding or other special event, or even to call someone in their social circle.

Asking permission is a sign of respect. If you have trouble asking for permission, it might indicate a struggle for dominance between you and your child's spouse. That struggle could be part of the trouble between you. Or it could be that you already feel so disrespected by them that you can't bear the loss of *self*-respect you perceive in asking for their permission. If these feelings are present, they might be getting in your way. Explore them with a therapist or other safe person so that you can regain enough psychological flexibility to employ effective behaviors.

Important: when you ask permission, don't disregard the response! Act in accordance with your child's partner's wishes. Not because they're always right or because they're monsters who need to be appeased, but because it's *their* life you're talking about. Asking permission in matters that belong to them — their wedding, marriage, children, home, friends, job, and so on — lets them know you're not trying to control anything that they have a right to control themselves. They need to know this in order to feel safe sharing their lives with you.

Opinion. Ask your child's spouse for his opinion on practical issues. "What do you think our son would like for Christmas?" "Where do you think we should celebrate our anniversary?" If you can, appeal to the spouse's interests and expertise. If you have a son-in-law who appears to know about nothing except beer and video games, ask for his opinion regarding beer or video games. But also ask for his opinion on random things like insurance companies, cars, fertilizer, or anything you're interested in learning about. It almost doesn't matter what you ask about; just engaging him in a respectful way can warm up chilly relations between you. Obviously, you'll want to avoid politics, religion, or any other area where you suspect you don't see eye to eye.

Preferences. Many times, parents will ask me what they should do in particular situations regarding an in-law, such as sending gifts or arranging accommodations when visiting. Often, the simple answer is to ask the in-law. Let's say you have a prickly daughter-in-law, and she and your son and grandchildren are coming for a long-awaited visit from out of town. They've already told you they're staying in a hotel. You might ask, "Would you like to have the kids stay with us, or do you prefer having them in the hotel with you?" or "Would you like to have Thanksgiving at the house, or should we all go out?

Permission, opinion, and preference. To get on somebody's good side and make yourself a desirable companion, ask for one of these regularly. If, at this point, you're thinking, "I only wish I could ask anything. They won't pick up the phone or return emails," see chapters 8 and 9 for ideas on how to change the picture.

When You're Caught between Your Kid(s) and Your Spouse

I hear regularly from mothers whose adult kids have cut them off because the mother stayed with a man whose behavior has had a negative impact on the child. Sometimes it's the father who's caught in the middle between his spouse and his child. In either case, usually the problem behavior of the targeted spouse has been going on to some degree since the child or children were young. Or maybe a new spouse reminds the kids uncomfortably of someone from childhood who hurt them. Or perhaps the kids are jealous of the parent's relationship, because they feel they never got enough attention from Mom or Dad to begin with.

For situations like this I recommend family therapy. Family knots and tangles are hard to pick apart without the help of someone who can take a bird's-eye view. As usual, look for a therapist who helps each family member not to feel judged and who brings compassion to each person's experience.

Regardless of whether your family seeks professional help, recognize that this isn't a problem you can solve by yourself. Don't play referee. That's not your job, it's way too stressful for you, and it doesn't work in the long run. Your child(ren) will just get more annoyed with you, and the bad feelings will tend to multiply.

Separate Relationships

Even if the bulk of animosity or silence is directed at your spouse, your kids might be looking for a heartfelt apology from you. Remember that a good apology includes a description of *why* your actions — or refusal to take action — was, or is, hurtful to them. As always, they need to know you understand their point of view.

Here's an example of an apology from the nontargeted spouse: "I haven't always been responsive to the feelings you've expressed about [your spouse or partner], and I imagine [or "I know," if they've told you explicitly] you've felt unsupported by me. I'm so sorry for that. I didn't know how to handle the difficulty between the two of you, and I'm afraid I wasn't there for you. I regret it. I want to do better from now on."

Such an apology from you is especially appropriate when your spouse or partner is not the child's parent. In this case, you should focus on repairing your own connection with your child. You might have to tolerate maintaining separate relationships with your partner and your child, because without a parent-child bond, there's little inherent incentive for either of them to mend that relationship. For that to happen, your partner will have to put in the lion's share of the effort.

Never tell your estranged child to try to get along with, or accept, someone who hurts or offends them — even their other parent. They're not motivated to do so: they've already shown an inclination to just avoid that person. Plus it puts them in the wrong for the way they feel, which creates an incentive for them to stay away from both of you.

Your Spouse, the Child's Parent

Let's assume for the rest of this section that your spouse is the other parent of your adult child. If you're still with this spouse, an apology from you obviously won't smooth out all the wrinkles, let alone make it possible for the family to coalesce. There's still the matter of the offending behavior. What if your spouse and child can't be in the same room together without being triggered by each other's behavior?

You might have tried to persuade your child to accept your partner the way he is, because that would solve the problem. But unless your partner has apologized and is willing to do so again if needed, *and* to make sincere efforts to change the offending behavior, that's like asking your child to respond to a letter that wasn't sent.

If you choose to stay with a spouse or partner who has a difficult relationship with your child, you have your reasons. Set a boundary around your own relationship with your partner, and if necessary, let your child know that even though you love her and you're truly sorry for the way she's been hurt by your partner, you need to have that relationship in your life. Don't get into debates about your spouse or otherwise justify your decision: you're an adult, with the right to choose whom you spend time with. (See chapter 12 for help with assertive communication.)

It's normal to wish your child could simply stop taking things so personally, but don't encourage him to do so. He won't be able to implement that advice. Instead, he'll conclude that you're choosing your spouse over him.

A United Front?

What if your spouse wants you to cut off contact until your child agrees to reconcile? In many of the couples I see, just one parent is targeted for estrangement by an adult child. The targeted parent grieves every time he's left out of phone calls or meetings. To him, continued contact by his spouse amounts to condoning the child's hurtful behavior. Why should the child get to enjoy contact with the other parent instead of suffering consequences from their hurtful actions? When you're the targeted one, it's as if you're at a family banquet with your hands tied behind your back. Everyone else is enjoying the meal, and they don't seem to care if you starve.

If you're in the middle and your targeted spouse is urging you to cut off contact with your child, validate your spouse's feelings. Rejection is a heavy burden to bear, and it's worse to be the only one. It's only natural for her to wish for some sort of consequences for the child. Cutting off contact can seem like a fair and reasonable response to your child's selective rejection. But responding to estrangement with more estrangement is not the answer. Give your spouse a hug, let her know you understand why she's hurt, and offer sympathy, but explain that cutting off your child will not solve the problem.

Adult children don't estrange themselves simply because they can get away with it. They have other reasons. Let me ask you this: If your spouse is the target, has he or she read this book? If not, why not? In any intergenerational family estrangement, the responsibility for setting and maintaining the tone of the relationship falls to the older person. Their extra years of experience presumably give them greater emotional maturity. Younger family members rely on them for guidance. If that's not currently the case, this may be a growth opportunity for your spouse.

Provide emotional support, but steadfastly refuse to make a bad situation worse by multiplying the estrangement by two.

Validate, with Boundaries

While you can't solve the problem between your spouse and your child yourself, you *can* provide simple emotional support to both of them — preferably with the help of a support network of your own. When your adult child complains about your partner, you can validate her feelings without throwing your spouse under the bus. Be curious instead of trying to explain away her grievances or express a different point of view. Find out exactly how your child feels about your partner. Invite her to talk to you openly about her feelings, without defensiveness, just as if she were complaining about your own behavior.

Help her identify the emotions that arise regarding your spouse, then acknowledge them with compassion: for example, "I can understand how your father's angry outbursts make you feel as though there's something wrong with you. No wonder it's so hard for you to be around him."

Validate your child's emotional response to your partner's behavior (e.g., he feels bad about himself when Dad criticizes him), rather than his opinion about the behavior (e.g., "Dad is so rude!"). This will help you avoid betraying your spouse when you support your child. Ironically, validating your child's strong negative feelings, without trying to change them, may increase his ability to cope with your spouse's behavior.

There's a saying in therapy: "What you resist, persists." Don't resist your child's negativity. Embrace it, and it will be soothed. Your compassionate acceptance will help to calm your child and make him emotionally stronger, to the point where he may spontaneously become more generous toward your spouse. If you've been practicing constructive wallowing — that is, embracing rather than running from painful feelings — you'll understand intuitively that giving deference to feelings makes them more, not less, manageable. This is as true for other people's feelings as it is for your own.

Remember: validate your child's emotions, not his or her judgments. If you tell your child you agree that your spouse is a jerk, you've put yourself in a bind. But saying you understand your child's strongly negative feelings about your spouse's behavior, and allowing him to express those feelings to you without any debate, shows you to be a good listener and a reliable parent.

If your child tries to hold your feet to the fire and get you to admit that your spouse is awful in some way, set a boundary: "I see the behaviors you're pointing out, and I understand why you find them offensive [if true]. My relationship with [spouse] is different from yours, and divorcing her is not an option. You don't have to spend any time with her if you don't want to. I just want to make sure that *you and I* have a strong and close relationship, and for you to feel like I have your back. That's the most important thing."

In summary:

- Don't play referee.
- Get family therapy.

- Recognize potential limits on nonfamilial bonds.
- Set boundaries around your relationship with your partner.
- Validate your child's feelings without requiring that he try to change them.
- Attend to your personal relationship with your child.

When You Suspect Mental Illness in Your Child

Sometimes I hear from parents who know or, more often, suspect that their estranged child has a mental illness. The child's condition appears to be contributing to, or causing, irrational thoughts and behavior that keep the estrangement in place.

A mental illness that causes a loss of cognitive and emotional functioning will affect all your child's relationships, not just those with his parents, extended family, or childhood friends. Among his spouse, coworkers, and newer friends, someone besides you will have noticed that something is very wrong. Your child's ability to hold a job, run a household, and maintain peer relationships will likely suffer if his condition meets the criteria of a serious mental illness.

It is possible that your child has some form of mental illness. About 20 percent of Americans do, according to the National Institute of Mental Health.[4] But even if your child is one of them, her condition, in itself, is not necessarily responsible for her reluctance to reconnect. Depression, anxiety, or bipolar disorder can certainly affect your child's communication with you. Depression in particular encourages isolation. But your child's general attitude toward your relationship is not usually determined entirely by brain chemistry gone haywire. Always assume you can have an influence on your relationship, and act accordingly. Engage with the person, not the illness.

About 4 percent of American adults have a serious mental illness causing substantial impairment of functioning.[5] If you're the parent of one of these adults, estrangement is probably the least of your worries. You're afraid for her physical well-being, her ability to care for herself, and possibly for her very life. Frighteningly, you no longer have the authority to insist that she get help. Unless your child is declared mentally incompetent, no one can force her to seek treatment, take medication, or keep appointments. It's devastating to feel so helpless when the stakes are this high. If your child isn't available to you, do you have an ally in her life who might be able to persuade her to seek help for her condition?

Whether your child is in treatment or not, the question remains: what does he need from you that you're in a position to give him? You can't make him well again just by loving him; if only you could. But you can treat your child with the compassion and patience he deserves. Remember, this is an illness, not a willful act of disrespect. No one chooses to suffer with a mental illness, any more than they would choose to get cancer.

Don't face a serious mental illness in your child alone. Educate yourself and connect with local support networks, and visit the website of the National Alliance on Mental Illness at www.nami.org.

If your child's mental and emotional health is less than ideal, but her condition doesn't qualify as severe, remember that mental illness is not a character flaw. It's not something your child is choosing out of weakness or spite. Instead, it's a condition that should elicit compassion in response. Separate the person from the illness, and apply your best parenting skills whenever you get the chance. You may not be able to heal your child, but you can make sure your relationship is not a source of added stress.

When There Are Financial Issues

Some of the parents who contact me for consultation regularly give substantial amounts of money to their adult children, despite chilly relations between them. For many of these families, money has become seemingly the only basis for connection. This leads to resentment and ambivalence on the part of parents, and probably their children as well. If you're in this situation, it will be hard for you to begin the work of separating financial issues from emotional ones without exploring your own attitudes and expectations about family and money.

Money plays a role in every family, from the ultra-rich to the very poor. The nature of that role, and the amount of influence it has in parent–adult child relationships, varies among families. Here's a message from one parent for whom money seems to have played a central and very disappointing role:

> I spent most of my life's savings on my children's college education, and then financing trips to see them after they moved 2,000 miles away. I never questioned doing this until now, and facing retirement with no savings, and no relationship with my wealthy son, feels like I have lost everything. I know it will only make him madder to hear this, but do parents have any right to a return on their investment and financial support of their children?

Now that he's an adult, you're no longer financially responsible for your child. And unless you had him sign a contract, you can't expect a return on any financial investment you've made in him.

My own mother sent her mother, my grandmother, hundreds of dollars a month until the end of her life. She did this not because her mother asked, but because she wanted to — because she cared for her mother and wanted her to be comfortable.

I feel grateful to my mom for so many reasons. I would love to give her buckets of money every week in her twilight years, even more than she did for my grandmother. But that impulse comes from my love and care for her, not a sense of obligation.

I don't "owe" my mother money: I don't feel I need to pay her back for all the money she's spent on me over the years. We don't have a business relationship. My mother isn't a bank, and I'm not her customer. When she and my dad spent money on me, they spent it because they wanted me to have the things and experiences the money could provide.

You've no doubt heard this before, and it might annoy you: children don't ask to be born. So, a priori, you and I owe our parents nothing. It's said that in China, if you save someone's life, you become responsible for them for as long as you live. Isn't that interesting? The person whose life you saved doesn't owe you anything. This strikes me as analogous to rearing a child. You created them — biologically, socially, or both. Therefore, according to the Chinese philosophy, you owe them! It's a different way of looking at things, but it gives you more control than if you feel your child owes you and isn't paying up.

The best investments parents can make in their children are time, energy, respect for their basic human dignity, and empathy. These are the most likely to pay dividends in the future (though as with all investments, there are no guarantees).

It's never too late to make such an investment. That's what this entire book is about — making good, solid investments in your relationship with your adult child. Money is not a necessary part of that equation. It can create complex relational problems and is best left on the periphery of parent–adult child relationships.

Emotions and Money

Financial problems between parents and adult children are caused by money, yet they're almost never *about* money. They're about expectations and, not surprisingly, emotional needs.

Meet Marvin, a fictional father with a teenaged son. When Marvin was growing up, his father, although very well-off financially, allowed Marvin to find his own way. Marvin got no financial help whatsoever from his parents. Nevertheless, he's managed to amass a great deal of wealth by his own talent and sustained effort.

When his son comes of age, Marvin could go in two different directions. He might think to himself, "What was good enough for me is good enough for my son. Let him find his own way in the world. He doesn't need my help."

Let's say he refuses to help his son, who can't understand why. All his son knows is that Marvin could easily help him financially, but won't. He's angry at Marvin for what feels like a dereliction of affection as well as fatherly duty.

If Marvin isn't in touch with his own feelings of anger at his father, who refused to help him when he was his son's age, or if he unconsciously judges himself for feeling that way, he might respond to his son's anger by labeling him lazy, selfish, or materialistic. Between his son's anger and Marvin's criticism, their relationship could get rocky.

Alternatively, let's say Marvin decides to do his son the favor that his own father never did for him. He provides copious financial help, which his son enjoys and comes to expect. If Marvin isn't in touch with his own feelings of envy and even resentment of his son's good fortune compared to his own at that age, he may become intensely concerned with his son's expectation of abundance, viewing it as a shameful lack of gratitude or ambition.

In both cases, Marvin's expectations of, and reactions to, his son's behavior are colored by unconscious feelings from his own childhood.

Sibling Rivalry

I've heard from more than a few parents about problems caused by money that went to one child and not another. Where there are complaints about unfairness around money, there are almost always complaints about other kinds of unequal treatment. The complaining child may feel less important and less loved. Even though this perception may be mistaken, it needs to be taken seriously. Something has given them the impression that they're worth less than their sibling(s) to you. Try to understand the aspects of your family's reality that gave them that view of themselves, and address what you can in the present.

Use the re-parenting principles to help your complaining child feel loved and important despite differences in your spending. Acknowledge their reality and apologize for everything you possibly can. Your love is worth more than money if you can show it, rather than tell it, to your child. Before you examine your financial relationship with your estranged child, take a long look at the give-and-take you experienced with your parents in your family of origin. There you'll find clues as to your own unmet needs and expectations, which may be affecting your financial relationship with your child.

Going into debt or even bankruptcy to help an adult child is a formula for resentment. If your sense of what's right or normal has gone off the rails, see a financial counselor for advice.

A regular counselor or therapist can also help to uncover unconscious beliefs about family and money. Get help sorting through this if it feels confusing or overwhelming.

If You're Called "Controlling"

How are you supposed to re-parent an adult child who accuses you of being intrusive, overbearing, overinvolved, or controlling? Surely showing interest and trying to meet their needs is in direct conflict with being less in their business?

For some parents, showing interest is not the problem. It's showing *too much* interest that's pushing their child away. If you relate to that description, focus like a laser on respecting your child's boundaries. This will mean showing interest only in what's important to *them*, not what's important to you.

Avoid all of the following:

Getting involved in their problems. If your child mentions financial constraints, don't leap to the rescue with "Shall I give you some money?" Wait and see if you're asked. She may just be sharing a challenge with you, not asking for help. If your adult child needs assistance, she can ask for it. This approach is not being mean or playing games; it's respecting her status as an adult. If she needs something from someone, including her parents, she must do the work of figuring out what she needs and making a clear request. Expecting anything less from your child would disrespect her.

Showing unsolicited concern. Your child has his own concerns about his affairs. They may be different from yours. If he doesn't mind that his girlfriend treats him badly, or that he's sorely underpaid at work, leave it alone. He won't appreciate your concern. On the contrary, it will probably irritate him. Concerns you have that your child doesn't share are more about you than they are about him. Is it torture to watch him grope his way through unnecessary difficulties? Yes. Will it improve your relationship to highlight potential threats that are invisible or trivial to him? No.

Offering advice. Parents dispense suggestions to their children as naturally — and for some, almost as frequently — as they exhale. Parenting entails guidance, especially when children are young: parents offer instruction, encouragement, admonition, recommendations, warnings, and other input. But it can be tough to know when to quit. Adulthood confers freedom from all that helpful supervision — or it should. Now your child gets to do whatever she feels like — even, I sincerely regret to say, if it messes up her life. It's a sad fact of parenting adults: you're totally invested in their well-being and powerless to improve it.

Well, maybe not absolutely powerless. You can add to your child's quality of life by making your best self always available to him as a warm, supportive presence. Even when the rough winds of life batter your child, you can be the rock he clings to in a storm. Wouldn't you rather be that rock than merely a source of unwanted advice?

It can take a lot of practice and many missteps, but your efforts at "underextending" your help, if sincere, will be noted. On the off-chance your child actually *asks* for your help or input, make sure she's really asking, not just telling you her situation.

Here's an example of behavior that some estranged children find stifling:

> **Child:** I'm going to ask [neighbor] to come over and help me take down the shed.

Parent: Why don't you ask [other people] as well, and make it a work party?

On the face of it, there's nothing wrong with the parent's response. It's merely a helpful suggestion. But when the vast majority of conversations between the child and the parent are characterized by helpful suggestions on the part of the parent, the child loses a sense of autonomy and control over his own life — and resents it.

If your child accuses you of being too much in their business, get familiar with two statements: "That's nice," and "I'm sorry to hear that." Here's what they look like in action:

Child: I'm going to ask [neighbor] to come over and help me take down the shed.
Parent: That's nice.

Child: I paid $150 for this haircut and I don't even like it.
Parent: I'm sorry to hear that.

If you feel like jumping out of your seat just reading these examples of the adult children dangling out there without any advice from their parents, this section is for you.

The Need to Help

What kinds of feelings arise in you when you don't get involved in solving your child's problems? Those feelings must be unpleasant if it's hard for you to resist helping. For some parents, being helpful is the only way they know to relate to their adult children. Their friendly suggestions may come from an unconscious fear of losing the relationship if they're not needed anymore. Subconsciously, they cling to the role of helper in order to remain relevant in their child's life. In addition, they may have gotten so comfortable in their role as involved parents that they don't know who else to be when they're around their child.

If this description fits you, even a little, your suggestions, support, and advice may be helping you more than your child. Also, be honest with yourself if you're using financial or other types of support as the price of admission to your child's life. You can forgive yourself for using the obvious or only lifeline you've got in order to stay in contact. But try substituting emotional support for offers of advice or financial help. It will take an open-ended application of effort on your part, but your child may very well come to appreciate your earnest and consistent emotional support. It's a rare resource in most people's lives.

Let your child's boundaries be sacrosanct. Listen to him, offer him emotional support ("You can do this," "You'll figure this out") and tolerate *not* helping him. With time, new habits become easier. And they have benefits. You'll find out who you are to him when you're not focused on helping. And you'll find out how resourceful and smart he is. You might both be pleasantly surprised. You can have a relationship based not on need but on plain and simple affection.

By the way, your child may behave as though she *wants* you to resume the old behavior. Don't be drawn by this. It's likely an unconscious test of your new boundaries or a sign of ambivalence about her independence. Either way, hold your boundaries firmly by refusing to offer advice, even when asked. "You're smart; you can figure this out yourself." is a valid response from the parent of an adult child who has complained of overinvolvement. If you say it with love and you mean it, it will hit the mark.

When Therapy Leads to Estrangement

Did your child turn against you after entering therapy? It happens all the time. Everything seemed fine before she went into therapy, but now all of a sudden your child is dissatisfied with the relationship. The facts are suggestive, but let's take a closer look.

If you've ever been in therapy, you know that clients are encouraged to reflect on their thoughts and feelings. Therapists ask a lot of questions: it's what we do. Even people who've never sat on a therapist's couch have memorized the Therapist Question: "And how do you feel about that?"

> Johnny: My parents want me to go to medical school.
> Therapist: And how do you feel about that?

The virtue of the Therapist Question lies in the fact that it may never have occurred to the client to consider his feelings about a particular topic before. Johnny might learn just by answering the question that he resents feeling pressured to choose a career he's not sure he wants. Did therapy create Johnny's resentment? No, but it did unlock it.

Imagine that your neighbor kept a wolf in her backyard. The wolf has always been chained and never caused problems. But last night someone came along and let the wolf out. Unfortunately, it ended up dining on one of your cats. Whom do you blame? Technically, it was the wolf that killed the cat. But wolves can't be sued or punished for being wolves, so you'll probably seek to lay the blame elsewhere.

You might be annoyed at your neighbor for keeping a wolf in the yard to begin with, but that person who came along and let it out? *That* person should definitely be held accountable, don't you think? That person is the therapist. Part of what we've been doing since the days of Sigmund Freud and Carl Jung is to "let the wolf out" of our clients' yards, in the form of their deepest, darkest, and truest emotions.

The emotional freedom created in the safe haven of the therapy room is necessary for healing and growth. But there's often fallout in a client's personal life as she comes to grips with resentments, disappointments, irritations, and other feelings that may have festered for years, or a lifetime. The old adage "Better out than in" is put to the test when clients begin to express themselves more fully in their relationships with others. Family members may be shocked at the change they see in their loved one. What they don't realize is that nothing's new on the inside. The only difference is that something is being expressed that wasn't visible before.

Ultimately, in therapy your child is moving toward greater authenticity, not baseless anger or heartlessness. It's disturbing to feel as though you don't recognize your child anymore. But although it's appropriate to grieve the loss of the person you used to know, this transformation signals the emergence of your child's authentic self, the person he or she truly is.

As for the question of whether therapists actively suggest to clients that they cut off their parents, I wish I could say that it never happens. I fear that sometimes it does. But I also have to say that if someone suggested to me that I cut off my only living parent, it simply wouldn't happen. Only if I already had a tense, conflict-ridden, or otherwise painful relationship with my mother would I be susceptible to such a suggestion. What about you? If I suggested you kick your child to the curb because of how she's acting, would you walk away from her? I hope not.

A Note to Therapists

If you're a therapist reading this, I hope you agree that it's not appropriate to advise people to cut off important relationships, for at least three reasons.

First, giving advice is not what we therapists do. We know that it usually does more harm than good by re-creating unhealthy power dynamics and curbing the client's self-efficacy. Advice is abundantly available from clients' family and friends; if it seems screamingly obvious to you that a client should cut a parent out of their lives, I assure you, someone else will suggest it.

Second, adult clients need to be, or become, capable of making such decisions themselves. If they're not yet able to do so, we can offer the emotional support and acceptance that a therapist's expertise *does* comprise. We can normalize their thoughts and feelings, ask clarifying questions, provide accurate empathy, and model tolerance of ambiguity. Our role is to witness, facilitate, and support our clients' growth, not to stunt it by providing them with our answers to life's complex questions.

Third, the ability to navigate and repair relationships with important others is a higher-level skill, and thus more valuable in the long run, than the ability to cut such people off. Yes, there are cases in which relationships are so damaging, and the chances of change so minuscule, that cutoff is the healthiest — and only — course of action. But again, this is a personal decision for the client to come to with the supportive acceptance of an otherwise neutral therapist, rather than by suggestion.

Clients value relationships. They want to develop skills in maintaining and enriching them, not to remain stuck or afraid. We can support clients in repairing important relationships only to the extent that we ourselves know how to do this. If we tend to cut and run from difficult dynamics in our personal lives, it will be harder to assist our clients in making the changes they wish to see. Before advising a client to cut ties with anyone, especially family, please consider your own biases and weigh them against your client's overarching goals.

If You're Ready to Let Go

What if you're at the end of the road? It's been years without contact, years without hope, and you want to make it official that you're letting go. Let me first say how sorry I am for the loss of your relationship with your child(ren). The notion that there might be more peace in letting go than in continuing to knock on a door that seems welded shut does cross the minds of many estranged parents from time to time. But for most, letting go permanently remains hypothetical.

If you're truly done, and you want to make a clean break, here are two things to think about doing.

Let Your Child Know

Contact your child to say that you won't be reaching out to them anymore, but that you will always be available if they change their mind about contacting you.

Even if right now you don't feel like making yourself available if they come back, tell them you'll be there anyway. That way, you're covered from here on out. You won't have to write again if and when your feelings change. Who knows how much time might go by in the meantime, and what the circumstances might be, if they come around in the future? Who knows how you both will feel then? The only way you'll reject them if they contact you in the future is if you don't manage to heal from, and make peace with, their rejection of you. And I hope that with the aid of this book and other support, you won't be in that position.

Here's an example of wording you could use when you're ready to send your final letter.

Dear _____,

I wanted to write and let you know that I won't be reaching out to you anymore. Please understand that this is not because I don't love you or don't want to reconnect with you. I'll always love you and never stop hoping for a chance to repair our relationship. But I'm backing off because it's not clear that my [emails, letters, calls, etc.] are welcome, and I'm afraid you might even find them distressing. So I won't be writing anymore, but I'll be thinking of you just as often, with love. No matter how much time passes, please know my door (and my heart) will always be open to you.

All my love,
Mom

Grieve

Not all parents reach the point of sending a letter like this. But if you do, this final message can set you free to grieve. Your note may be a little longer than this, but try to keep it as short as you possibly can. Remember that shorter messages are more likely to be read fully — and repeatedly — than long ones. You don't want your child seeing your message as a self-centered ramble. The longer your message, the more self-centered it will appear, no matter what words you use. This is unfortunate, but it's true. For best results, keep it short.

Grieving is not a linear process. It comes and goes, waxes and wanes, and can take you by surprise at any time. At various points in the future, you'll be reminded of your child(ren). When that happens, put words to what comes up for you. You can do this silently, but use complete sentences. Here's an example:

I'm seeing a little boy who looks so much like my son did at that age. I'm feeling sad and nostalgic. I'm appreciating the time in my life when I had a little boy to cherish. I'm feeling so sad now that he's lost to me forever.

You may continue to experience emotions about your child for the rest of your life. Those feelings can coexist with, rather than derail, your enjoyment of the life you have. If you talk yourself through your feelings in this way, it will help them pass through you as quickly as possible and dissipate...until they're triggered again. Actively create positive relationships and experiences for yourself — not to try to replace your child, because that's not possible, but rather to avail yourself of all that remains that's good and useful and healthy for yourself and others.

11 RECONCILIATION

Even entrenched estrangements can and do come to an end. I've heard of adult children who reached out to a parent after more than thirty years of silence. By that time, parent and child may have become strangers to each other. But sometimes, that sad development can give rise to new possibilities.

It's typical to act without thinking in the company of first-degree relatives. It's usually a sign of comfort and connection — or familiarity, again in the literal sense of the word. Regrettably, it may also be how you became estranged from your child in the first place. You weren't constantly on guard against doing or saying the wrong thing. You just did and said what came naturally.

Once you're speaking again, and enjoying more frequent contact with your child, that's when it hits you: this is not the same relationship you used to have. In fact, you're building a new one, one that feels good to both of you, day by day. Understanding the special challenges of reconciliation after estrangement will help you relax and realize that nothing is necessarily wrong if things feel a little clumsy or uncomfortable right now.

Walking on Eggshells

If you feel like you're walking on eggshells with your estranged adult child now, it's because your relationship is no longer familiar. You have to be vigilant. In some ways it's beneficial to feel awkward and self-conscious, because it means you're being mindful about how you interact with your child. Isn't that better than reverting to your comfort zone, which includes the same old behavior patterns, and unwittingly damaging the relationship?

As you gradually become more at ease in your new rapport with your child, that eggshell feeling will become less and less acute. You'll have a better sense of what to do, and what not to do, for the benefit of the relationship.

The Learning Curve

When learning anything new, including unaccustomed ways of relating to an adult child, we go through four stages of consciousness and competence.[1]

In the beginning, we don't know what we don't know. This is the *unconscious incompetence* stage. It's where the roots of estrangement lie. Parents behave in the ways that come naturally, and to the extent that their behavior fails to mesh with their children's needs, the relationship may be damaged without the parent's desire or knowledge.

In the second stage, we become aware that we need to do something different, but we don't know what or how. This is called *conscious incompetence*. This stage ushers in the first sensations of walking on eggshells. It's extremely uncomfortable to be in this stage with your child: you know you're making mistakes, but you aren't sure how to fix them.

As you acquire new skills and begin to use them, you enter the next phase of learning, called *conscious competence*. Although you now have tools, information, and ideas for what and how to change, you're not yet expert at using them. You still feel as though you're walking on eggshells — aware of every word you say to your child and anxious about applying new skills properly.

In the fourth and final stage of learning, you've finally internalized the new skills and tools. They've become routine. You no longer walk on eggshells, because you do and say the right things without having to think about it. This final stage, which not everyone reaches, is called *unconscious competence*. People at the top of their professions, be they comedians, surgeons, or athletes, have achieved this level of learning. They make complicated, difficult feats look deceptively easy.

Because parent-child relationships are formed over years and decades, not weeks and months, it can also take years to turn a parent-child relationship around. Because real change begins only in the second stage, that of conscious incompetence, you can expect to be walking on eggshells for most of that time. As John Maxwell astutely observed, everything worthwhile is uphill.[2] Get comfortable with the discomfort of walking on eggshells. It's part of the process.

Focus on the Future

Unless your child wants to talk about the past — in which case, absolutely go down that road with him — your messaging is most potent when it brings the relationship into the present and nudges it gently but surely toward a better future. Don't be shy about letting your child know you intend to play a positive role in her life from today forward. Check out these two statements:

"All I ever wanted was for you to be happy."
"I want to support your happiness."

Which one sounds more powerful? More responsible? More optimistic?

All of us have self-protective skins that keep us from making bold, positive statements like the second one above. And of course, you don't want to be pushy or intrusive. There's a line between being proactive in the relationship and being overbearing. But there's also a line between respecting your child's autonomy and being too passive. Somewhere in between is the sweet spot.

If you say something to your child about your relationship that makes you feel a little vulnerable, your communication is probably falling in that middle ground — not too pushy and not passive, either. "I could help you with the open house, if you like. I'd be happy to do some baking for it," is an example of this kind of communication.

Pepper your offerings with qualifiers like "If that's okay with you," "If you like," and "How would that be for you?" Don't ignore a reaction to something you're saying. Check in by saying something like, "You went quiet. How do you feel about what I just said?" Keep your tone curious and calm. The Parent of an adult child is still an authority figure, but not authoritarian. It's never going to be "your way or the highway" when you talk to your now-adult child. If you get the sense that you're asking for too much, back off. Give your child time to bring the subject up again if he wants to. Otherwise, let it go. Be assertive, not aggressive. I talk more about assertiveness in the next chapter.

Expressing Remorse (but Not Too Much)

In the course of rebuilding your relationship, your child may say or imply that he's been hurt. You might feel defensive, or you might feel so terrible about it that you cry inconsolably, possibly while sobbing, "I was such a terrible parent!"

I've had more than one adult child tell me in therapy that her mom or dad reacts with tears or self-recrimination if she expresses disappointment or annoyance. A sensitive adult child may feel terribly guilty hurting her parent like this, a fact which she eventually begins to resent. She wants to be able to communicate honestly with her parents without their imploding in shame. The guilt and resentment motivate her to avoid discussing important topics with her parents at all. Over time, this leads to more and more emotional distance between them.

When important conversations can't happen because of a child's fear of setting the parent off emotionally, what might have started out as a cautious reconciliation could devolve back into estrangement.

If you tend to respond with high emotion when confronted by your child about your parenting, communication style, or other behaviors, realize you're demonstrating how your behavior has affected *you*, rather than how it has affected him. This reaction violates the child's need for visibility and validation. If you feel you owe your child an apology for past behavior, review "How to Apologize" in chapter 8.

Staying Alert

Once you're back in touch with your estranged child, keep meetings and phone calls brief at first. There are three reasons why I recommend this. First, shorter periods of contact allow for pinpoint concentration on your objectives. Second, if you're together too long, you and your child may slip into the old, unpleasant patterns of interaction that led to the original estrangement. Those are dangerous. Third, remember the wisdom of show business: "Always leave them wanting more." Let your child look forward to your next contact, rather than needing time to recover from too much togetherness.

During the first few years of reconciliation — and it does take years to create a new relationship — prepare for a phone or in-person meeting as you would for a professional interview. Be strategic, not emotional, in your approach. Prepare to stay "on message." You don't have to memorize anything, but practice your Parent stance with your spouse or a close friend.

It's admittedly grueling to have to think so hard about each meeting after reconciliation, but you're building a new relationship now, day by day. That takes presence of mind and conscious effort. It's work. The harder you work now, the easier it will be over time to navigate this new relationship you've built so carefully.

Your objective in any contact with your child, regardless of the stated purpose of the meeting, is to become trustworthy again by playing the role of the Parent and meeting their emotional needs. Essentially, this means:

- listening well
- showing that you care more about your child's thoughts and feelings than your own

It would be lovely just to be able to kick back and enjoy spending time together. Isn't that what family is supposed to be about? But your family has undergone a damaging rift, and the rules of engagement have changed. You have an important new role, one that requires attention and consistency. Eventually, depending on the work you put in now, you'll start to develop more freedom and flexibility in your relationship.

Listening Well

Unless you've been accused of asking too many questions, feel free to ask your child not-too-personal questions about their lives. Listen *carefully* to everything they say. They're giving you the information you need to be close to them again. If you're on the phone, feel free to take notes. Get to know their thoughts and feelings, and use the information to offer visibility, acceptance, validation, appreciation, and support.

They're taking a cooking class? Wonderful. How do they like it? When did they develop an interest in cooking? What are they learning to cook? Be positive about what they're positive about, but don't try to turn something around if they're taking a negative attitude. Share in the negativity: "Oh, that's terrible. That's really too bad." This is significant: you don't need to fix their attitude if they feel bad about something, just understand and validate their feelings. It's not normal or necessary to be happy all the time. Give them implicit permission to be angry, disappointed, or sad by not overreacting to these feelings.

Listening is a skill most of us think we're better at than we actually are. There may be considerable time between conversations with your child; instead of losing or wasting all that time, use it to rehearse the skills that will make you more effective on that happy day when you're in touch again. Practice listening to other people. Listening is a biggie. No one can do it really well without practice. As a therapist, I listen for a living, so I get a lot of practice. But I'm still not as good at it as I'd like to be, especially with family. A sort of hack I use, which you can use with your child, is to take special note of any emotional content. For example, rather than trying to memorize the details of your son's new diet as he's telling you about it, take note of how hopeful and optimistic he seems. Reflect those feelings back ("You sound excited about this diet"), and he'll be impressed that you were "really listening."

If you've been accused by your child of asking too many questions, try sharing information about yourself instead. This might feel awkward if you're not used to talking about yourself without an invitation. But awkward means you're doing something different, which in this case is a good thing. Try telling your child about something in which there might be overlap in your lives. If your daughter just had a baby, for instance, but she feels "interrogated" when asked how she's doing, you can reveal something like, "When I had my first baby, I was absolutely exhausted all the time. I probably got three hours of sleep a night, if that." Instead of asking questions, let your sharing draw her out.

Here's another example: "When I lost my job at XYZ, that was one of the hardest times of my life. I didn't know what we were going to do. It's a very difficult thing, to lose a job."

Take mental notes if you're meeting in person, so you can follow up on fertile topics later. The more you listen and take in everything your child has to say, the more topics of conversation you'll have for next time. The best subject to talk with your child about is the one that interests him most.

If you're invited to your child's house, pay attention to your surroundings. Do they have a collection of books, shot glasses, or ceramic frogs? Are they planting a garden? Do they have pets? All of these are fodder for present or future conversation.

A caveat: stalkers follow their victims and find out everything they can about them, including their activities, their schedule, and their taste for ceramic frogs. If you've ever been accused of stalking your child, dial back your conversation about her and her activities or possessions. Listen, nod, and share relevant details about yourself instead.

Before you pick up the phone or go to meet your child, review the list of the Parent's responsibilities, specifically this one:

> *The Parent is dedicated to the welfare of the Child, and shows interest and delight in the Child. The Child is not required to reciprocate.*

Ahead of any meeting with your child, arrange to spend time with someone who makes you feel seen, heard, and valued. Don't look to your child to meet these needs, but *do* get them met appropriately.

Remember that the Parent is not a doormat, but a voluntary caregiver who gladly approaches the Child and fills their bucket. Go into every encounter with your child with your own bucket as full as you can get it. That way, you'll be poised to give, give, and give some more without needing anything in return. It's like having a conversation with a three-year-old; you have to do all the work. (I'm not trying to insult your adult child by comparing her with a toddler, but simply giving you a mental tool for implementing your re-parenting strategy.)

Handling Complaints

Sometimes therapy can kick off a deluge of complaints from an adult child and even mark the beginning of renewed estrangement. When this happens, as we've seen, it's not because the therapist has brainwashed her into thinking she should be upset with you. Remember, people don't go into therapy because they're wildly happy: they do it because they have emotional pain about something. As we saw in chapter 10, putting words to their feelings helps therapy clients make sense of those feelings and gives them a way to communicate about their needs — possibly for the first time in their lives.

As I noted before, we as a society are not good at talking about feelings. Consider the responses of this reader's mother:

> The problem is mostly my mother whose favorite lines are, "Oh don't be ridiculous, you couldn't really feel that way. I am a much better mother than that," and "My God, you are too sensitive. You don't need help, you can handle it."

It may be Mom's defensiveness talking there, but it could also be that she's learned to devalue all emotions — both her own and others'. You don't have to be insensitive or unloving to have this dismissive attitude toward emotions; you just need to have been raised in an environment where how you felt didn't matter. Take feelings seriously — yours and your child's. Don't ever get into a debate about whether someone "should" feel a certain way. Feelings are not a matter of choice, and therefore they can't be right or wrong.

If They Give You Something to Read

Did your child give you an article or a book to read that's supposed to explain how they feel or what they think you did wrong? If so, did you read it and discuss it with them? Your doormat alarm ("I'm being treated like a doormat! I have to stand up for myself!") may have gone off, preventing you from being receptive to the information.

If your child did suggest that you read something, that's a good sign: if they didn't value your relationship, they wouldn't be offering you information to help you repair it. When adult children provide information like that, it's not for incrimination, but for successful reconciliation.

Read anything your child gives you with an open mind. Search for ways in which the shoe fits, not the ways in which it doesn't. Try to see things from your child's point of view, and find ways to let her know that you get it. You've got to step into her shoes to genuinely understand where she's coming from. You also have to put on your Parent hat and turn off that doormat alarm. Remember, your child is not trying to attack you: she's trying to help mend the relationship you share.

I'll say it again: your child is not trying to make you feel bad about yourself. Assuming it's not purely a developmental phase that's keeping her away, what she wants is for you to understand something that will help her meet an important need and stay in your life for the long term. It may even be something that, when addressed, can help you meet a need in yourself.

Keep Responding to Emotional Needs

Complaints are emotional needs in disguise. Your child may not have the language to "own" his feelings the way we talked about in chapter 3, so it's up to you as the Parent to view the complaint as a request, rather than as the criticism it might resemble.

It's like when your children were infants and they cried: they couldn't say, "Please change my diaper," or "I need a nap now," so you had to figure out what they needed. It may seem ridiculous to have to do that with an adult child, but on the other hand, it gives you a simple recipe for responding to complaints. Just ask yourself, "What's the emotional need here that I can meet right now?"

Things can't change between you until one of you puts the other's needs first. As the person who's taken on the role of the Parent, you get to do the heavy lifting. Take heart! This is a message from a parent who found success:

> I focus only on her and talk only about her. After all, in my 60's
> it doesn't matter about me trying to explain why and how I did
> the things I did when she was growing up. Having my daughter
> in my life is the most important thing.

Talking about the Past

This may sound strange, but you're lucky if your child is willing to talk to you about something unpleasant that happened in the past. Even if they're dripping with venom about it, or seem either totally irrational or completely indifferent now, it's a good sign that they're willing to talk about it at all. They're giving you a chance to be the Parent about something. It's an opportunity to right what came across as a wrong the first time around.

Decline to be put off by your child's anger, blame, or unreasonableness about it. They're back in the role of the Child, and the most effective response to someone — anyone — taking on that role is to step into the role of the Parent and de-escalate any potential conflict. If you're hurt by your child's words or behavior, there's nothing wrong with your reaction. Make sure to give yourself a hug or get one from someone else, and acknowledge how hurt you feel. But don't do it with your child. Don't retaliate, and don't expect an apology. Take the time for self-care, apologize to yourself, and when you feel stronger, return to the task of taking your child's perspective.

Your child's complaint is not really about the past. Don't debate or argue about what did or didn't happen. It's an easy mistake to make. Instead, think about what your child needs from you *in the present moment* as she tells you her story. You can't change the past, but you can offer her a good experience in the present, where she's feeling hurt. Will you be here for her now, even if she believes you weren't there for her back then? This is how you turn a relationship around. Give her what she needs today, and you won't have to argue about yesterday. Rather than defending your past actions, take positive actions in the present.

A heartfelt apology that includes an understanding of your child's pain, and excludes explanations, justifications, or denials, is always appropriate and will act as a balm. (See "How to Apologize" in chapter 8.) It can be the beginning of communication if there's been little or none. The facts of what actually happened are irrelevant to relationship repair: focusing on those will hinder your progress. If your child has negative feelings about something, treat those feelings as the only relevant facts.

The same is true for you, by the way. Your feelings are not debatable, any more than your child's are. But when it comes to interactions with your estranged child, you must let someone else (a spouse, friend, or counselor) acknowledge your feelings. Don't seek acknowledgment from your child.

Everything you say and do matters when your child brings up the past with you. Even if you do a stellar job of putting his needs first in a particular interaction, he may continue for a time to protect himself by refusing to trust you until you show consistency. That's to be expected, so don't be discouraged.

Focus on what's needed according to the Parent's role responsibilities, and trust the process. Never seek reassurance from your child. It's okay to ask, "Did I understand you correctly?" if it serves to meet her needs. But, "Do you still think I'm horrible?" is not at all constructive from her point of view. Try to avoid questions like this that give your child too much power.

Estranged adult children will need time to process the new attitudes and behaviors you're bringing to the table. They'll need to see consistency in order to trust you. So when you're talking about something that's a sore spot between you, use the role responsibilities, not the lack of a warm response, as your confirmation that you're getting it right.

Holding Your Boundaries

The difference between an estranged parent and an *abused* estranged parent is how well they maintain their own boundaries. It's no walk in the park, having to defend your personal limits. But it is up to each of us to do it.

In my work as a therapist, I occasionally have clients who constantly test the boundaries of our relationship. They ask me for special favors, like discounted rates or extra time, or they behave in unexpected ways that require me to figure out an appropriate and ethical response. These clients consume more of my time and energy than all the others combined, and I feel resentful every time they surprise me with a new way to test my boundaries. But the fact is, they're doing nothing wrong. I'm resentful only because I hate having my boundaries tested. I dislike having to defend them. But no one else is to blame for my feelings about that.

Think for a moment about boundaries in general. They're just like borders; one can cross them, but only with permission. If people succeed in entering a country illegally in plain sight of the border guards, who's to blame — the determined immigrants, or the border guards whose job it was to stop and vet them? As long as a country has something to offer, there will be people willing to test the strength of its borders. If a boundary is to be meaningful, it must be actively monitored and, when necessary, defended.

Even if your child has made a unilateral decision to limit or cut off contact with you, you still have boundaries to maintain. It's up to you to inform others, including family members, of what your boundaries are. There's no sense in blaming an adult child or anyone else for crossing boundaries you haven't marked out, let alone defended.

It certainly feels like poor treatment (some even say it's abusive) when your child won't communicate with you, but a lack of contact is not technically a boundary violation. A country can keep other countries from selling their goods within its borders, but it can't force them to sell their goods in that country. We get to draw lines around ourselves, like borders. We can keep certain behaviors *out*, but we don't get to control how others behave. Calls, texts, emails, and visits are voluntary for adults, including your adult child(ren).

Yet there *are* behaviors you can and should stand up to. Are you allowing your child (or anyone else) to call you names or curse at you? Does your estranged child have unlimited access to your financial or other resources? Do others feel free to talk right in front of you about getting together with your estranged child? If so, your border guards are asleep at their posts.

The Parent always seeks a balance between love and discipline. Your boundaries must be held, but in a calm, almost professional manner. The border patrol does its best to avoid hiring guards too eager to bust heads. They want sentries who know the rules and can maintain their cool while doing their jobs. Similarly, the defense of your personal boundaries must be matter-of-fact, not emotionally reactive or punitive. No busted heads need occur when you hold off a boundary invasion. You may feel angry, as I do, when someone tests your boundaries. But they're allowed to test them. It's your job to make sure your boundaries are secure.

Here are a few examples of what it might look like to hold your own boundaries:

> "I want to hear what you have to say, but please don't call me names."
>
> "I want you to have what you need, but I'm not going to give you that amount of money."
>
> "You may not realize this, but when you talk about getting together with [estranged child], it hurts me. Would you mind not talking about that in front of me?"

It might seem strange to think about maintaining your boundaries when you're the one who's been cut off. Especially if contact is infrequent or nonexistent, you might feel as if you have to take whatever you can get from your child. That's not so. Setting good boundaries will keep you from feeling abused. When managed well, good boundaries can improve all your relationships.

Reconciliation with Only One Parent

It's hard to be pushed away by your child at all, but when you're the *only* parent in the family being ignored, it feels even more personal. A scenario I hear about repeatedly concerns the divorced mother who raised a son without any help from his father. When the son reaches his late teens or early twenties, suddenly he wants nothing to do with the mother who raised him. Instead, he reaches out to his father, and the two become close. Mom finds herself shut out, wondering how and why this happened.

For some young men who longed for their fathers when they were kids (a longing they might or might not have expressed aloud), the reconnection with Dad corresponds with a rejection of Mom. There may be a multitude of reasons for this, but one aspect may be the development of the son's identity as a man.

Both fathers and mothers can be targeted in this way, and not only after divorce. Still-married parents can become divided over an estrangement that resolves with reconciliation for only one of them. As we saw in chapter 10, the targeted parent often wishes the favored parent would refuse contact with the child until the child reconciles with both parents. This impulse to demand a united front is a natural one, but it's not a good strategy for healing estrangement. The only person sadder than an estranged parent whose spouse still has contact with her adult child is an estranged parent with no point of connection to the child at all. She has no idea what's going on in her child's life and can't be certain that messages sent will be received.

Don't ask your spouse to cut off contact with your child. You might ask her to convey your love, but don't ask her to try to get your child to reconcile with you. If her own relationship with your child feels tenuous, she might not even be able to convey your good wishes right now. The "favored" parent is often more like the "tolerated" parent: she's walking on eggshells herself. I've heard of cases where the mere mention of the targeted parent caused the child to withdraw.

If you're still estranged after your child reconciles with your spouse, give it time. Assure your spouse that it's okay for her to bond with your child. Their renewed contact is a possible bridge between you and your child. Your leading hope for your own reconciliation is the strength of your spouse's relationship with your child. If your child feels well supported by your spouse, he will have more emotional resources with which to meet you halfway in your continuing efforts to reconcile. In time, your spouse might be able to convey positive messages from you to your child, to prime him for reconnection. Time and your spouse's bond with your child can both be to your advantage.

12 GIFTS FOR YOURSELF AND YOUR CHILD

By now you might have started thinking not only about how to be with your child, but about how to be fully present in your other relationships as well. How might you incorporate aspects of the Parent role with your spouse or partner, friends, siblings, even coworkers? It's interesting to ponder how your relationships might change, even subtly, when you step into this powerful role. Still, the most important person in your life, the one who most needs the rational, loving, generous, and wise energy of the Parent, is you.

Being Your Own Parent

The Parent is your highest, most centered, and most peaceful self, the union of your wisdom, compassion, patience, and objectivity. You can think of the Parent as your essential self, free of ego, anxiety, or even personality — or simply as your very best self.

As we've seen, developing the Parent requires embracing the role of the Child, too, with its delightful capacity for learning, receiving love, and experiencing joy. Make sure your bucket of emotional needs is as full as can be before you try to fill anyone else's bucket. Some of the self-care practices described in chapter 4 will help you with this task, as will working with a compassionate counselor or therapist.

I don't know of any way to sustain the Parent role without also getting to be the Child somewhere, somehow, with someone, sometimes. Balance out your Parent responsibilities by giving to yourself as you would give to the Child. The contents of this chapter are among the most important in this book. They'll help you build up your inner Parent by nurturing the Child in you and strengthen the Parent directly by developing assertiveness. These skills will serve you in all your relationships, including, of course, the one you share with your adult child(ren).

Enhancing Your Self-Esteem

Many parents with adult children are, to say the least, skeptical of self-esteem. Attitudes vary, but here are some comments I've heard in the course of my career:

"Isn't that what ruined our kids — too much self-esteem?"
"I'm an adult. I don't need to worry about self-esteem."
"There's no such thing; it's a made-up phrase and a fad."

In my experience, however, low self-esteem is a silent but hugely influential factor in estrangement. When you're constantly doubting your own worth, feelings of self-protection, denial, and defensiveness are never far away. Typical self-protection strategies impair the ability of both parent and adult child to connect safely. Self-esteem that's intact and healthy is one of the greatest advantages you can have in communicating effectively with your child.

Self-esteem is often defined in terms of self-evaluation: how do we rate ourselves and our abilities? But evaluative definitions lead to misconceptions, even among psychologists. Have you ever known someone who bragged openly and frequently about how great he was, belittling others in the process? Did you think, "That guy has way too much self-esteem"? That's not self-esteem; it's arrogance, conceit, or narcissism. You can easily have too much of those, but there's no such thing as too much self-esteem. That would be like too much health; it makes no sense.

True self-esteem is not based on achievements, abilities, or appearance. If you point out their accomplishments or positive personal qualities, people with low self-esteem can agree with you, intellectually. "Yes, I guess I am loyal to my friends." "Sure, I'm a decent golfer." But such assessments don't really touch them at their core. Their low self-esteem remains stuck where it is, because it goes deeper than the level of behavior, which is where achievements and good deeds reside.

The Opposite of Shame

Healthy self-esteem can best be described in terms of its opposite, which is baseless shame. What we call low self-esteem is experienced as a chronic feeling that something is wrong with us. Despite the absence of any firm evidence, there it is anyway, the secret slogan of low self-esteem: *There's something wrong with me.* If your self-esteem has been injured, you'll recognize this sinking feeling. Its real name is baseless shame. It's the type of shame that lives at the core of a person, feels like a part of her, but has no basis in reality.

Shame is imposed on all of us, mostly unavoidably, by normal socialization and conditioning. "Don't eat that! It's dirty." "Would you stop that racket?" "Look what you did to your dress." Because our behavior doesn't always get a positive reaction, we learn early in life that we're acceptable if we meet certain conditions. When we fail, we develop shame. It can be argued that a certain amount of shame is good for us; it keeps us from doing things that are considered antisocial, inconsiderate, or immoral. You might call this other type "functional shame." It serves the function of steering us away from inappropriate behavior.

Functional shame is not the problem. The underpinning of low self-esteem is a vast store of baseless shame — shame for which there is no good reason. Where does all that shame come from, if it has no basis? And why is it still hanging around now that we're not children anymore?

When you were born, you showed up with all those needs we've talked about. You had no shame whatsoever as you took your first breath and cried out for nurturing. As a youngster, you wanted to be valued, to be seen for who you were, to be cherished by someone, and to belong. To the extent that those perfectly normal needs were neglected or thwarted in your early years, you began to feel more and more ashamed — not of your behavior, but of *yourself*. You figured the people around you must be right if they thought you weren't worthy of their time, attention, or affection. You couldn't help but conclude that there must be something wrong with you. But there wasn't. That mistaken but enduring assumption is an injury that occurred when you didn't get what you needed and deserved.

Healthy self-esteem is either the relative absence of this early injury, or the result of its having healed to the point where you no longer believe there's something inherently wrong with you. If you've been injured, healing is required to repair (and thereby raise) your self-esteem. If you've never consciously engaged in healing your self-esteem before, it's still injured. You carry unnecessary shame.

Parts of ourselves that are damaged when we're young don't spontaneously regenerate. Instead, they become more fractured over time. What you were able to tolerate at age twenty-five can feel overwhelming by the time you're sixty-five. Self-esteem is one of these components that don't spontaneously heal. I wonder how many midlife crises are really emotional wounds from childhood that surface after a prolonged period of neglect. But there is a way forward, and for many it means confronting the devastating lie "There's something wrong with me."

You started your life with healthy self-esteem. Infants generally enter the world emotionally intact. They don't think they're better than anyone else, but they don't think they're worse, either. They don't assume everything they do is great; you'll notice they get very upset if they fail at some task they've set for themselves. They just haven't been injured enough yet to believe there's something inherently wrong with them.

People with healthy self-esteem trust in their basic goodness, and although they strive to do well, they don't expect themselves to be great at everything. They try their best when they do something, and they refuse to see failure as proof that they're unworthy human beings. Instead, they see it as a signal that they need to do something differently next time. For these lucky folks, trying and failing builds self-esteem better than not trying at all.

For people with injured self-esteem, however, trying something new or difficult feels dangerous. They might fail, and failure feels like confirmation that there really *is* something wrong with them. Attempting to reconnect with your estranged adult child when you have injured self-esteem might be one of those heart-in-mouth adventures. But this one is just too important not to face.

Self-Esteem Builders

Re-parenting your child, or yourself for that matter, requires a minimum level of self-esteem to be sustainable. Especially if you don't want to succumb to feeling like a doormat, you need enough self-esteem to be able to say, "I'm up to the difficult task of meeting the needs of another. I have needs too, and I'll make a point of getting them met elsewhere, or meeting them myself." In the beginning, you'll have to adopt an attitude of blind faith that there is really nothing wrong with you. Then you can actively address low self-esteem in a multitude of ways, with kindness and self-compassion.

The right counseling relationship is like rocket fuel for self-esteem. Review the section on therapy toward the end of chapter 7, and also try some of the following self-esteem-building activities:

Smile, don't frown, when viewing your reflection in the mirror. Frowning at yourself reinforces the falsehood that there's something wrong with you.

Who was the first person to give you a look like that? Don't repeat that hurtful behavior. As Bob Newhart said in a very funny sketch about therapy, just stop it! You don't deserve dirty looks from yourself or anyone else. Treat yourself as if you were worthy of a smile. If contempt makes this difficult, just notice the contempt and wonder where it came from. It doesn't belong to you.

Don't apologize to anyone for how much you cry. You're allowed. Say it with me: "I am allowed to cry as much as I want." No one gets hurt by your crying. If someone is uncomfortable, that's hard luck for them. You don't have to pull yourself together for someone else's comfort. Crying is good for you. It releases stress. If you're kind to yourself while you cry, it also relieves and serves to process the emotions behind the tears. But only if you're kind to yourself about it. For a step-by-step exercise to help you process what you're feeling, see the TRUTH technique in my book *Constructive Wallowing*.[1]

Get on top of your relationship with food. Why am I talking about food in a section on self-esteem in a book for estranged parents? Because eating is something we do multiple times a day that both reflects and affects our relationship with ourselves. If you usually feel bad about yourself around food, your self-esteem is constantly under attack. Disordered eating — constant dieting, binge eating, and so on — isn't about food, it's about emotions. Healing from emotional injuries can set your eating back on track and halt the daily assault on your self-worth. Get help from an eating disorder therapist if your relationship to food feels negative. Changing this will benefit every other area of your life.

Correct people who guess at what you're feeling and get it wrong. We all do it: guessing at other people's feelings is a commonplace and usually innocent pastime. "I bet you're thrilled your nasty coworker got fired," is an example. So is, "You look angry." Observers sometimes hit the nail on the head, but often they get it wrong. Use these episodes to get to know yourself better. Think about the label that's just been put on you.

How well does it fit at this moment? Maybe you were thinking about a serious subject, suddenly realizing it requires your attention. You're not angry at all, but concerned. Correct the guesser, even if only in your mind, when he or she misinterprets how you feel. It's a subtle way of telling yourself that what you really feel is important.

Try something you want to do that's unlikely to work. Invite failure. Embrace mental discomfort. Most people who are afraid to fail have an unconscious belief that they won't be able to tolerate it. The only way to find out if you can tolerate failure is to fail. Please don't court catastrophe in order to test this! Keep your experiment manageable. For example, apply for a job that's a bit of a stretch, or audition for a local play. All great achievers have survived failure. There's some truth to the adage "What doesn't kill you makes you stronger," at least when it comes to the hard knocks in life that shape who we become. Inviting failure may be scary, but defeat can be less agonizing when it's anticipated with an open mind.

Accept help, or a favor, graciously. How many offers of assistance have you batted away, saying, "Thanks, but I'll do it myself"? If you're like me, you reflexively say no when someone offers to help you. Why do we do this? It's a habit, but that doesn't explain it away. I do it because I don't want to feel bad about "making" the other person do something they don't have to do. Especially if the favor takes them out of their way, I get anxious. I'd rather skip the help and avoid the anxiety.

Tolerating those feelings instead opens us up to receiving. If we tolerate them and get through the initial protest inside our own heads, we'll be able to receive not only the help that's offered but eventually also the message that we're worth it.

Send loving thoughts to every part of your body. Your body is your avatar. It's the incarnation and representation of your spirit. If you hate your body, it's tricky to distinguish between that and hating *yourself*. Try sending love to each part of your body every day. Say, "I love you, toes," and go from there. Don't worry if you don't mean it. The mere fact that you're taking the time to say kind words to your body demonstrates more esteem for yourself than if you didn't bother. Let your inner critic scoff, but don't let it win. Every body deserves to be loved.

Take one tiny step toward a cherished dream. If you have a goal or aspiration for the next phase of your life, what are you doing to make it happen? If the answer is "Not much," it may be that it feels better to hold it as a possibility "someday" than to reach for it now and realize you can't have it. Taking a small step toward your goal — like making a phone call or doing a quick internet search — is a sneaky way of convincing your subconscious that your personal desires are worth striving for. Yes, even at the risk of failure. Prove to your deepest self you're worthy of your own efforts by daring to take action. Self-esteem itself is an action. Esteem yourself by putting your goals at the top, not the bottom, of your daily to-do list.

Speak up when asked about your preferences. People with injured self-esteem often don't know themselves very well. And it's a tall order to hold someone you don't even know in high esteem. Get more familiar with yourself. You receive a built-in self-esteem exercise anytime someone asks for your opinion. Make up an answer if you're not sure; it's that important. "Where should we go for lunch?" "Are you a morning or a night person?" "Do you like playing board games?" These may be trivial topics, but each nevertheless provides an opportunity to build your self-knowledge. Make a decision and take a stand, even if it turns out to be wrong. Any statements you end up retracting, or restaurants you wish you hadn't picked, provide just as much information as if you'd nailed the response the first time.

Set and hold a boundary. This is graduate-level practice for those with injured self-esteem. When you're not convinced you're allowed to have boundaries in the first place, defending them is a stretch. Read some books or articles about boundaries. Once you have an understanding of what boundaries are and how to hold them, you'll have to supply the courage to practice what you've learned. If you do, it will be worth every drop of sweat on your brow as you take those steps. The self-respect inherent in boundary setting will crowd out baseless shame; the two can't coexist within you. Self-respect is a light that chases away the shadow of shame.

If you're a saver, spend a bit more and get something you like. Saving money is a good thing; if you're careful about spending, I commend you. But the ancient Greek ideal of moderation, not to mention the concept of yin and yang, requires a bit of spending alongside all that thrift. And so might your self-esteem. Is there something you'd enjoy having, that you could easily afford but haven't acquired because you don't strictly need it? Think about that policy: you're only allowed to have things you absolutely need. Turned around, that means you're *not* allowed, even as an adult, to acquire something just because it would make you happy. That's not a message conducive to self-esteem. Treat yourself as you would a good friend, and give yourself a gift once in a while.

If you're a spender, save with a purpose. Some of us are more spendthrift than thrifty. Money comes in, and it soon goes out again. Many families who struggle to live within their means have no choice about this. But some people don't manage to save no matter how much money comes in.* If this describes you, saving doesn't come naturally, and it isn't easy. That's why I recommend it. The right kind of self-discipline — the kind that makes you genuinely better off, not just feeling as though you checked the right boxes — is a form of self-esteem. Healthy self-esteem thrives on your setting and meeting reasonable standards, including managing money in a way that benefits you both today and

---

* There are many causes of overspending, and they can be complex. You might benefit from therapy to discover why you overspend and/or undersave. Caring friends, online resources, and support groups are also potential allies and supporters if you want to change your spending habits.

in the future. When you successfully save toward a planned purchase, you'll know you did something for yourself that was extremely difficult, but (here's the good part) you're worth it.

Accept compliments with a smile and a simple "Thank you." How do you habitually react when someone offers you a compliment? Do you ignore it, deflect it, or turn it back on the giver? Or do you simply say thank you? Accepting compliments is another of those freebie sets of mental calisthenics that present themselves now and then to help you practice receiving. This is one of those techniques classified under the heading "Act as if you were, and you will be." Practice at home. Tell yourself, "You look very nice today," and then reply, "Thanks! I appreciate the compliment." You're taking a step just by saying those words. Make sure you smile. Even if you cringe inside as you do this, the exchange may convince your subconscious that not only is there nothing wrong with you, but you're actually pretty cool.

Have that awkward conversation you've been avoiding. There are certain kinds of conversations it takes guts to initiate. Breaking up with someone is, for most of us, one of them. Apologizing to your adult child may be another. Each time you put yourself in the line of fire to speak or hear a bitter truth, you're telling yourself, "This is difficult, but it's important, and I'm strong enough to withstand the discomfort of it. If it doesn't go well, I can apologize and ask for a do-over." If that doesn't make you at least a little bit proud of yourself, I don't know what will.

Conversely, avoiding necessary but painful conversations reinforces the notion "I can't do this; there must be something wrong with me," or perhaps "Whatever's wrong with me will be revealed if I open myself up to an honest conversation." Either way, avoiding awkward conversations (or, as the business author Susan Scott calls them, "fierce" conversations) leaves you feeling incompetent, frustrated, and ashamed.[2]

Have you heard of parkour? It's a sport that involves moving around, through, over, and under naturally occurring obstacles in an urban setting. It's a sound substitute for the artificially induced exercise you get from machines at the gym. Parkour is a good analogy for using day-to-day events and conversations to build your self-esteem. Do some emotional parkour as you go about your day, using spontaneous conversations and events to strengthen injured self-esteem.

As a general guideline, anything that requires you to actively accept yourself as you are, or to treat yourself as you would a valued friend, is a salve for injured self-esteem. Once your self-esteem starts to heal, and unneeded shame to dissipate, your bucket will fill up more quickly from self-care and through your other relationships. It may even grow in capacity, so that you can play the Parent to your adult child more easily and for longer periods.

Feeling Is Healing

Parents hate it when their children are in pain; yet when their children hurt *them*, the human being inside the parent may feel like lashing out in self-defense. What a complex experience. You love your child, but she's wounding you with her cruel or unreasonable behavior. She's your child — younger, with less experience and maturity — yet she seems so powerful. If you feel a kaleidoscope of emotions, you're normal. Being human means having emotions, reacting to the ups and downs of fate as well as to your own shifting perceptions.

Nobody wants to sit around steeped in emotional pain or confusion. Maybe that's why the number one question I hear from my clients is "What should I do now?" Most estranged parents focus on the tactics involved in solving the problem of estrangement, and on next steps, because it hurts too much to stop and just feel the feelings. It seems better to try to take action to fix them.

In reality, the best answer to what to do next is often simply to pause and notice the uncertainty, or the fact that you're in pain. Failing to pay attention to yourself makes you more and more emotionally depleted, less and less able to do what's necessary to repair the relationship. The longer you try to outrun the pain you're in by focusing on concrete actions, the more resentment builds up in your heart toward your child. You can't help but view him or her as the reason for your worsening condition.

Imagine that someone has physically hurt you. The wound is serious, but instead of seeking medical attention you run around trying to get this person to somehow undo the injury. Meanwhile, left untreated, the wound grows worse instead of getting better. What's the most sensible step to take before this injury starts to take a toll on your functioning?

This section is about how to attend to the emotional wounds of estrangement so they don't send you into a vortex of pain and powerlessness. Obsessing, worrying, ruminating — all of these are the brain's attempts to fix how we feel inside. The trouble is that feelings can't be fixed in this way. If you're in pain over your relationship with your child, it's too late to fix your feelings. You're already wounded. The appropriate response to the immediate problem of emotional pain is to get quiet and listen to it.

Feeling Abandoned

Gary was a fifty-five-year-old divorced father with a twenty-four-year-old daughter, Bonnie. According to Gary, Bonnie had wanted nothing to do with him since his divorce ten years earlier from her mother. Bonnie didn't acknowledge him on Father's Day or his birthday, nor did she show any interest in getting together for holidays. But occasionally she would reach out and say hello, as if everything were fine between them. Gary was devastated by what he perceived as her ongoing rejection of a "real relationship" with him. He vacillated between being angry with Bonnie and blaming himself for the state of their relationship. By the time Gary came to me for help, he was afraid to have any contact with his daughter in case his angry feelings showed in their interactions.

I asked Gary about all the feelings that came up when he thought about his daughter. The most intense emotion for him was a feeling of abandonment. Gary had been adopted when he was six, after spending most of his life in foster homes. Despite being well loved and cared for by his adoptive family, Gary's early feelings surrounding being abandoned by his birth mother had never resolved. When Bonnie created distance between them, those feelings erupted in full force. They affected Gary's ability to play the Parent role, since his emotions trapped him in a childlike state.

In therapy, Gary identified and consciously experienced the long-standing feelings of abandonment that Bonnie's behavior had triggered. This freed up inner resources he'd been using to keep his uncomfortable emotions in check, giving him more energy and clarity than before. It also convinced him that he could survive being abandoned. The fact was, Gary *had* survived abandonment. What we fear most in relationships is what's happened to us before. (If it hadn't already happened, we wouldn't know how painful it is, and we wouldn't be so fearful.)

Ultimately, to his surprise and chagrin, Gary came to understand that Bonnie had felt abandoned by *him*. She'd been angry with him during and after the divorce. Ten years on, she simply didn't know how to reconnect. She needed him to help make it happen. Because of his feelings of abandonment and the anger that accompanied and masked those feelings, he'd been neglecting to reach out to her, expecting her to initiate contact. Now that his emotions were no longer controlling his behavior, Gary was able to begin making positive, consistent efforts toward strengthening his relationship with Bonnie. I'm pleased to say that last year she took him to lunch on Father's Day for the very first time.

If you want to see the situation clearly, and to marshal enough resources to act in a purposeful, strategic way, feeling your feelings is not optional. In our culture, we expect to make things happen by putting our emotions aside and applying effort. But this only makes things harder than they need to be. Unacknowledged feelings act like chewing gum in the gears of our behavior; they have a destructive impact we're not aware of.

Take your attention off your child and bring it to yourself. What are you feeling right now? Sad? Angry? Remorseful? Abandoned? Go back to those lists of feeling words from chapter 3 and label your experience. Tell yourself whatever it is you're feeling, like "I feel invisible and lonely. My child is the most important person in my life, and he won't even talk to me. I feel worthless and sad." Consciously experience those feelings so that they stop chasing you. Far from being a waste of time, feeling your feelings in this deliberate way is the most productive use of the time while you're apart from your child. (Again, see the TRUTH technique in my book *Constructive Wallowing* for instructions on how to do this.)

Increasing Assertiveness

Each of us has thoughts, feelings, opinions, preferences, and needs that won't necessarily jibe with those of important others. Sometimes there will be inevitable conflicts to navigate. The presence of conflict doesn't mean a relationship has come to an end, or even that it's unhealthy. It's how conflict is handled that makes relationships healthy or unhealthy.

When conflict entails threats of (or actual) physical violence, unproductive silence, name-calling or character attacks, it's damaging and unproductive. Such behaviors don't bring people closer or build trust. Also, talking to Person B about a problem you're having with Person A instead of talking to Person A directly about the problem (called *triangulation*, because Person B forms a triangle with you and Person A) can erode trust and goodwill between all three people. Even though there's no overt aggression, there's a quiet erosion of bonds.

When we don't know a better way to handle conflict and we don't want to be aggressive, we tend to avoid confrontation in the interest of lessening potential damage. Ironically, the harder we work to avoid conflict in important relationships, the less we tend to feel close and secure in them.

Instead of avoiding confrontation, we can practice assertive communication. This can help us in many situations:

- handling conflict
- structuring important conversations

- expressing our needs
- holding our boundaries
- improving our self-esteem
- knowing each other better
- trusting each other more

So what does assertiveness look like? I'll offer a few ideas here, but please explore the topic further online or at your local library. Better yet, take a class or workshop. I taught assertiveness to various groups for years because I wanted to spread the word about its effect on quality of life. Once learned and practiced consistently, assertiveness is a powerful skill.*

What Assertiveness Looks Like

Unlike communication that's passive (suffering in silence), or aggressive ("You always/never do _____!" or "You're such a _____!"), or passive-aggressive ("forgetting" to do something you resent being asked to do), assertiveness calmly and politely states your boundaries and needs in a way that respects the other person as well as yourself.

Assertive communication is *direct*, meaning you speak to the person you need to address, not someone else; centered on communicating your *own* thoughts and feelings; *respectful* and *responsive*; and *firm*, meaning your position doesn't change just because someone else doesn't like it.

The examples below show how Assertive Anne handles herself.

Scenario 1

Anne: May I have this salad with the dressing on the side?
Waiter: The salad comes already dressed.

---

* My understanding of assertive communication is based primarily on Ann Dickson, *A Woman in Your Own Right: Assertiveness and You* (London: Quartet Books, 1982).

Anne: I didn't realize that. Is it possible to get it with the dressing on the side?

Waiter: I'll ask the chef.

Anne: Thank you.

Scenario 2

Friend: Can I borrow that book when you've finished reading it?

Anne: No, the last two books I lent you never made it back to me.

Friend: I promise I'll return this one right away. Honest.

Anne: I know you have good intentions, but the answer is still no.

Friend: It's just a book!

Anne: It may be just a book, and I don't want to hurt your feelings, but I'm still not willing to lend it.

Scenario 3

Someone stands in front of Anne, who's waiting in line at the checkout counter.

Anne: Hi. I'm next in line.

Rude person: (*Ignores her*)

Anne: Excuse me; I'm next in line.

Rude person: What's your problem?

Anne: You stepped in front of me even though I was here first. I'm next in line.

Rude person: (*Ignores her*)

Anne (*To cashier*): I'm next in line even though this person is standing in front of me.

In scenario 3, Anne appeals to an authority figure — in this case, the cashier — only after getting nowhere with direct communication. Being assertive should work for you easily nine out of ten times — when you're dealing with people outside the family. With family members, plan on getting resistance nine times out of ten when you first start using this style of communication.

Scenario 4

Checkout clerk: Would you like add a dollar to your purchase for charity?

Anne: No.

It can be empowering to utter the simple word *no*, without excuses or apologies. You can smile pleasantly while you say it. But it's not necessary to dress up your answer with extra words.

When you know how to speak and act assertively, you feel more in control when situations arise. It becomes easier to respond, rather than react. In order to act assertively, you have to believe that you're entitled to your position, whatever it is, and to know your position: what you want, what you'll tolerate, and so on.

These principles may sound simple, but they can perplex the best of us in practice. Try reading a book or taking a class about assertiveness with a friend, and practice the exercises together.

Healthy Entitlement

Consider the assertion above: "You're entitled to your position." The terms *entitled* and *a sense of entitlement* both have negative connotations for many people. But it's important for adults to have a strong enough sense of entitlement to claim and act on the rights we hold, and to protect our personal boundaries. It's only an overreaching of entitlement that makes the concept questionable.

The idea of entitlement is distasteful mostly to those who mistakenly believe they're not entitled to anything. If you're nervous or skeptical about entitlement, that's all right. All I ask is that you open your mind to the possibility that more is due to you than you've been taking. Following is a list of some of the rights you have that you might not have thought about. You can choose whether, when, and with whom to exercise them. Sometimes exercising your rights will bring consequences. Every action you take has repercussions — but so does every action you *don't* take.

Claiming these rights is optional, and especially with your estranged child, you'll probably make a conscious choice *not* to exercise some of them. Whether you claim the right or not, as an adult, you're entitled to do all of the following:

- put your needs first
- pick your friends
- decide based on emotion, not logic
- refuse to answer questions you don't want to answer
- change your mind
- choose how you spend your time
- choose how you spend your money
- seek better health, or not
- make requests — even unreasonable ones
- refuse requests — even reasonable ones

This list isn't exhaustive; it's just a sampling of your freedoms. How does reading them make you feel? If any of these seem wrong to you, try putting this in front: "I don't have the right to..." Does it seem more appropriate *not* to be allowed? What's your source of information about what you're due as an adult? Is the information accurate? How well does it serve you? What might happen if you claimed the license to all the rights mentioned above?

Embracing assertiveness can be a challenge at the best of times, let alone when you're asserting rights you aren't used to exercising. Practice first in situations where it's easier for you, and work up to ones that feel more challenging.

Even if you succeed in developing a healthy sense of entitlement, you still have to make decisions about where you stand, what you want, and what you will and won't put up with. Don't wait till you're in the middle of a conversation to try to figure those out. Take the time you have between contact with your child to think about these things. Tease apart your longing for connection from your need to set good boundaries.

If you find it hard to be assertive, forgive yourself. You learned somewhere along the line that it wasn't appropriate for you to assert your rights. But you can learn differently. It just takes courage, practice, and time.

PUTTING IT ALL TOGETHER

You've spent some time pondering your family history and how it affects your view (and perhaps your child's view) of relationships. You've learned about the normal developmental processes of differentiation and individuation that play a role in our behavior throughout our lives. You've contemplated the needs we all share, which continuously affect our relationships with both others and ourselves.

You know how important it is to get good at dealing with, and talking about, emotions. You've become familiar with the role responsibilities of the Parent and the Child. You're more in touch than ever with your emotional needs and have some clear ideas about how to take care of yourself. You've got guidelines for bringing back the Parent while offering your inner Child what she or he needs. You've read specific advice about how to handle contact with your adult child when you're both ready.

We've talked about coping with silence and other specific situations, and about why you need and deserve tons of support. You've had a crash course in developing emotional literacy, building your self-esteem, and developing assertiveness — all valuable for anyone daring to take on the demanding role of the Parent. I hope you've become convinced that even when you're not in contact with your child, there's plenty of work you can do in the service of improving that relation-ship. You've perhaps come to share my view that your relationship with yourself is the foundation for the one you share with your child.

The aim of this book was to provide you with a set of tools for your relationship toolkit. To your project of reconciliation with your child, you bring the courage and the openness to do whatever is required to make it happen, within your personal boundaries. In reading these chapters you've put yourself through a constructive self-exploration and come out the other side. It's still possible that no matter what you do or how well you do it, your child may not come back to you. If that happens, as dreadful as it is, you will survive. You might even thrive. To a certain extent, that's up to you.

While reading, you've undoubtedly brought your own insights, ideas, and tools to bear on the subject. These also form a part of your enhanced toolkit. Nothing is required of you that you don't either al-ready have or have access to.

Now that you're equipped with all these resources, this may be the end of our time together. However, if you would like to consult with me about anything in these pages, I'm available for brief, short-term online or telephone consultation anywhere in the world. Visit TinaGilbertson .com/consultation to learn more. You may also benefit from joining my friendly, active, and positive community at ReconnectionClub.com. There you can connect with other estranged parents and me, partake of courses, workshops, and other resources that I've created, listen to interviews with other experts, and participate in group Q&A calls. I look forward to welcoming you to the Club.

ACKNOWLEDGMENTS

I have to start by acknowledging the many therapy and consultation clients and members of the Reconnection Club who have opened their hearts to me during some of the most painful times of their lives. This book was born from their experiences and insights, their questions, struggles, and accomplishments.

To these folks I say, you inspire me every day, and it's a privilege to work with you.

My literary agent, Janet Rosen, urged me for years to write this book before I finally did. When the time was ripe, she searched tirelessly for just the right publisher. If you're reading this book, it's largely because of Janet's enthusiasm and tenacity. Janet works with Sheree Bykofsky of the eponymous literary agency. Sheree is a warm and knowledgeable agent whose clients love her, and for good reason. Thank you both for sticking with me all these years.

Thank you to Georgia Hughes, our champion at New World Library. Our short time working together was as smooth and pleasant as colored glass. In her colleague Jason Gardner I found an editor with the two most essential editorial qualities: a cheeky sense of humor and a sophisticated knowledge of the industry. To the extent that this book meets or exceeds readers' expectations, it's due to Jason's expert handling.

Many thanks to all my colleagues and friends, especially Lisa Voisin and Jessica Graves, for your openhearted support and input, both during this project and beyond.

To my small but mighty blended family — Mum, Charles, Mary, Natha, Michael, Jen, and Kieran — you are precious to me, and all of you have contributed to my contentment and success.

Lastly, I have my beloved husband, Mike Witt, to thank for being the joy in my heart, the fuel in my tank, and the best life partner I could ask for. You're the reason I can actually sit down and write a book.

NOTES

Introduction

1. Ben Sasse, *The Vanishing American Adult: Our Coming-of-Age Crisis — and How to Rebuild a Culture of Self-Reliance* (New York: St. Martin's Press, 2017).

Chapter 1: Faces of Estrangement

1. Kylie Agllias, *Family Estrangement: A Matter of Perspective* (London: Routledge, 2017), 4.
2. Megan Gilligan, J. Jill Suitor, and Karl Pillemer, "Estrangement between Mothers and Adult Children: The Role of Norms and Values," *Journal of Marriage and Family* 77 (August 2015): 914.
3. Richard P. Conti, "Family Estrangement: Establishing a Prevalence Rate," *Journal of Psychology and Behavioral Science* 3, no. 2 (December 2015): 34.
4. Kristina Scharp and Elizabeth Dorrance Hall, "Family Marginalization, Alienation and Estrangement: Questioning the Nonvoluntary Status of Family Relationships," *Annals of the International Communication Association* 14, no. 1 (2017): 35.
5. Conti, "Family Estrangement," 31.
6. Leo Sher, "Parental Alienation and Suicide in Men," *Psychiatria Danubina* 27, no. 3 (2015): 288.

7. Kristen Carr, Amanda Holman, Jenna Abetz, Jody Koenig Kellas, and
    Elizabeth Vagnoni, "Giving Voice to the Silence of Family Estrangement:
    Comparing Reasons of Estranged Parents and Adult Children in a Non-
    matched Sample," *Journal of Family Communication* 15 (2015): 134.

8. Lucy Blake, "Parents and Children Who Are Estranged in Adulthood: A
    Review and Discussion of the Literature," *Journal of Family Theory and
    Review* 9 (December 2017): 528.

9. Blake, "Parents and Children," 530.

10. Blake, "Parents and Children," 529.

11. Carr et al., "Giving Voice," 137–39.

12. Parents_Survey_7_2018.pdf and AdultChild_Summary_7_2018.pdf:
    Survey results posted on Estranged Stories, https://estrangedstories.ning
    .com/, accessed June 10, 2018.

13. Blake, "Parents and Children," 529.

14. Kristina Scharp and Rachel M. McLaren, "Uncertainty Issues and Man-
    agement in Adult Children's Stories of Their Estrangement with Their
    Parents," *Journal of Social and Personal Relationships* 35, no. 6 (2017): 812.

15. Amanda J. Shallcross, Allison S. Troy, Matthew Boland, and Iris B. Mauss,
    "Let It Be: Accepting Negative Emotional Experiences Predicts Decreased
    Negative Affect and Depressive Symptoms," *Behaviour Research and Ther-
    apy* 48 (2010): 928.

16. Blake, "Parents and Children," 529–30.

Chapter 2: Family History

1. Amy J. L. Baker, "The Long-Term Effects of Parental Alienation on Adult
    Children: A Qualitative Research Study," *American Journal of Family Ther-
    apy* 33 (2005): 293–301.

2. Baker, "Long-Term Effects of Parental Alienation."

3. Ivan Boszormenyi-Nagy and Geraldine M. Spark, *Invisible Loyalties: Rec-
    iprocity in Intergenerational Family Therapy* (New York: Brunner/Mazel,
    1984), 11, 25, 32–33, 37–41.

4. Dara M. Ibrahim, Ronald P. Rohner, Rhiannon L. Smith, and Kaitlin
    M. Flannery, "Adults' Remembrances of Parental Acceptance-Rejection
    Predict Current Rejection Sensitivity in Adulthood," *Family and Consumer
    Sciences Research Journal* 44, no. 1 (September 2015): 52.

5. Corine De Ruiter and Marinus H. Van Ijzendoorn, "Attachment and

Cognition: A Review of the Literature," *International Journal of Educational Research* 19 (1993): 530–31.

6. Cassidy J. D. Jones and P. R. Shaver, "Adult Attachment Style and Parenting," in *Attachment Theory and Research: New Directions and Emerging Themes*, edited by J. A. Simpson and W. S. Rholes (New York: Guilford Press, 2015), 234–60.

7. John Byng-Hall, "Creating a Secure Family Base: Some Implications of Attachment Theory for Family Therapy," *Family Process* 34 (1995): 5.

8. Jones and Shaver, "Adult Attachment Style and Parenting," 2015.

9. Nanu Elena Doinita and Nijloveanu Dorina Maria, "Attachment and Parenting Styles," *Procedia: Social and Behavioral Sciences* 203 (2015): 200.

10. Mario Mikulincer, Phillip R. Shaver, Omri Gillath, and Rachel A. Nitzberg, "Attachment, Caregiving, and Altruism: Boosting Attachment Security Increases Compassion and Helping," *Journal of Personality and Social Psychology* 89, no. 5 (2005): 818.

11. Bessel Van der Kolk, "Developmental Trauma Disorder," *Psychiatric Annals* 35, no. 5 (May 2005): 402.

12. Vincent Felitti, Robert F. Anda, Dale Nordenberg, David F. Williamson, Alison M. Spitz, Valerie Edwards, Mary P. Koss, and James S. Marks, "Relationship of Childhood Abuse and Household Dysfunction to Many of the Leading Causes of Death in Adults," *American Journal of Preventive Medicine* 14, no. 4 (1998): 245–58.

13. "What Is Domestic Violence?" National Domestic Violence Hotline, www.thehotline.org/is-this-abuse/abuse-defined, accessed June 14, 2019.

14. Michael J. Sheridan, "A Proposed Intergenerational Model of Substance Abuse, Family Functioning, and Abuse/Neglect," *Child Abuse and Neglect* 19, no. 5 (1995): 520.

15. Marina Barnard and Neil McKeganey, "The Impact of Parental Problem Drug Use on Children: What Is the Problem and What Can Be Done to Help?" *Addiction* 99 (2004): 553.

16. Nancy J. Kepple, "Does Parental Substance Use Always Engender Risk for Children? Comparing Incident Rate Ratios of Abusive and Neglectful Behaviors across Substance Use Behavior Patterns," *Child Abuse and Neglect* 76 (2018): 52.

17. Christine Walsh, Harriet L. MacMillan, and Ellen Jamieson, "The Relationship between Parental Substance Abuse and Child Maltreatment," *Child Abuse and Neglect* 27 (2003): 1410–12.

Chapter 3: Lost in Translation

1. Rick Peterson and Stephen Green, *Families First — Keys to Successful Family Functioning: Communication*, Virginia Cooperative Extension Publication 350-092 (2009), available at www.pubs.ext.vt.edu/350/350-092/350-092.html.
2. David M. Keating, Jessica C. Russell, Jennifer Cornacchione, and Sandi W. Smith, "Family Communication Patterns and Difficult Family Conversations," *Journal of Applied Communication Research* 41, no. 2 (2013): 175.
3. Peterson and Green, *Families First*, 1.
4. Amanda J. Shallcross, Allison S. Troy, Matthew Boland, and Iris B. Mauss, "Let It Be: Accepting Negative Emotional Experiences Predicts Decreased Negative Affect and Depressive Symptoms," *Behaviour Research and Therapy* 48 (2010): 926–27.

Chapter 4: Unmet Needs

1. *Supernanny* (US version), starring Jo Frost, produced by Ricochet Entertainment, January 2005–March 2011.
2. Alexander R. Lyon, "Current State of Knowledge on Takotsubo Syndrome: A Position Statement from the Task Force on Takotsubo Syndrome of the Heart Failure Association of the European Society of Cardiology," *European Journal of Heart Failure* 18 (2016): 16–17.
3. J. Eric Gentry, Certified Clinical Trauma Professional (CCTP) Intensive Training Course, live training through PESI in Denver, Colorado, January 31–February 1, 2019.
4. Tina Gilbertson, *Constructive Wallowing: How to Beat Bad Feelings by Letting Yourself Have Them* (Berkeley: Cleis Press, 2014), 9–13.

Chapter 5: Independence

1. Stephen A. Anderson and Ronald M. Sabatelli, "Differentiating Differentiation and Individuation: Conceptual and Operation Challenges," *American Journal of Family Therapy* 18, no. 1 (Spring 1990): 35.
2. *Nature*, " My Life as a Turkey," written by Rachael Teel and Joe Hutto, directed by David Allen, aired November 15, 2011, on PBS, www.pbs.org/video/nature-my-life-as-a-turkey.
3. Kristina Scharp, personal communication, January 21, 2019.

Chapter 7: Filling Everyone's Buckets

1. Tim Gilbertson, *Constructive Wallowing: How to Beat Bad Feelings by Letting Yourself Have Them* (Berkeley: Cleis Press, 2014) 117–24.
2. Rachel L. Ruttan, Mary-Hunter McDonnell, and Loran F. Nordgern, "Having 'Been There' Doesn't Mean I Care: When Prior Experience Reduces Compassion for Emotional Distress," *Journal of Personality and Social Psychology* 108, no. 4 (2015): 610–22.

Chapter 8: Contact

1. Amy J. L. Baker, *Adult Children of Parental Alienation Syndrome: Breaking the Ties That Bind* (New York: W. W. Norton, 2007): 212–13.
2. Amy J. L. Baker and Douglas C. Darnall, "A Construct Study of the Eight Symptoms of Severe Parental Alienation Syndrome: A Survey of Parental Experiences," *Journal of Divorce and Remarriage* 47, no. 1–2 (2007): 56–57.
3. Harriet Lerner, "The Power of Apologizing," *Psychotherapy Networker,* March–April 2018, 44.

Chapter 10: Special Circumstances

1. Amy J. L. Baker, *Adult Children of Parental Alienation Syndrome: Breaking the Ties That Bind* (New York: W. W. Norton, 2007): 37–38.
2. See also the website of the National Domestic Violence Hotline, specifically www.thehotline.org/help/help-for-friends-and-family.
3. Deanna Brann, personal communication, March 26, 2019.
4. Data from 2017 National Survey on Drug Use and Health, cited in "Mental Illness," National Institute of Mental Health, www.nimh.nih.gov/health/statistics/mental-illness.shtml, accessed June 19, 2019.
5. "Mental Illness."

Chapter 11: Reconciliation

1. Anne Grodzins Lipow, "Why Training Doesn't Stick: Who Is to Blame?" *Library Trends* 38, no. 1 (Summer 1989): 64–65.
2. John Maxwell, "Today's Friday Challenge Word Is: Everything Worthwhile

Is Uphill," John Maxwell Team, http://johnmaxwellteam.com/2017
-everything-worthwhile-is-uphill/, accessed August 19, 2019.

Chapter 12: Gifts for Yourself and Your Child

1. Tina Gilbertson, *Constructive Wallowing: How to Beat Bad Feelings by Letting Yourself Have Them* (Berkeley: Cleis Press, 2014), 117–24.

2. Susan Scott, *Fierce Conversations: Achieving Success at Work and in Life One Conversation at a Time* (London: Piatkus, 2017).

BIBLIOGRAPHY

Agllias, Kylie. "Difference, Choice, and Punishment: Parental Beliefs and Understandings about Adult Child Estrangement." *Australian Social Work* 68, no. 1 (2015): 115–29.

———. *Family Estrangement: A Matter of Perspective*. London: Routledge, 2017.

Anderson, Stephen A., and Ronald M. Sabatelli. "Differentiating Differentiation and Individuation: Conceptual and Operation Challenges." *American Journal of Family Therapy* 18, no. 1 (Spring 1990): 32–50.

Baker, Amy J. L. "The Long-Term Effects of Parental Alienation on Adult Children: A Qualitative Research Study." *American Journal of Family Therapy* 33 (2005): 293–301.

———. *Adult Children of Parental Alienation Syndrome: Breaking the Ties That Bind*. New York: W. W. Norton, 2007.

Baker, Amy J. L., and Douglas C. Darnall. "A Construct Study of the Eight Symptoms of Severe Parental Alienation Syndrome: A Survey of Parental Experiences." *Journal of Divorce and Remarriage* 47, no. 1–2 (2007): 55–75.

Barnard, Marina, and Neil McKeganey. "The Impact of Parental Problem Drug Use on Children: What Is the Problem and What Can Be Done to Help?" *Addiction* 99 (2004): 552–59.

Barrett, Lisa Feldman, James Gross, Tamlin Conner Christensen, and Michael Benvenuto. "Knowing What You're Feeling and Knowing What to Do about It: Mapping the Relation between Emotion Differentiation and Emotion Regulation." *Cognition and Emotion* 15, no. 6 (2001): 713–24.

Blake, Lucy. "Parents and Children Who Are Estranged in Adulthood: A Review and Discussion of the Literature." *Journal of Family Theory and Review* 9 (December 2017): 521–36.

Brann, Deanna. *Reluctantly Related: Secrets to Getting Along with Your Mother-in-Law or Daughter-in-Law.* Knoxville, TN: Ambergris Publishing, 2013.

Byng-Hall, John. "Creating a Secure Family Base: Some Implications of Attachment Theory for Family Therapy." *Family Process* 34 (1995): 45–58.

Carr, Kristen, Amanda Holman, Jenna Abetz, Jody Koenig Kellas, and Elizabeth Vagnoni. "Giving Voice to the Silence of Family Estrangement: Comparing Reasons of Estranged Parents and Adult Children in a Non-matched Sample," *Journal of Family Communication* 15 (2015): 130–40.

Clarke, Edward J., Mar Preston, Jo Raksin, and Vern L. Bengtson. "Types of Conflicts and Tensions between Older Parents and Adult Children." *Gerontologist* 39, no. 3, 261–70.

Conti, Richard P. "Family Estrangement: Establishing a Prevalence Rate." *Journal of Psychology and Behavioral Science* 3, no. 2 (December 2015): 28–35.

De Ruiter, Corine, and Marinus H. Van Ijzendoorn. "Attachment and Cognition: A Review of the Literature," *International Journal of Educational Research* 19 (1993): 525–40.

Dickson, Anne. *A Woman in Your Own Right: Assertiveness and You.* London: Quartet Books, 1982.

Doinita, Nanu Elena, and Nijloveanu Dorina Maria. "Attachment and Parenting Styles." *Procedia: Social and Behavioral Sciences* 203 (2015): 199–204.

Felitti, Vincent, Robert F. Anda, Dale Nordenberg, David F. Williamson, Alison M. Spitz, Valerie Edwards, Mary P. Koss, and James S. Marks. "Relationship of Childhood Abuse and Household Dysfunction to Many of the Leading Causes of Death in Adults." *American Journal of Preventive Medicine* 14, no. 4 (1998): 245–58.

Ford, Brett Q., Phoebe Lam, Oliver P. John, and Iris B. Mauss. "The Psychological Health Benefits of Accepting Negative Emotions and Thoughts: Laboratory, Diary, and Longitudinal Evidence." *Journal of Personality and Social Psychology* 115, no. 6 (December 2018): 1075–92.

Gilbertson, Tina. *Constructive Wallowing: How to Beat Bad Feelings by Letting Yourself Have Them.* Berkeley: Cleis Press, 2014.

Gilligan, Megan, J. Jill Suitor, and Karl Pillemer. "Estrangement between Mothers and Adult Children: The Role of Norms and Values." *Journal of Marriage and Family* 77 (August 2015): 908–20.

Grodzins Lipow, Anne. "Why Training Doesn't Stick: Who Is to Blame?" *Library Trends* 38, no. 1 (Summer 1989): 62–72.

Gross, James J., and Robert W. Levenson. "Hiding Feelings: The Acute Effects of Inhibiting Negative and Positive Emotion." *Journal of Abnormal Psychology* 106, no. 1 (1997): 95–103.

Holt, Stephanie, Helen Buckley, and Sadhbh Whelan. "The Impact of Exposure to Domestic Violence on Children and Young People: A Review of the Literature." *Child Abuse and Neglect* 32 (2008): 797–810.

Ibrahim, Dara M., Ronald P. Rohner, Rhiannon L. Smith, and Kaitlin M. Flannery. "Adults' Remembrances of Parental Acceptance-Rejection Predict Current Rejection Sensitivity in Adulthood," *Family and Consumer Sciences Research Journal* 44, no. 1 (September 2015): 51–62.

Jerrome, Dorothy. "Family Estrangement: Parents and Children Who 'Lose Touch.'" *Journal of Family Therapy* 16 (1994): 241–58.

Jones, Cassidy J. D., and P. R. Shaver. "Adult Attachment Style and Parenting." In *Attachment Theory and Research: New Directions and Emerging Themes*, edited by J. A. Rholes, 234–60. New York: Guilford Press, 2015.

Keating, David M., Jessica C. Russell, Jennifer Cornacchione, and Sandi W. Smith. "Family Communication Patterns and Difficult Family Conversations." *Journal of Applied Communication Research* 41, no. 2 (2013): 160–80.

Kepple, Nancy J. "Does Parental Substance Use Always Engender Risk for Children? Comparing Incident Rate Ratios of Abusive and Neglectful Behaviors across Substance Use Behavior Patterns." *Child Abuse and Neglect* 76 (2018): 44–55.

Lerner, Harriet. "The Power of Apologizing." *Psychotherapy Networker*, March–April 2018, 40–47.

Lyon, Alexander R. "Current State of Knowledge on Takotsubo Syndrome: A Position Statement from the Task Force on Takotsubo Syndrome of the Heart Failure Association of the European Society of Cardiology." *European Journal of Heart Failure* 18 (2016): 8–27.

Malinosky-Rummell, Robin, and David J. Hansen. "Long-Term Consequences of Childhood Physical Abuse." *Psychological Bulletin* 114, no. 1 (1993): 68–79.

Mikulincer, Mario, Phillip R. Shaver, Omri Gillath, and Rachel A. Nitzberg.

"Attachment, Caregiving, and Altruism: Boosting Attachment Security Increases Compassion and Helping." *Journal of Personality and Social Psychology* 89, no. 5 (2005): 817–39.

Murphy, Anne, Miriam Steele, Shanta Rishi Dube, Jordan Bate, Karen Bonuck, Paul Meissner, Hannah Goldman, and Howard Steele. "Adverse Childhood Experiences (ACEs) Questionnaire and Adult Attachment Interview (AAI): Implications for Parent-Child Relationships." *Child Abuse and Neglect* 38 (2014): 224–33.

Peterson, Rick, and Stephen Green. *Families First — Keys to Successful Family Functioning: Communication.* Virginia Cooperative Extension Publication 350-092 (2009).

Ruttan, Rachel L., Mary-Hunter McDonnell, and Loran F. Nordgern. "Having 'Been There' Doesn't Mean I Care: When Prior Experience Reduces Compassion for Emotional Distress." *Journal of Personality and Social Psychology* 108, no. 4 (2015): 610–22.

Sasse, Ben. *The Vanishing American Adult: Our Coming-of-Age Crisis — and How to Rebuild a Culture of Self-Reliance.* New York: St. Martin's Press, 2017.

Scharp, Kristina, and Elizabeth Dorrance Hall. "Family Marginalization, Alienation and Estrangement: Questioning the Nonvoluntary Status of Family Relationships." *Annals of the International Communication Association* 14, no. 1 (2017): 28–45.

Scharp, Kristina, and Rachel M. McLaren. "Uncertainty Issues and Management in Adult Children's Stories of Their Estrangement with Their Parents." *Journal of Social and Personal Relationships* 35, no. 6 (2017): 811–30.

Scharp, Kristina M., and Lindsey J. Thomas. "Family 'Bonds': Making Meaning of Parent-Child Relationships in Estrangement Narratives." *Journal of Family Communication* 16, no. 1 (2016): 32–50.

Scharp, Kristina, Lindsey Thomas, and Christina Paxman. "'It Was the Straw That Broke the Camel's Back': Exploring the Distancing Processes Communicatively Constructed in Parent-Child Estrangement Backstories." *Journal of Family Communication* 15 (2015): 330–48.

Scott, Susan. *Fierce Conversations: Achieving Success at Work and in Life One Conversation at a Time.* London: Piatkus, 2017.

Shallcross, Amanda J., Allison S. Troy, Matthew Boland, and Iris B. Mauss. "Let It Be: Accepting Negative Emotional Experiences Predicts Decreased

Negative Affect and Depressive Symptoms." *Behaviour Research and Therapy* 48 (2010): 921–29.

Sher, Leo. "Parental Alienation and Suicide in Men." *Psychiatria Danubina* 27, no. 3 (2015): 288–89.

Sheridan, Michael J. "A Proposed Intergenerational Model of Substance Abuse, Family Functioning, and Abuse/Neglect." *Child Abuse and Neglect* 19, no. 5 (1995): 519–30.

Van der Kolk, Bessel. "Developmental Trauma Disorder." *Psychiatric Annals* 35, no. 5 (May 2005): 401–8.

Walsh, Christine, Harriet L. MacMillan, and Ellen Jamieson. "The Relationship between Parental Substance Abuse and Child Maltreatment." *Child Abuse and Neglect* 27 (2003): 1409–25.

Williams, Kipling D., Wendelyn J. Shore, and John E. Grahe. "The Silent Treatment: Perceptions of Its Behaviors and Associated Feelings." *Group Processes and Intergroup Relations* 1, no. 2 (1998): 117–41.

INDEX

ABOUT THE AUTHOR

No one ever says to a six-year-old, "You'll make a great psychotherapist one day." Consequently, it took Tina Gilbertson a good portion of her life to discover her calling. For about fifteen years, Tina worked in media — first on the editorial staff at a local newspaper in her home town of Vancouver, BC, and later in book publishing and television in New York City. She even spent ten years pursuing an acting career, with an early *X Files* appearance as an "under five" (meaning she spoke fewer than five lines). She spent about nine years too many on acting before deciding it wasn't for her.

Tina's accidental exposure to therapy — she lived in Manhattan, so it was practically required that she find a therapist — led to an epiphany. Although she was creative, her greatest satisfaction came from helping people. She felt at home in the therapy room, and when she thought about trading the client's chair for the therapist's, she knew she had finally found her path. Decision made, she moved back to the Pacific Northwest to be closer to her parents and graduated with a master's degree in counseling psychology at the age of forty. She went directly into private practice and has never looked back.

Meanwhile, Tina had met her now-husband, Mike, and acquired a stepdaughter, Jennifer. In 2007, with family life in place and a career selected, she embarked on a quest to make her greatest contribution to the world, both personally and professionally. In addressing parent-adult child estrangement, she found it. She now focuses exclusively on this issue as a therapist, speaker, and consultant. She has appeared as an expert in hundreds of media outlets, including the *Washington Post*, the *Chicago Tribune, Forbes, Glamour, Redbook*, and *Real Simple*.

Tina's forays into acting and other creative pursuits now serve her in her roles as a writer, speaker, and content creator. She's the co-founder, along with her husband, Mike, of ReconnectionClub.com, a website dedicated to educating and supporting parents of estranged adult children. She is also the creator and host of the *Reconnection Club Podcast*, available in all major podcast directories. For more information, visit http://reconnectionclub.com/podcast.

Tina is available for a limited number of consultation appointments by distance. Learn more at http://tinagilbertson.com/consultation.